WORD GLOSS

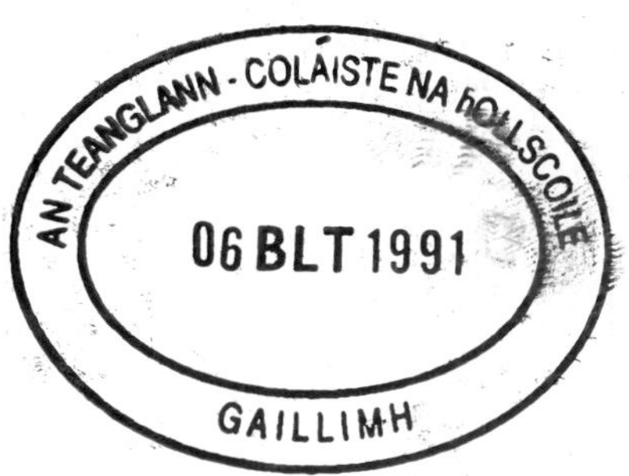

WORD GLOSS

JIM O'DONNELL

Institute of Public Administration
in association with
Irish Permanent Building Society

First published 1990
Institute of Public Administration
57-61 Lansdowne Road
Dublin, Ireland
Tel: (01) 697011 (Publications)
Fax: (01) 698644

ISBN 1-872002-45-5

Cover and title pages designed by
Gerard Butler Design
Typeset in 11/12 Bembo
by Brunswick Press Limited, Dublin
Printed by Aston Colour Press Limited

To the women in my life—
Mary, Jane, Rebecca, Sarah, Aisling
et al.

Contents

Foreword
by Brian Farrell

Words are the common currency of our communication. We use them, exchange them, discard them. We draw on a rich treasury of words, gathered up over the centuries and millennia of human experience; accumulated, adapted, applied and transformed in use. Too often we speak and write them without much regard for, or even knowledge of, their roots and meanings. Yet it is precisely that discriminating awareness of the root-meanings of words which distinguishes the educated, the discerning, the critical élite.

For long enough, that élite was a social class, preserving their secret word-strength through a classical education. That was not an experience shared with the majority. Today barriers of class and, to some extent, education are breaking down. Latin and Greek have almost disappeared from the curriculum; English is often taught without much regard for either subtlety or syntax. Words, like over-used and badly-rubbed coins, are losing the distinctive sharpness and definition with which they were freshly-minted.

This volume offers an exciting opportunity to a wide audience to recover something of a lost world, to regain forgotten grounds of significance, to explore the sources and the nuances of the vast panoply of words that we use, read and hear. *Wordgloss* is an invitation to share in the textured abundance of a great cultural heritage. This fascinating and revealing collection of words — some current and apparently commonplace, others seemingly esoteric and alien — is brilliantly arranged to encourage the reader to a fuller understanding of that enigmatic aphorism of Wittgenstein: 'the limits of my language are the limits of my world'. Because this is not just a collection, not another inert reference book or glorified dictionary. It is, I believe, a unique experiment: a challenge to the reader to interact with the words on the page, to experience them and be stimulated to pursue them.

Jim O'Donnell has constructed an adventure-playground with words and concepts that leads to a fuller appreciation, and therefore a more exact and powerful command, of language. This is a collection of words that every educated person should know and understand. These are words that many of us use. They are the stock terms of current affairs and economics, of journalism and finance. Through a deeper awareness of their origins we can come to a better understanding of the world in which we live. Confidence and assurance about our vocabulary are surely what Carlyle meant by his admonition: 'Be not a slave of words'. Knowledge of their derivation can release us from the tyranny of imprecise and incoherent language; it can make us free to express ourselves more fully.

Only a wordsmith of style and substance could have conceived and executed this handsome glossary. It required a writer of experience, concern and exactitude. It also demanded a man who knew his own mind. Jim O'Donnell has written and published widely and well on public affairs. He has edited the work of many other authors. He has been fertile in producing the ideas out of which books are made. All of that experience of, sensitivity to, and precision with words shines in these pages. This is word-craft of a high order that never intimidates but leads the reader on to turn the page. It is the accomplished work of a writer with a fine feeling for words and a rich familiarity with them in varied fields.

The selection ranges over wide categories. There are words drawn from law and political science, from philosophy and the arts, from science and technology. Latin and Greek tags and literary allusions rub shoulders with the language of the Sunday heavies. Connections, often surprising connections, are made and there are verbal and visual illustrations to enhance a text marked, above all, by clarity.

This is a book for virtually all ages. It will be welcome on the student's desk and beside the crossword puzzle. It is for the expert and the amateur alike. The politician and the speech-writer, the civil servant and the teacher, the journalist and public relations practitioner will find it a valuable and intriguing treasure-hoard. This is a book for all who wish, and need, to savour words to the full. It can also be seen as a contribution to a significant part of the continuing mission of the Institute of Public Administration: to provide us all with an enriched and shared vocabulary through which we can talk to each other about public affairs.

September 1990

Preface

Wordgloss seeks to increase your delight in words, especially those used in discussing public affairs.

The work gathers its flow from the confluence of two major streams of interest. The first stream has its source in the need people feel to understand the words and concepts used in the discussion of public affairs in the media. What does a journalist mean when he or she refers to 'a draconian measure', 'an apocryphal story', 'an iconoclastic figure', '*laissez faire* policies', 'the balance of payments', a company's 'viability', 'the hidden curriculum', 'forensic evidence', or 'the mixed economy'?

The fact is that the discussion of public affairs ranges over a wide spectrum of specialised areas. Politics, law, environment, health, education, finance, taxation, the economy, history, statistics — those are among the most important. Since most of us do not have the opportunity of making studies in all the areas, it follows that we do not start out with a good grasp of all the vocabulary. We depend on encountering some words a number of times in different contexts to define them for us — a process that of its nature does not ensure exactitude. There are many words and terms that occur so infrequently that we may never define them — yet they are the ones most apt to express certain important ideas. 'Dialectical', 'analogical', 'paradigm' 'ideology', 'hypothetical', '*sine qua non*' are examples.

People concerned about this issue have pinned their hopes on the development of social and political studies in post-primary schools. For some twenty-five years we in the Institute of Public Administration have made a sustained effort to support the teaching of Civics — we published *How Ireland is Governed* to provide Civics teachers with a reference on the institutions of government, and the monthly *Young Citizen* to provide students with information on, and lively discussion of, public affairs. However, it is common knowledge that Civics, owing to the pressure of examinations — it is an unexamined subject — has not been given the profile in the curriculum which it clearly should have.

The task of spreading an understanding of public affairs, a fundamental duty of a democratic society, now falls largely on informal processes — discussion among people when they meet, articles in newspapers and magazines, public affairs programmes on radio and television. Through these channels words and concepts come sweeping over us — 'exchequer', 'Zionism', 'radical', 'conservative', 'Machiavellian', 'doctrinaire', 'macroeconomics', 'paparazzi', 'suffrage', 'the Rome Treaties', 'fiscal rectitude', *status quo ante*, 'cornucopia' — and we are left clutching at their meaning, and perhaps never fully grasping it. *Wordgloss* aims to offer everyone the capacity to swim assuredly with that current.

The other major stream of interest has its source in the feeling many people have that their grip on language is not as sure as it should be. One finds that academics are expressing increasing concern at the drop in the standard of English of students taking their courses; teachers in commercial colleges are responding to the same phenomenon when they say they have no difficulty in placing a student in employment if his or her English is good.

A number of reasons is advanced to explain this condition. Grammar is no longer being taught as intensively as it was. The competition for the attention of people that comes from the electronic media means that people read far less. Moreover, the words they hear are usually more loosely deployed than those that appear in print. The most telling reason is, I believe, that fact that Latin and Greek are no longer taught extensively in post-primary schools.

Up to the 1960s most students took Latin in the Leaving and about ten per cent took Greek. Currently less than two per cent take Latin and less then twenty-five students — an almost sub-optical percentage — take Greek. The nature of English makes this significant.

Broadly speaking, English consists of a store of simple Anglo-Saxon words that describe everyday things — man, woman, boy, dog, cat, house, rain — and a store of complex words, derived from Latin and Greek, that convey sophisticated experience — feminism, democracy, monopoly, nepotism, geology, alibi, stereotype, and so on. In understanding the latter, it is a great help to have studied Latin and Greek, but it is not essential. An adequate understanding of the roots of the words and how they came to have their present meaning can be given in English. Words that appear difficult can frequently be broken down into two or more simple root words. Thus 'democracy' is a combination of two Greek words: *dēmos* 'people' and *kratein* 'to rule'. Moreover, in modern society whenever scientists or specialists of any kind seek to fashion a new word to describe a new process or idea they almost invariably search through the glittering database of the classical languages which even on the threshold of the third millennium is not found wanting. *Wordgloss* aims to provide those who have never studied Latin or Greek — nearly everyone under forty years of age, it would appear from the statistics — with some of the great advantages of such study.

The confluence of these interests is made possible by the fact that in the discussion of public affairs a preponderance of the concepts we use are derived from Latin and Greek. The Greeks of classical times, two thousand five hundred years ago, did not invent public affairs but they were the first to write about them. Their level of discourse was so sophisticated that their vocabulary serves us today. The Romans, who for hundreds of years maintained one of the greatest of empires, borrowed much of their thought from the Greeks but also invented many political, especially legal, terms that still inform the English language.

In order that its current is ample to carry a broad enough understanding of public affairs the text receives many small contributions from other languages — 'apartheid' (from Afrikaans), 'blitz' and 'ersatz' (from German), 'Yankee' (from Dutch), 'slogan' from (Irish), *'coup d'état'* (from French) are examples.

Wordgloss consists of words drawn from a number of sub-sets. One sub-set is of key political concepts such as democracy, socialism, communism, secularism, fascism, capitalism, liberalism, conservatism. Another consists of key institutions, such as the constitution, the President, the Taoiseach, the cabinet, the Dáil and the Seanad. Another consists of legal terms such as law, Act, crime, injunction, jury, statute. There are also sub-sets of philosophical, economic, social and historical terms. Given the provenance of the book a sub-set of Latin expressions, so hallowed that they are preserved in their original language (examples are *ad hoc, in camera, de facto, sub rosa, ultra vires*), is also explained. In addition a number of unusual words, based mainly on Greek, that crop up in the discussion of public affairs — though they are not peculiar to it — is set forth (words such as 'ephemeral', 'neophyte', 'apocryphal', 'polemical', 'strategy', 'hegemony').

In selecting the words I consulted textbooks, monitored newspapers and magazines, and drew upon the experience of publishing widely in the area of public affairs.

Wordgloss employs the concept of public affairs to identify the population of words to be glossed, to select a limited — and therefore manageable — perspective within which to gloss them, and to provide a content that is of its nature useful for everyday living. It uses the knowledge that the teaching of Latin and Greek is in catastrophic decline to fix upon a simple, direct address to the reader — 'this word means this', 'that word means that' — which otherwise might not be possible. It uses the aim of fixing words in the memory of the reader to define its style.

It is a well-known memory-training technique to associate what you wish to remember with something else whose vividness and concreteness you will more easily remember; and so *Wordgloss* uses stories and graphics. Memory is also helped where items are clustered. Words such as anarchy, oligarchy and hierarchy are clustered under the suffix *-archy*; words such as fratricide, matricide and regicide are clustered under the suffix *-cide*. Some words are twinned with their opposites, for example monopoly and monopsony, orthodox and heterodox. *Wordgloss* also clusters words that belong to a family. Thus under 'vote' you will find suffrage, constituencies, franchise, poll and hustings.

Another important support to the memory is repetition; so I have deliberately used throughout the work words defined in special articles, so as to give further examples of usage. Since interest is the hunting-dog of memory, I have used Irish experience, where appropriate, to make the text appeal more sharply to Irish readers (for whom this edition has been prepared).

ACKNOWLEDGEMENTS

A work such as *Wordgloss* draws on a wide range of resources. First of all, there is the work of countless previous authors, encyclopaedists and lexicographers. When Dr Johnson said: 'A man will turn over half a library to make one book' one would surely be forgiven for assuming that he — great dictionary-maker that he was — was thinking especially of those who write books about words.

Wordgloss also benefits greatly from the advice and scholarship of the great number of people I consulted. Some I asked to comment on the text generally, others I asked to comment on those parts in which they had a specialised interest. While any errors are my responsibility — I collected, interpreted and composed the material — much of the text's gloss is attributable to the interest and kindness of those readers. They include: Viv Abbott, T.J. Barrington, John Blackwell, Professor Basil Chubb, Michael Colley, Professor John Coolahan, Donal de Buitleir, Sean de Fréine, George Eaton, Desmond Egan, Professor Brian Farrell, Donal Flanagan, Grainne Flynn, Miriam Hederman O'Brien, Jack Henderson, Frank Holohan, Professor John Jackson, Tim Kelly, Finola Kennedy, Brendan Kiernan, Professor Patrick Lynch, Sean MacCarthy, John McGinty, Padraig McGowan, Senator Maurice Manning, Alex Miller, Fergal O'Connor OP, Micheál Ó hÓdhráin, Fr Gerry Rice, Mervyn Taylor, TD, Bernard Treacy OP, Tom Turley, Tony White, Jonathan Williams.

The two people I exploited most were probably Fergal O'Connor, Socratic master, who raised his lamp to throw light on what I needed to see, and Jack Henderson, the architect of the Classical Studies syllabus of the Department of Education, who, through his large knowledge of the literature, helped me convey a deeper sense of the classical period — surely one of the sunniest afternoons in human experience.

A number of my colleagues in the Institute took a positive interest in the work and I am grateful to them. John Gallagher, the Institute's director general, readily appreciated that *Wordgloss* could promote one of the Institute's basic aims of fostering mutual understanding between the public and public servants, but his enthusiasm had its source, I believe, in the fact that he is the son of a former and distinguished Classics teacher in St Flannan's College, Ennis (*sequiturque patrem non passibus aequis* — see page 177). Patricia Brown, Frank Litton, Declan McDonagh, Michael Mulreany and Frank Ryan read the text or parts of it and made useful suggestions. Mary

Prendergast, our librarian, and her staff, with the professionalism and courtesy for which they are renowned, provided a great number of the references upon which a work such as *Wordgloss* must draw. It is pleasant to record the commensal involvement of the Institute's publishing staff. Iain Mac Aulay and Maurice Flanagan read the text and commented on it, and helped in the picture research and production generally. A small part of the word processing was done by Anne Murphy and Sarah Blair, but the bulk of it was done by Dolores Meagher who, sustained by her own literary enthusiasms, successfully completed a task that must at times have seemed Sisyphean (see page 223) because the text was necessarily a continuously developing one.

ILLUSTRATIONS

In identifying and acquiring graphic materials I was greatly helped by Dr Pat Donlon, Director of the National Library, and Eugene Hogan and Dr Noel Kissane on the staff of the library. David Lawlor of An Post had the picture of the statue of Cú Chulainn specially generated for *Wordgloss*. Bro Paul, SVD, editor of *The Word*, a long-standing friend, dug generously into his resources. William Aliaga-Kelly did most of the special photography. E.F. O'Donnell did some of the picture research in London. I am grateful to all of them as well as to the staff of the Graeco-Roman Department of the British Museum who gave me a desk and a chair — and the freedom to search through their treasures.

The publishers are very grateful to the following for supplying illustrations: APSO 247, Bord Failte 25, Chester Beatty Library, Dublin 118, 171, 186, The British Tourist Authority 47 (The Cenotaph), Dublin Port 31, The Embassy of the United States of America, Dublin 103, European Commission 36, 92, 93, 94, 95, 96, Fine Gael 191 (Dukes), The Green Party 192 (Garland), *Irish Press* 195, 196, 240 (De Valera), *The Irish Times* 19, 27, 108, 135 (Whitaker), 149, 191 (Haughey), 240 (Costello), Lensmen 53, 142, 191 (Spring), 196, 240 (Cosgrave), National Film Archive, London 26 (The Hunchback of Notre Dame), National Library of Ireland 35, 60, 70, 71, 76, 105, 119 (Emmet) 163, 200, 223 (MacEoin), 249, Novosti Press Agency, Moscow 116, Progressive Democrats 192 (O'Malley), *The Word*, Divine Word Missionaries, Maynooth 120, Workers' Party 192 (De Rossa).

The publishers wish to thank the following for permission to reproduce illustrations: Allied Irish Bank 211, Archivi Alinari 68, 144, Board of Trinity College, Dublin 11, British Museum 185, 194, 224, 238, 250, Camera Press 47, Central Bank of Ireland 86, Commissioners of Public Works, Ireland 102, 148, Hulton-Deutsch Collection, 15, 17, 33, 41, 46, 55, 64, 75, 101, 105 (Davison), 117, 130, 139, 152, 165, 177, 246, 257, 265, 266, The Irish Stock Exchange 233, Municipal Gallery of Modern Art 54 (Lane, Gregory), Museo del Prado 62, National Gallery, London 54, National Museums and Galleries of Merseyside 215, National Museum of Ireland 156, 212, National Portrait Gallery, London 18, 28, 41, 79, 88, 119, 135, 162, 183, 190, RTE 181, 261, An Post 170, 262, Turner Entertainment Co. (© RKO Radio Pictures, Inc. Ren. 1967 RKO General, Inc.) 26 (The Hunchback of Notre Dame).

The publishers have sought to clear permission for all illustrations not in the public domain.

For their work in laying out the pages I must thank Jennifer McCaw and Paul Bray.

The Irish Permanent Building Society, whose generous support has enabled us to present the text to the reader in the most effective manner, deserve the final word of thanks.

Using Wordgloss

1. The small letter o found throughout the text before a word or phrase, e.g. °government, °*sine qua non*, indicates that the word (or a closely related form of it) or the phrase is explained elsewhere in the text. You will locate the explanation by consulting the word or phrase in the index and searching the page whose number is given in italic.
2. Latin and Greek nouns are quoted in their nominative and genitive cases (thus the Latin word for a 'judge' *judex, judicis* and the Greek word for 'light' *phōs, phōtos*) because the words derived from them are usually derived from the genitive form (thus 'judicial' and 'photo'.)
3. The straight dash above a vowel in a Greek word indicates the long form of the vowel. *Wordgloss* conforms to this technicality partly to help restrain the reader from concluding that an s ending indicates a plural (thus *politēs*, the Greek word for 'citizen' would otherwise appear as *polites*).
4. The Greek *k* and *u* transliterate into English as c and y respectively.
5. Statements in quotations which illustrate usage were originated for this text save for a small number of attributed ones which were drawn from printed sources.
6. For the sake of directness words are referred to as words rather than nouns, adjectives, verbs, adverbs etc., except in a small number of cases where distinctions are necessary. For the same reason a certain amount of repetition is allowed in the text.
7. *Wordgloss* uses an alphabetically-ordered dictionary style of presentation. The body of the text, however, is frequently associative rather than linear in its development because *Wordgloss* is primarily pedagogic in intent.
8. Marginal glosses are used to supplement the body of the text and are placed as close as possible to the word glossed. Captions are also developed opportunistically.
9. To help the reader track down items of information the index is a detailed one.

aboriginal
pertaining to the earliest °inhabitants or things

A (*ab* before a vowel) is a Latin word meaning 'from'. *Origo, originis* is a Latin word meaning 'beginning' or 'origin' from which we also derive 'original' and 'originally'. The aborigines of Latium, the district around Rome, were a tribe called the Latini — hence the word 'Latin'. The aborigines of Australia, sometimes offensively referred to as 'abos', are the race which occupied that continent before the Europeans discovered it. The American Indians are the aborigines of North America. The Caribs (after whom the Caribbean is called) were the aborigines of the West Indies.

The term 'aborigines' tends to be used to suggest a °primitive race. When the °colonists had respect for the race in possession, they would refer to them as the 'indigenous' people (*indi* is a strengthened form of the Latin word *in* meaning 'in' and *gignere*, from which we derive the *gen* particle, is a Latin word 'to produce'); or they might refer to them as 'the natives' (from the Latin word *nasci* which means 'to be born'). Natives who violently resisted the colonists were called savages. 'Savage' comes by way of the °modern French word *sauvage* from the Old French *salvage*. *Silva,* from which *salvage* was derived, is the Latin word for 'a wood'; woods were uncleared areas and therefore wild.

civilised
Civilis is a Latin word meaning 'pertaining to a citizen' i.e. a city-dweller, in its orignial sense; 'civilisation' which contrasts with '°barbarism', is characterised by the peaceful coming together of groups of people to achieve objectives individuals could not achieve alone — cities with their elaborate °economic, °social and °cultural oganisation have always been regarded as °centres of civilisation

From the sixteenth °century on, as the colonising Europeans encountered primitive peoples in the Americas, in Australasia, and in the South Seas generally, they developed the concept of the noble savage — a condition of °human existence that seemed to display °excellences of life which civilised man had lost. Throughout man's °history, the notion of an early °era when life was lived in perfect harmony with nature has been part of his thought and °mythology — thus the Greeks and Romans harked back to a Golden Age, the Hebrews to the Garden of Eden; and with the discovery of the noble savage a modern form of primitivism found expression in such literature as Longfellow's *Song of Hiawatha* (1855). The concept of the noble savage is explicitly referred to in *The Conquest of Granada* by John Dryden (1631–1700):

I am as free as nature first made man,
Ere the base laws of °servitude began,
When wild in woods the noble savage ran.

The Golden Age of the Greeks — a paradise on earth, with ease, plenty and pleasure. 'Paradise' derives from an Old Persian word, *pairidaeza*, meaning 'a pleasure-ground' which the Greeks borrowed in the form *paradeisos*. Thus Xenophon writing in his *Anabasis* tells us of the Persian king Cyrus: '[He] had a palace there and a large pleasure-ground [*paradeisos*] full of wild animals, which he used to hunt on horseback . . . . . Through the middle of the pleasure-ground the river Meander flows.' (The Meander was a proverbially slow, winding river — it gave us the word 'to meander')

The concept of the noble savage sprang from a positive view of the human condition. It appealed to certain thinkers (as well as to °sentimentalists) because it seemed to °contradict the °Biblical °doctrine of Original Sin: they believed that in undermining revealed religion the concept would undermine the °political thinking based on it — and encourage the development of new political thinking based on reason rather than °tradition.

positive
-ive is a Latin suffix indicating 'a tending towards'. *Posit* is a Latin formation meaning 'something placed'. Positive in its basic sense means 'definite'; here it means 'marked by the presence of good qualities'. Its opposite is 'negative' (*negare* is the Latin word 'to deny')

In their discussions about the origins of society (and therefore of the basis of authority in human affairs) modern °philosophers developed the notion of the °state of nature. This they viewed in either a positive or negative manner. Thus Jean Jacques Rousseau (1712-78), one of the most °influential of modern political thinkers, interpreted the state of nature in a positive way, asserting the natural goodness, equality and °freedom of men and women — in stark contrast to the conditions of his own time. He traced the corruption of society to the development in men of *amour propre* (self-esteem) and of the drive to assert their own worth before and against other men.

Agriculture and °metallurgy, by leading to the establishment of °private property, provided a °physical means of asserting one's °social position — the more you owned the more you were respected. States, Rousseau believed, were brought into being by the wealthy to provide the means of protecting private property — that is why they were not concerned with liberty and equality. The poor assented to the arrangements for the sake of security.

His remedy was a new social contract under which the general will would be expressed through a °vote on all °laws by the body of free and equal citizens; it would be the duty of the state executive (in whatever form it took) to apply the laws equally to all.

the executive is the branch of government concerned to execute, that is, carry out, laws, plans, agreements etc. (*ex* is a Latin word meaning 'out', *sequi* is a Latin word 'to follow')

The English philosopher Thomas Hobbes (1588–1679) took a negative view of man in the state of nature — men with their contrary desires were naturally prone to violence and injustice; a sovereign power, in whatever form, is needed to impose order and stability; the state is a creation of man — it may be well or badly built.

A people respected °ostensibly because they have been in possession of a particular territory from time immemorial, but in reality because they are powerful, may be described as 'autochthonous' (*autos* is the Greek for 'self', *chthōn* is the Greek for 'land' — autochthonous, therefore, means 'sprung from the land itself').

academic
as a noun, a professional member of the staff of a °university or other institution of higher learning; as an adjective, impractical and theoretical; or pertaining to an institution of higher learning

Outside Athens in ancient times there was a garden which was linked with a legendary hero called Academus. When in 387 BC the °philosopher Plato established a school there, it came to be called the Academy. The ten-year course of studies that Plato laid down was aimed not at helping the students make a living but at making them examine the world and man's place in it. It was said that the Academy was so solemnly dedicated to study that it was forbidden to laugh there.

The Latin poet Horace made a famous reference to Plato's Academy: *Atque inter silvās Academi quaerere verum* — 'And seek truth in the groves of Academus'. Milton echoed this in *Paradise Regained*:

Socrates (c.470–399 BC) and Plato (429–c.347 BC). 'Platonic', as in 'a Platonic relationship', is applied to a purely spiritual love for someone of the opposite sex. We rely largely on Plato for °biographical °material on Socrates; Platonic love was a °synonym for Socratic love — the kind of non-sexual interest in young men that Plato shows Socrates as having; °originally, therefore, the term applied to the quality of love without particular reference to women

The groves of Academe,
Plato's retirement, where the °Attic bird
Trills her thick-warbled notes the summer long.

'Academe' (also sometimes 'academia') is used to refer to a university environment.

Plato's Academy continued for nine hundred years and so had a °history longer than any university that exists today. It was closed by the Emperor Justinian — because it was the last stronghold of the ancient °pagan learning — in 529 AD, round about the time the great Irish °monastic schools were being established. How Irish learning might have developed had those °centres survived till our own time is, of course, an academic question.

Act
a °law made by the °Oireachtas (also called a °statute) as distinct from a law based on the common law i.e. customary practice

Agere, from which 'act' is derived, is the Latin word 'to do' — an act is 'a thing done', in this instance by the °legislature. (The word 'actor' usually describes a male member of the cast of a play but it may also be used simply to describe someone who does something.) The word's association with °legislation goes back to Roman times when a daily account of the various matters brought before the °senate, the opinions of the chief speakers, and the decisions of the house was published under the title *Acta Senatus*.

Most Acts start off as Bills prepared in a °civil service department under the supervision of a minister. The °legal advice of the Attorney General is sought. The Bill is cast in a °technically perfect legal form by an expert on the Attorney General's staff called a °parliamentary draftsman. Leave to introduce a Bill is sought in either House of the °Oireachtas and, if it is given, the Bill is printed and circulated to members.

The debate on the Bill proceeds through a number of stages; amendments may be made to it. It is then sent for debate to the other House. A Bill amended by the °Seanad is always sent back to the °Dáil for its approval. When a Bill, other than a Bill to amend the °constitution, is passed or deemed to be passed by both Houses, it is sent to the °President for his or her signature.

The President signs the Bill not earlier than the fifth day and not later than the seventh day after the date on which the Bill is presented to him or her unless a motion requesting the President's earlier signature is agreed to by the Seanad, or unless he or she decides to refer it to the Supreme Court to test its constitutionality.

If a °majority of the Seanad and not less than one-third of the Dáil °petition the President to decline to sign a Bill on the ground that it contains a proposal of such importance that the will of the people thereon ought to be ascertained, the President may accede to the request after consultation with the Council of State and may sign only when the proposal has been approved by the people in a °referendum or by a new Dáil after a dissolution and a general °election.

A Bill to amend the constitution, passed or deemed to be passed by both Houses and approved at a

referendum, is signed forthwith by the President. The President °promulgates the law by having a notice published in the *Iris Oifigiúil*, the official gazette. The signed copy of the Bill, now called an Act, is kept in the office of the Supreme Court.

ad hoc
for this purpose

Ad is a Latin word meaning 'to' or 'for'. *Hoc* is a Latin word meaning 'this thing'. The expression is frequently used about committees. An *ad hoc* committee is a °temporary committee set up to do a particular task. It is disbanded when the task is done. Used of arrangements — *ad hoc* arrangements — it °connotes improvisation.

ad nauseam
to the point of causing sickness

Ad is a Latin word meaning 'to' or 'for'. *Nauseam* is a form of *nausea* the Latin word for 'seasickness'. A bore often creates his or her effect by going on *ad nauseam* about a °topic of exceedingly limited °interest to the hearer(s). *Nausea* is itself derived from the Greek word *nausia* also meaning 'seasickness' which in turn derives from the Greek word for a ship *naus* (hence 'nautical'). *Navis* is the Latin word for a ship (hence 'naval' and 'navigator').

ad rem
to the point, pertinent

Ad is a Latin word meaning 'to' or 'for'. *Rem* is a form of the Latin word *res* meaning 'thing' or 'matter'. A speaker who makes pertinent or relevant points is said to speak *ad rem*.

advocatus diaboli
the devil's advocate

canonise
means the °criterion for establishing what books are divinely inspired and by transference the list of such books (*kanōn* means 'a measuring rod' in Greek) To *canonise* is to list °officially a dead °person among the saints

Before the Pope canonises a saint, a very long, thorough examination of the °candidate's life is carried out. One °official is assigned the task of arguing against the proposal to canonise. He is known as the *advocatus diaboli* (*advocatus* means 'advocate', one who pleads the cause of another, from the Latin word *advocare* 'to call in'; *diaboli* is a form of *diabolus*, the Latin word for 'devil', from which we derive 'diabolical'). *Advocatus diaboli* may be applied generally to anyone who tests an argument by arguing the opposite case. Thus, 'Acting as *advocatus diaboli*, I put it to you that ....' Sometimes when the term is applied to someone who takes the °unpopular side of an argument, there is a suggestion that he or she is simply being argumentative.

aegis
protection, patronage

In this drawing of a statue of Pallas Athene at Dresden, the aegis is the goatskin itself. Note the Gorgon's head

Aix, aigos is the Greek word for 'a goat'. The *aegis* was the goatskin covering on the shield of Zeus, the chief of the Greek gods, often transferred to mean the shield itself. To be under the aegis of Zeus was to be protected, and therefore favoured, by Zeus. In Homer's *Iliad*, the °epic poem which tells of the °Trojan War, the gods and goddesses are depicted as showing great interest in the affairs of °mortals, even to the extent of intervening in battle. Thus Apollo and Pallas Athene borrow the shield to protect their heroes. Homer describes the shield as follows:

> Athene, daughter of aegis-bearing Zeus ... equipped herself for the terrible business of war with the arms of Zeus the Cloud-Gatherer. About her shoulders she threw the dreaded tasselled aegis, all round which the figure of Panic was depicted, while within it was Strife and Valour and blood-chilling Rout; within it, too, was the head of the ghastly monster Gorgon, fearful and terrible, the emblem of aegis-bearing Zeus.

Time has long ago leached the divine potency from the word. Nowadays you might find yourself attending a conference held under the aegis of the °Confederation of Irish Industry.

affidavit
a written statement, given under oath, that may be produced in evidence in court

Affidare is a late Latin word meaning 'to swear to'.

a fortiori
with all the more reason

A (*ab* before a vowel) is a Latin word meaning 'from'. *Fortis* is the Latin word for 'strong'. *Fortior* is a form of it that means 'stronger'. The expression is used in the context of °logical argument. Thus someone might assert: 'If I would not let my best friend drive my car, *a fortiori* I would not let a complete stranger drive it!'

agenda
things to be done; items of business requiring consideration or decision at a meeting

Agere is the Latin word 'to do'. *Agenda* is a form of the word which means 'things to be done'. A *hidden agenda* is the °objective or objectives that an individual or °cabal wishes to achieve through group action without letting the rest of the group know.

In the discussion of °education the concept of 'the hidden °curriculum' occurs. A school curriculum lays down, for everybody to see, the °subjects to be pursued by the students — Irish, English, °Science etc. However, in the way in which it teaches the subjects, in the atmosphere it creates, in the extra-curricular (*extra* means 'outside' in Latin) activities it arranges, a school may seek to achieve certain hidden objectives such as °moral courage, honesty, persistence, conformity. The set of such objectives pursued by a school is called 'the hidden curriculum'.

agent provocateur
someone secretly employed to induce others to engage in disruptive or provocative actions

Agent is the French word for 'agent' derived from the Latin word *agere* 'to do'. *Provocateur* is a French word meaning 'provoking'. °Governments have been known to use *agents provocateurs* to provide them with excuses to move their police forces against certain groups.

agrarian
relating to land

Ager, agri is the Latin word for 'field'. Agrarian unrest in Ireland climaxed at the end of the last °century with the activities of the Land League founded by Michael Davitt in County Mayo in 1879. Things settled down after a series of Land °Acts transferred ownership from the landlords to the tenants.

alias
an assumed name

context
— the setting in which something occurs (*con* is a Latin particle meaning 'with', *texere* is a Latin word 'to weave')

Alias is a Latin word meaning 'on other occasions'. It is usually used in a °legal context and specifically where an accused has used a name other than his or her own to establish a new identity in order to facilitate the committing of a crime (thus in court an accused might be identified as 'Tom Brown *alias* Tom Green').

For various reasons writers may use a name other than their own but this is called a *pen name* (in French *nom de guerre*, in pseudo-French *nom de plume*), not an alias. Thus one of the greatest novelists in English, George Eliot, the author of *Middlemarch*, was a woman, Mary Ann Evans.

If you wish to send a message to someone without revealing your name, you may use a *pseudonym* — a false name — or no name at all, and so remain *anonymous*. *Onoma* is the Greek word for 'name'. *A* (*an* before a vowel) is a Greek prefix that negatives a word. *Pseudos* is the Greek word for 'false'. A *synonym* is a word that means the same thing as another word: 'lift' and 'elevator' are synonyms (*sun*, transliterated *syn* in English, is a Greek word meaning 'with').

alibi
the plea that a person was elsewhere at the time of an alleged °act

Alibi is a Latin word meaning 'elsewhere'. In day-to-day usage alibi has been reduced to any kind of excuse.

alienation
a feeling of being cut off from others

Alienus is a Latin word meaning 'belonging to another' and conveys the sense of estrangement which is the essence of 'alienation'. (An alien is someone who is not a citizen of the country in which he or she resides but who belongs to another country.) Alienation, like many other terms, came into vogue with the spread of °Marxism. It was borrowed from Hegel.

For Marx, the °capitalist system produced a crippling sense of alienation in the industrial worker by such effects as estranging the worker from the °product of his labour (it was not his) and from his fellow-workers (because it distinguished between types of labour and created a °competitive labour market). The worker, Marx asserted, could achieve his °human potential only if he were released from the capitalist system.

Broadly speaking, alienation is used in °modern °social thinking to describe the sense of °isolation the individual feels in modern society (adversely contrasted with the warmth of the extended families and the small communities of earlier times). The word *anomie* is used in this sense too. Derived from the Greek negative particle *a* and *nomos* the Greek word for 'law', it conveys the feeling of hopelessness that follows upon the loss of meaning and purpose in a prevailing °culture. The Greek historian, Thucydides, in his famous account of the plague in Athens uses this word to describe the behaviour of the Athenians at that time:

> The plague first introduced into the city a greater lawlessness [*anomia*]. For, where men hitherto practised concealment, they now showed a more careless daring. They saw how sudden was the change of °fortune in the case both of those who were prosperous and suddenly died, and of those who before had nothing, but in a moment were in possession of the property of others. And so they resolved to get out of life the pleasures which could be had speedily and would satisfy their lusts, regarding their bodies and their wealth alike as transitory.

'Anomie' also conveys the feeling of inability to identify with a particular form of °political, social or religious culture (it could be applied, for example, to the inability of French °aristocrats to accept the new °bourgeois culture after the Revolution).

In law, alienation means the disposal of property. Property which cannot °legally be disposed of, because it would deprive one's heirs, is referred to as 'inalienable'.

inalienable
In is a Latin negative prefix; *alienus* is a Latin word meaning 'belonging to another' — inalienable, then, means 'incapable of being transferred to another' and therefore 'incapable of being taken away'; *imprescriptible* 'not capable of being limited by law' from *im*, a Latin prefix that negatives a word, and *praescribere,* a Latin word meaning 'to lay down as a rule' — is a °synonym for 'inalienable' and is also used in relation to rights

alphabet
the letters of a language set forth in a fixed order

Alpha is the first letter of the Greek alphabet and *beta* is the second. The Greek alphabet is derived from the Phoenician °script (the Phoenicians were °Semitic traders, descendants of the Canaanites). Alpha is derived from the Semitic *aleph* meaning 'ox', originally 'ox-head', represented as . The Greeks, who did not know the meaning of *aleph,* thought the letter looked better standing up — hence A. Beta is derived from the Semitic *beth. Beth* means 'house' (as in Bethlehem — 'house of bread' — so called because it was in a prosperous grain-growing area) and was represented as — hence B.

A	α	alpha
B	β	beta
Ω	ω	ōmega

Alphanumeric is used to describe a typewriter, computer or other machine that uses both letters and numbers (*numerus* is the Latin word for 'number').

Omega is the last letter of the Greek alphabet; when

God is called 'the Alpha and the Omega' what is meant is that He is the beginning and the end (of all things).

Γ	γ	gamma
Δ	δ	delta
Ι	ι	iota
Χ	χ	chī
Ρ	ρ	rho

Gamma is the third letter of the Greek alphabet. Gamma rays are penetrating radiation given off by radioactive substances. (There are three major kinds of radiation — alpha, beta and gamma; a fourth kind is called X-ray.)

Delta is the fourth letter of the Greek alphabet. In Aldous Huxley's *Brave New World* the deltas are the lowest grade of worker (it was customary for °academics to rate their students' work using the first four letters of the Greek alphabet, alpha being highest grade, delta lowest). The °capital form of delta is triangular and so aeroplanes with triangular wings are described as delta-winged. An alluvial tract at the mouth of a river is called a delta (because that of the Nile was delta-shaped).

Iota is the Greek letter i, the smallest in the alphabet. It is used as a word meaning 'something very small'. Thus, 'The bargaining was very tough but he did not concede one iota'. One of the bitterest schisms in the early church occurred because of an iota of difference between two sides — that between those who believed the Father and Son were of the same (*homos* in Greek) substance and those who believed they were of like (*homoios* in Greek) substance. (Schism is the Anglicisation of *schisma*, a Greek word for 'a split' derived from the word *schizein* 'to split'; from that word we also derive 'schizophrenia', a condition in which the mind — Greek *phrēn* — divides itself between reality and illusion.)

The Chi-Rho page from the Book of Kells

Chi (for ch) is the twenty-second letter of the Greek alphabet and *rho* (for r) is the seventeenth. Combined, they form the first three letters of Christ's name: so the *chi* superimposed on the *rho* was used as a monogram for Christ. One of the most famous pages in the Book of Kells — the Chi-Rho page — is lovingly devoted to this monogram.

The Russians use the Cyrillic alphabet, which is based on the Greek alphabet, because they were converted in the ninth °century by St Cyril and other Greek °Orthodox Christians who brought writing to them.

ambivalent
having at one and the same time opposing attitudes towards an °object

Ambi- is a Latin prefix meaning 'on both sides'. *Valere* is a Latin word 'to be strong'. To be ambivalent is to be strong on both sides, to be for and against something at the same time. Thus, 'We have always been ambivalent about °emigration, on the one hand lamenting the departure each year of thousands of °energetic, bright young people and on the other failing to take the kind of °radical °economic and °social measures necessary to staunch it'.

Ambiguous, applied to statements, now means 'capable of more than one meaning' although it °originally meant capable of two meanings (from *ambi-* and *agere* the Latin word 'to drive'). *Equivocal* is a °synonym for ambiguous (*aequi-* is a Latin prefix meaning 'equal', *vox, vocis* is the Latin word for 'voice'). People often resort to ambiguity (or equivocation) to avoid giving a lie direct.

amnesty
a general pardon extended to a large group of people

A is a Greek prefix that negatives a word. *Mnēstis* is a Greek word meaning 'remembrance'. An amnesty is a self-conscious overlooking of past wrongs. The °victor often grants an amnesty to the defeated so as to put behind the rancour of war (indeed the weaker side may make the granting of an amnesty a °*sine qua non* of surrender).

Amnesty International is the name of the independent worldwide movement that works impartially for the release of all prisoners of conscience, for fair and prompt trials for °political prisoners, and for an end to torture and execution.

Amnesia, derived from the same word as amnesty, is the clinical condition of loss of memory (*memoria* is the Latin word for 'memory').

analogy
a correspondence in certain respects between things otherwise different

Analogia was a term used by Greek mathematicians to °denote 'equality of ratios' (*ana* is a Greek word meaning 'with' and *logos* is a Greek word meaning 'word', 'reason' or, as here, 'ratio'). The term 'analogue', in America 'analog', is still used in °scientific fields. In common speech an analogy is often used to convince us that there is a correspondence between a process we know well and one we do not know well. Thus, 'There is an analogy between how a row breaks out between youngsters and how a war breaks out between °nations'.

classified
Classis is a Latin word for 'an assembly', a group, a class: to classify is to put in groups that have some characteristic in common. 'Classical' pertains to something first class. The Greek word *taxis* means 'rank': 'taxonomy' means the act or principles of ranking or classifying

In the theory of language, words are classified as univocal, equivocal, or analogical. A word is *univocal* if it has the same core meaning in all its uses — thus the word 'cow' means the same when it is used of many different cows (*unus* is the Latin word for 'one' and *vox, vocis* is the Latin word for 'voice'). A word is *equivocal* when it can have different meanings in the same usage — thus 'His aunt brought him to see the *picture'* (*aequus* is the Latin word for 'equal'). To equivocate in argument is to draw inferences from different uses of the same word or concept within a discussion without acknowledging the shift of meaning (jokes hinge on equivocation and therefore are often untranslatable). A word is *analogical* when it has a core meaning that varies with usage — thus the meaning of the word 'good' differs when it is applied to a field and a boy. Awareness of the analogical character of words protects us from false inferences.

An *allegory* is a form of analogy (*allos* is a Greek word meaning 'other', *agoreuein* is a Greek word 'to speak'). Among the most famous allegories in literature are Aesop's Fables. The concept is especially important in °Biblical studies where it may be argued that certain texts, for example *Genesis*, should be understood allegorically rather than literally. *Simile* is probably the most common form of analogy (*similis* is the Latin word for 'like' from which we also derive 'similar' and 'assimilate'). Thus, 'He ran like the hammers of hell'. *Metaphor* is a more daring form of analogy than simile (*meta* is a Greek word meaning 'with' and *pherein* is a Greek word 'to carry'), where we say something is not like, but is, something else. Thus, 'She was the apple of his eye'.

Analogy allows us to understand one thing in terms of another and thereby makes possible many different sorts of discourse. Thus one proceeds to some understanding of God by using words derived from the created world — we say He is wise or good, but not in the way °humans are wise or good. More generally, the analogical character of thought and discourse points to the fact that the human mind attains knowledge and understanding indirectly, that is, it knows of one thing in terms of others. But it is this very feature that allows us to equivocate in our discourse — to intend a meaning other than the apparent one. We must also be careful not to draw false inferences from analogies. We cannot infer from the fact that a good typewriter makes little noise that a good rocket launcher makes little noise.

anarchism
a °political °doctrine which holds that °governments should be abolished and in their place a co-operative system established

A (*an* before a vowel) is a Greek prefix which negatives a word. *Archein* is a Greek word 'to rule'. Anarchists prize °freedom (not disorder). They feel that °humans, °social animals, should be free to combine with their fellows on a voluntary basis (but anarchists have differed in their ideas on how this should be done). Because they see the °modern °state as forcing people to work together (and as providing an °apparatus which some people can use to force others to do what they want), they regard it as intrinsically evil. Since governments seek to impose control from the °centre, anarchists lay stress on °local control.

century
derives from the Latin *centum* 'a hundred'. A *centurion* was a Roman officer who commanded a hundred men. A *centenarian* is someone who is a hundred or more years old

In the nineteenth century, some anarchists sought to promote their beliefs through violence, often of a singularly desperate kind such as the °assassination of °Tsar Alexander II of Russia in 1881. Such °acts gave anarchists their °dominant °popular image of swarthy °conspirators priming a bomb in a cellar. Other anarchists have sought to promote their beliefs by non-violent means such as °civil disobedience, non-co-operation, strikes.

Pierre Joseph Proudhon (1809–65), a Frenchman, is regarded as the first modern anarchist. He called his form of anarchism 'mutualism' because he envisaged in place of the °bourgeois state a collection of autonomous communities co-operating with one another for their mutual benefit ('autonomous' means 'self-governing' from the Greek words *autos* meaning 'self' and *nomos* meaning 'law'). His emphasis on the rights of the individual rather than those of the collective brought

Proudhon

him into conflict with Marx who emphasised the need for a strong °central authority.

Anarchists have never formed a very significant movement. However, they provided °Marx with the idea of 'the withering away of the °state' as the °ultimate condition of °communism, and, in combination with °*syndicalists* (people who believed trade union power should be used to destroy the bourgeois state), they were °influential in France and Italy before World War I and in Spain before and during the °civil war (1936-39).

Religious principle has also been adduced in support of anarchism. The great Russian novelist Leo Tolstoy (1828–1910) was a religious anarchist: he felt the state was inconsistent with love, the °quintessential Christian virtue. In modern times one finds religious anarchists of a different kind — people who find the °*institutional* church unhelpful and seek to practise their religion outside it.

anomaly
irregularity, abnormality

A (*an* before a vowel) is a Greek prefix that negatives a word. *Homalos* is the Greek word for 'even'. °Bureaucrats and other people who draw up general rules for systems or °organisations must have sufficient imagination to foresee anomalies if they are to do their work effectively.

anticlerical
opposed to the clergy or their power

Anti is a Greek word meaning 'against'. *Klērikos* is a Greek word meaning 'chosen by lot'. In the early Church leaders were chosen by lot. Indeed that was how Matthias was selected to replace Judas as one of the Twelve Apostles — 'the lot fell upon Matthias'. Later the word 'cleric' was used to describe those set apart from the laity to minister to the Church.

After the conversion of the Roman Emperor Constantine in the fourth °century, Christianity became the °state religion and the authority of clerics in °temporal affairs developed. After the fall of the Roman °Empire, the clergy, in combination with strong °local leaders, brought order and a degree of stability out of the chaos of the Dark Ages and helped in the development of the °feudal system. (*Chaos* is a Greek word meaning the °primal state of the universe, the formless void before the creation of the ordered °universe — the °cosmos: 'In the beginning there was Chaos, vast and dark....' — Hesiod, *Theogony* °c. 700 BC.)

The relationship that developed between Church and °State, though often subject to great strain, was, broadly speaking, symbiotic. However, a general questioning of authority both °secular and °ecclesiastical was a °characteristic of the °humanist °tradition that became marked during the French Enlightenment (the period between the death of Louis X1V in 1715 and the French °Revolution in 1789). Thereafter, kings were deposed and, throughout Europe in the eighteenth and nineteenth centuries, anticlericalism was a notable feature of °civic °culture.

symbiotic
means 'mutually beneficial', literally 'pertaining to a living with' — *sym* is derived from the Greek word *sun* meaning 'with' and *biotic* from the Greek word *bios* meaning 'life'

In °modern times, with the effective separation of Church and State, anticlericalism is seldom more than the expression of the disaffection of individuals with elements of Church policy or practice. The word 'clerk', meaning someone who keeps accounts, is also derived from *klērikos*: in °medieval times it was only the clerics who, broadly speaking, could read, write and compute.

anti-Semitism
hatred of the Jewish race

Shem was one of the three sons of Noah. Abraham, from whom the Jews derive their race ('our father Abraham') was one of the many descendants of Shem. The term 'Semitic', therefore, strictly applies to other races as well as the Jews. *Anti* is a Greek word meaning 'against'. Anti-Jewish feeling was common among Christians, who blamed the Jews for the death of Christ. This was a religious rather than a racial prejudice. (However, racism was displayed by the Spanish Inquisition in its especial zeal to test the °bona fides of converted Jews.) It was not until 1965 that the Catholic Church formally declared that, while authorities of the Jews and those who followed their lead pressed for the death of Christ, all the Jews then living and their descendants, including the Jews of today, could not be blamed for the death of Christ, that is, were not guilty of °deicide.

Hatred of the Jews because of their race rather than their religion, a persistent °historical °phenomenon,

culminate
— to reach the highest point (*culmen, culminis* is the Latin word for 'roof' and therefore 'summit'; *apex* is another Latin word for 'top'; *acmē* is a Greek word for 'top' — thus, 'He reached the acme of his profession')

culminated in the °Holocaust — the °physical destruction of the Jews decided on by the °Nazis as the Final Solution of the Jewish problem at the Wannsee Conference in Berlin in 1942. Many reasons have been advanced for the strange phenomenon of anti-Semitism. In general, the Jews sought, wherever they were, to maintain their religious and °cultural identity. This, combined with their desire to return to the Holy Land, gave those in whose countries they settled a basis for seeing them as °alien.

In Poland and Russia, where there were large numbers of impoverished Jews, the Jews were a convenient °minority to blame for °political or °economic setbacks. Thus in 1905, following the defeat of Russia by the Japanese, the °Czarist police published a forged document called *The Protocols of the Elders of °Zion.* This purported to reveal a Jewish °conspiracy to enslave the world. It later fed Hitler's lunatic °fantasies about the Jews (*luna* is the Latin word for 'moon'; in ancient times the moon was thought to make people mad).

In Western Europe and America many Jews achieved glittering °material success and were conspicuous in art, literature, music, medicine, °science, thought: the envy this provoked in some people was visited upon the whole race of Jews. As Barnet Litvinoff in his book *The*

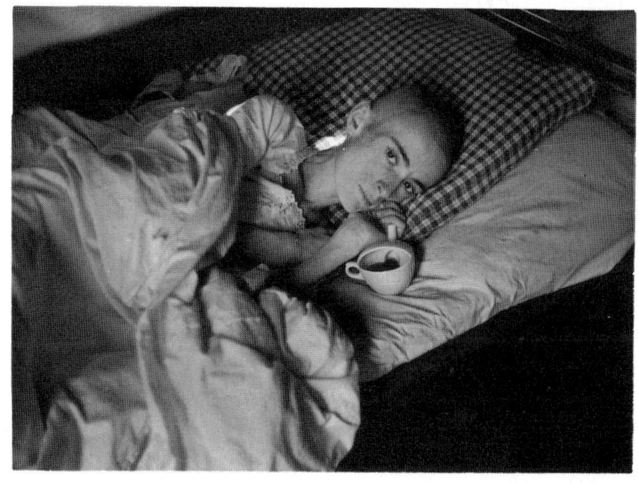

Belsen concentration camp 1945 — a survivor of the Final Solution. ('Survivor' °derives from the French *survivre*; *sur* derives from the Latin *super* 'over' or 'beyond', *vivre* derives from the Latin *vivere* 'to live'. 'Final' derives from the Latin *finis* 'an end' or 'a limit'. Hence 'define', 'confine', and 'infinite' — without limit)

Burning Bush: anti-semitism and world history °epigrammatically puts it: 'Wealth was not equally shared among the Jews, only the resentment attaching to it'. Most perniciously of all, at the beginning of this °century certain °pseudo-scientific theories about race were developed which suggested that the Jews were degenerate (*degenerare* is the Latin word 'to depart from its kind', 'to be inclined to become base'). These theories became part of Nazi °ideology.

James Joyce (1882–1941) had many Jewish friends. When the writer fled Paris in 1940, one of these, Paul Léon, returned to Joyce's flat, sorted out his papers and placed them for safekeeping with the Irish °legation in the city. They are now held in the °National °Library of Ireland. °Tragically, Léon was caught in a °Nazi round-up of Jews shortly afterwards and sent to a concentration camp where he died in 1942. He had delayed his departure from Paris until his son had sat his baccalauréat examination

Ireland's Jewish °population is tiny — hardly more than two thousand of the °Republic's citizens are Jews. But the Jewish °contribution to Irish life is disproportionately large. Thus °currently three of the °Dáil's 166 deputies and two of the sixty or so members of the °judiciary are Jewish. While Ireland has been notably free of anti-Semitism there was a number of outbreaks of anti-Jewish violence in Limerick and Cork at the end of the last and the beginning of the present century. Arthur Griffith was anti-Jewish. Moreover, it has been said that the explicit mention of the Jewish °congregations in the article on religion in °*Bunreacht na hÉireann* was a deliberate challenge by de Valera, a °conservative Catholic, to the anti-Semitism of the °vociferous supporters of extreme °right wing Catholic thought in the thirties.

A °mordant view of Irish tolerance is given at the beginning of Joyce's *Ulysses*, the hero of which is a Dublin Jew, Leopold Bloom. Mr Deasy, Orangeman and Christian gentleman, is speaking to Stephen:

> — I just wanted to say, he said. Ireland, they say, has the honour of being the only country which never persecuted the Jews. Do you know why ?
> He frowned sternly on the bright air.
> — Why, sir ? Stephen asked, beginning to smile.
> — Because she never let them in, Mr Deasy said solemnly.

apartheid
the unique system of unequal separation of

Apartheid means 'separateness' in Afrikaans. The word gained °universal °currency after the °election of the present °National Party of Afrikaners in 1948. °Legislation

'races' established by the white authorities of South Africa solely on the basis of skin colour

was passed to cover nearly every aspect of life in order to maintain white supremacy and °economic privilege through the °disenfranchisement and oppression of the °majority black °population who constitute 85 per cent of the population. Black Africans have no °vote, while there are separate racial chambers for 'coloureds' and Indians. Every South African is °classified by race and black Africans are divided into ten groups. Race °determines where people may live, freedom of movement and access to °education and °social benefits. The United °Nations has described apartheid as a 'crime against °humanity'.

Nelson Mandela, the African °National Congress (ANC) leader, in °Leinster House to address the °Dáil, July 1990. His release earlier that year, after twenty-seven years in a South African prison, seemed to signal the ending of apartheid

apocalyptic
relating to the final destruction of the world

Apo is a Greek prefix meaning 'from' or 'un-' like the Latin *a* and *ab*. *Calyptein* is the Greek word 'to cover'. *Apocalyptic* refers °primarily to the last book of the New Testament, *The Apocalypse*, or *The Book of Revelation* as it is called in English, where a °graphic account is given of the destruction of the world. The word is frequently used nowadays to describe the conditions that would attend the unleashing of a °nuclear war. *Armageddon*, the name of the imaginary battlefield on which the climactic struggle between good and evil is conceived to take place in *The Apocalypse,* is often used as a °symbol of the destruction of the world.

'The Four Horsemen of the Apocalypse' by Dürer. Described in *The Apocalypse*, they bring war, pestilence, famine and death. In the left-hand corner death has struck down a king who is being drawn into the jaws of hell. The °dynamism of the cavalcade was without precedent in °European °graphic °art — and made Dürer famous almost overnight. 'Cavalcade' means a company of riders, and derives from *caballus* the Latin for 'horse' from which we also derive 'cavalry', 'cavalier', and 'chivalry', as well as the Irish *capall. Equus,* another Latin word for 'horse' gives us 'equestrian' (which is opposed to 'pedestrian' meaning 'someone on foot' — *pes, pedis* is the Latin word for 'foot'). The Greek for 'horse' is *hippos* — thus a hippopotamus is a river-horse (*potamos* is the Greek for 'river'), a hippodrome is a course for horse races (*dromos* is the Greek for 'race' or 'course')

apocryphal
fictitious,
sham

Apocruptein is the Greek word 'to hide away' from which 'apocryphal' is derived. Apart from the four gospels and other works in the list of recognised writings (the °canon) of the New Testament, there were writings which purported to tell us more about the life of Christ, especially his youth, which is only summarily treated in the canonical writings. These works were hidden away because they were of dubious °origin and so were called *apocrypha*. The word occurs nowadays often in discussion of the °character of °public figures: many of the stories told about them are said to be apocryphal.

apotheosis
deification; deified ideal or highest development

The apotheosis of Germanicus. In his left hand he holds the °cornucopia and Victory is placing a laurel crown upon him. (The Greeks and Romans awarded laurel crowns to victorious athletes and generals — hence the proverbial admonition to a successful person not to rest on his or her laurels)

The Greek suffix *-osis* °denotes process or condition. Thus, hypnosis is the condition resembling deep sleep °produced by hypnotism (*hypnos* is the Greek word for 'sleep'). *Theos* is the Greek word for 'god'. Among the Romans, apotheosis signified the elevation of a deceased emperor to divine honours, that is, the deification of the emperor (*deus* is the Latin word for 'god' and the *fication* element derives from *facere* the Latin word 'to make').

When an emperor died he was given a splendid funeral. In addition, a wax image resembling him in every detail was made and exposed to view in the °imperial palace for seven days. Then, with solemn religious ceremony, the image was borne through Rome to the Campus Martius where it was placed on a great pile of wood which was set alight. As the flames mounted, an eagle was released from the pile of wood, soaring, so the Romans believed, to carry the emperor's soul from earth to heaven. From that time the emperor was worshipped with Jupiter and the other gods. The practice naturally invited satire. The °philosopher Seneca, who was exiled by the Emperor Claudius, wrote a skit on the deification of that emperor called *The Apocolocyntosis* (that is, the Pumpkinification) *of Claudius*, which is extant.

We use 'apotheosis' in a figurative sense. Thus, 'In his painting of the coronation of Napoleon — possibly his °masterpiece — David apotheosized the French emperor'.

Jupiter was the Roman equivalent of Zeus, the chief of the Greek gods. The eagle — the king of the birds — was associated with Jupiter. The Romans used the eagle as a °symbol of their imperial power — a practice in which they were to be imitated (in the first instance by Charlemagne when he was crowned as the first Holy Roman Emperor in 800.) The largest planet in the solar system is named °felicitously after Jupiter.

This modern rendering of the eagle as a symbol of °state hangs on the wall behind the °rostrum in the Bundestag, Bonn

Jove, as in the exclamation 'By Jove!', derives from a form of Jupiter. 'Jovial' is derived from Jove and means 'good-humoured' because °astrologers believed those born under the °influence of the planet Jupiter were °fated to be cheerful like the sportive god; in contrast, those born under the influence of the planet Saturn were fated to be saturnine, that is, heavy and gloomy in temperament — Saturn was the old god of agriculture whom the Romans equated with Cronus (the father of Zeus), haunted by the knowledge that one of his children would usurp him. We refer to the satellites of Jupiter as the Jovian moons: 'satellite' derives from the Latin word *satelles, satellitis* meaning 'attendant' or 'servant' — hence also the expression 'a satellite °state'.

a priori

pertaining to reasoning that proceeds from causes to effects. Reasoning that proceeds from effects to causes is called *a posteriori*

A is a Latin word meaning 'from'. *Priori* is a form of the Latin word *prior* meaning 'before. *A priori* literally means 'from something previous'. *Posteriori* is a form of the Latin word *posterior* meaning 'later'. *A posteriori* literally means 'from something later'.

Logicians use the term 'a priori' to describe an argument or process of reasoning which starts from some assumed general abstract definitions or theorems and moves to conclusions which it is hoped will reveal to us some knowledge of the world. This mode of reasoning is also called 'deductive' (*de* is a Latin particle meaning 'from', *ducere* is a Latin word 'to lead'). It is typical of mathematics and science (theorems and laws lead to conclusions) and is an integral part of all theory construction.

Logicians use the term 'a posteriori' to describe an argument or process of reasoning which starts from our concrete beliefs about the world and seeks to derive more general and abstract truths from them. This mode of reasoning is also called 'inductive' (*in* is a Latin particle meaning 'in'). It is typical of °philosophic, artistic and °moral reasoning and is an intrinsic part of the preparatory work of scientific thinking also. In practice, our thinking is always a combination of both types of reasoning.

abstract
means °literally 'drawn away' (from the Latin *abs* 'away from' and *trahere* 'to draw'). In this context it means 'existing only as a °mental concept' as opposed to something *concrete*, that is, 'existing in a °mass' from the Latin *con* meaning 'with' or 'together' and *crescere* 'to grow'

logician
— a master of the science of reasoning (*logos* is the Greek word for 'word' and 'reason')

°Philosophers have used the two terms in their efforts

to understand the nature of °human knowledge. Does our knowledge of the world presuppose some given ideas or beliefs which are innate or at least not dependent on what we call experience (a priori knowledge) or is all our knowledge derived from what we call experience (a posteriori knowledge) ?

innate
means 'inborn' or 'inherent' from the Latin *in* 'in' and *natus* 'born'; *native* (Latin *nativus*) means 'born in'

Some philosophers have argued that there must be some given principles or categories present to the mind for it to begin to work at all. There are two versions of this theory. The more extreme argues that all knowledge which merits the name is simply a deduction from some innate ideas and beliefs (thus the rationalists). The other version of the theory sees these innate ideas or categories as a precondition for experience — one needs the concepts of space and time, for example, before one can understand the world in such terms. These categories are, as it were, part of the furniture of the mind but their content is filled out by experience. They make experience possible. (Thus the constructionists.)

Other philosophers (the realists) reject the idea of innate knowledge whether of ideas or categories. For them, all knowledge is derived °ultimately from experience (a posteriori). The mind constructs its °ideas and beliefs in its endeavours to know the world. There is nothing in the mind that has not come to it in its encounter with the world. But the way things are in the mind is different to the way things are in the world. For these philosophers our world is a linguistic world (*lingua* is the Latin word for 'tongue') and our language is a worldly language. What we know is the real world. Ideas and language are simply the °media in and through which we experience the world.

relativism
— the °doctrine that knowledge is relative, °i.e. it derives its meaning by reference to something else (*relativus* is a late Latin word meaning 'having reference to' which is itself derived from *referre* 'to carry back'). *Absolute* is the opposite of 'relative' and means 'existing without relation to anything else' (*absolutus* is a Latin word meaning 'loosened from')

The idealists, in contrast, believe that what we know are our ideas and that therefore we have no direct knowledge of the world. Among idealists we have three schools — rationalists, °empiricists and mixed — the last-mentioned believe that some aspects of knowledge are innate and that others derive from experience.

Behind all a priori theories of the °origins of knowledge lies the desire for °certitude and for foundations to all our thinking. In that way, such theorists seek to ensure against relativism.

archive
records or the place they are kept in

The word °originally applied to °public records: *archeion* is the Greek word for 'public office' (derived from *archein* the word 'to rule').

-archy
anarchy, autarchy, hierarchy, matriarchy, monarchy, oligarchy, patriarchy — these are all concepts whose common ending *-archy* derives from the Greek word *archein* 'to rule'

Anarchy is the absence of °government — it is disorder (*a* — *an* before a vowel — is a Greek prefix that negatives a word).

Autarchy is rule by a single °person (*autos* is 'self' in Greek).

Hierarchy is rule by priests (*hieros* means 'sacred' in Greek). In time 'hierarchy' has come to mean the group of priests who rule the Church — the bishops — and also the pyramidal structure through which °organisations are usually managed.

Matriarchy is rule by a woman or mother (*mater* is 'mother' in Latin and in Doric Greek).

Monarchy is rule by a king or queen, emperor or empress (*monos* in Greek means 'alone').

Oligarchy is rule by a small group (*oligos* means 'few' in Greek).

Patriarchy is rule by a man or father (*pater* is 'father' in Greek and in Latin).

argumentum ad hominem
a point directed against the man (rather than against his argument)

Argumentum is the Latin word for 'proof'. *Ad* is a Latin word meaning 'to' 'for' or, as here, 'against'. *Hominem* is a form of the Latin word *homo* meaning 'man'. In °logic an *argumentum ad hominem* is a fallacy because it fails to address the points made by the other person and instead attacks his or her °character or background. Nonetheless since it plays on the hearers' prejudices it is often effective.

Two ancient °orators excelled in the use of this technique — Demosthenes, the Athenian, in his speeches against King Philip of Macedon (called, therefore, the Philippics) and Cicero, the Roman, against many opponents, °legal and °political, for example his Philippics, modelled on Demosthenes, delivered against Mark Antony.

assassinate
to kill treacherously

The word is derived from groups called the Assassins, who terrorised parts of Persia and Syria in the eleventh

°century. They got their name from their practice of taking hashish (cannabis) before they attacked. The word usually °connotes a deadly attack on a °person of some authority. George Bernard Shaw in *The Rejected Statement* observed that 'Assassination is the extreme form of °censorship'.

The assassination of Julius Caesar

astronaut
an American space-traveller

Astron is the Greek word for 'star'. *Nautēs* is the Greek word for 'sailor'. An astronaut explores the stars. The Russians call their space-travellers 'cosmonauts' (*cosmos* is the Greek word for '°universe').

asylum
a place of refuge

A is a Greek prefix that negatives a word. *Sulē* is the Greek word for 'right of seizure'. The ancient Greeks set aside certain places, such as °temples, where fugitives,

The Little Scellig off the coast of Kerry, one of the most important bird sanctuaries in the country, where 22,000 pairs of gannets nest. The °state has established sixty-five wildfowl sanctuaries where the shooting of birds is prohibited. In addition, the Irish Wildbird Conservancy owns and manages a number of nature sanctuaries

whatever their crime, could claim sanctuary. Up to quite recent times the word was applied to °psychiatric hospitals and homes for handicapped people. It now usually crops up in the °media in terms of someone fleeing a repressive °regime and seeking asylum in a friendly country.

'Sanctuary' derives from the Latin *sanctuarium* 'a holy place'. Under °medieval Church law a fugitive from justice or a debtor was immune from arrest if he or she gained access to a church or other sacred place. Thus in *The Hunchback of Notre Dame,* the film based on Victor Hugo's novel about medieval Paris *Notre Dame de Paris*, Quasimodo snatches the gypsy girl Esmeralda from the square in front of the °cathedral where she is being prepared for °public execution and carries her off to the sanctuary of the cathedral — 'Sanctuary! Sanctuary!'.

Charles Laughton as the hunchback. Robespierre and many of the leaders of the French °Revolution were °deists. They turned Notre Dame into a °temple of Reason, then into a temple to the Supreme Being, and finally into a store for food. The stonework fell into disrepair. Hugo's novel, published in 1831, gave an impetus (a thrust: *impetus* means 'attack' in Latin) to the movement to restore the building. Between 1845 and 1864 the °cathedral was restored to its pristine condition (*pristinus* is a Latin word meaning '°original' or 'former')

In recent times there has come into being in the US a loose association of people willing to give refuge in their homes or churches to fugitives from °political oppression in Latin America, who have entered the US illegally. It is called the Sanctuary Movement.

atavism
a reversion to °primitive behaviour

Avus is the Latin word for 'grandfather', *atavus* is the Latin word for 'great-great-great-grandfather' i.e. ancestor. °Psychologists believe that beneath the veneer of °civilisation there lurks in every one of us a set of responses — atavistic responses — genetically transmitted from ancient times awaiting the stimulus of exceptional circumstances such as extreme danger.

(*Avunculus*, from which we derive 'avuncular', as in 'He had an avuncular manner', is the Latin word for 'uncle'. The *unculus* suffix denotes a diminutive form of the word it is attached to — in this case *avus*. *Avunculus* literally means 'little grandfather'. *Homo* is the Latin word for 'man'. *Homunculus* means 'a tiny man' or 'dwarf'. The English 'uncle' comes from the French *oncle* which comes from the Latin *avunculus*.)

atom
in general, the smallest particle of matter

A is a Greek prefix that negatives a word; *tom* comes from the Greek word *temnein* 'to cut'. An atom is that which cannot be cut further. The Greek °philosopher, Democritus, developed an atomic theory 2,500 years ago: atoms were the basic building blocks of both body and soul. The story is told that Democritus put out his own eyes so that he could devote himself more fully to philosophical contemplation. He was accused of insanity and the great doctor, Hippocrates (who enunciated the famous Hippocratic oath that doctors have ever since accepted as their basic °code) was sent to examine his disorder. The physician did so and afterwards declared that Democritus was not mad but his accusers were.

Walton

°Modern physics is based on atomic theory. However, °scientists discovered that what they called 'atoms' could be split — they discovered a °sub-atomic world. (It was an Irish scientist, E.T.S. Walton, who set the course for

Cockcroft

the development of nuclear physics when, along with Sir John Douglas Cockcroft, he developed the first nuclear particle generator in 1931 — a feat for which they jointly won the Nobel Prize for Physics in 1951.)

Sub-atomic is °etymological nonsense (because it presupposes that that which cannot be cut further *can* be cut further). Scientists save the concept by defining an atom as the smallest subdivision of an element that retains the chemical properties of the element. At the sub-atomic level we find the densest part of the atom — the nucleus, derived from *nux, nucis* the Latin word for a nut.

Ek is a Greek word meaning 'out': *-ectomy*, a suffix meaning 'a cutting out', occurs in surgery °e.g. appendectomy (a cutting out of the appendix), hysterectomy (a cutting out of the womb; *hystera* is the Greek word for *uterus* which is the Latin word for 'womb'; *hysteria* is a °state of giddy emotionalism the Greeks associated with women — the Greeks in general were male °chauvinists), mastectomy (a cutting out of the breast — *mastos* is 'breast' in Greek).

-itis is a Greek suffix indicating 'disease' or 'inflammation' — hence 'appendicitis' and 'mastitis'. *Algos* is a Greek word for 'pain', hence 'neuralgia' (a pain along a nerve — *neuron* is the Greek word for 'nerve') and 'nostalgia' (°originally home-sickness — *nostos* is the Greek word for 'a return home'). An analgesic is a pain-killer (*a* — *an* before a vowel — is a Greek particle that negatives a word; an *anodyne* is also a pain-killer — *odynē* is another Greek word for 'pain').

auspices
patronage

The future, although often referred to as foreseeable — 'the foreseeable future' — is not foreseeable. People nonetheless seek reassurance about the future, especially when they are about to embark on some great enterprise. In ancient times they looked for signs from the gods who were believed to control everything that happens.

The kings of Rome had the power to consult the gods by means of *auspicia* (plural form of *auspicium*, derived from *avis*, the Latin word for 'bird' and *spicere*, the Latin word 'to observe'), literally 'bird-watchings'.

Typically, the king would go in the middle of the night to a high place, usually a hill, accompanied by an *augur*, a professional interpreter of signs. They would pitch a tent (*tabernaculum*) there. At day-break the king would observe the pattern of the flight of birds across a pre-selected tract of sky called a *templum*. The augur interpreted these signs (*omen, ominis* is the Latin word for 'sign' from which we derive 'ominous') declaring them to be either good omens ('auspicious') or bad omens ('inauspicious').

Auspices were taken before any °major proceeding. Action followed only when the auspices (that is, the gods) were favourable. To proceed under unfavourable auspices would be deemed sacrilegious. When the *auspicia* were duly observed, the augur declared them *inaugurata* and the battle or other action began. Thus 'inaugurate' is a solemn, even portentous, word for 'commence', which in turn is a solemn, and often portentous, word for 'begin' (as in 'Uncle Peadar commenced shuffling the cards before he inaugurated the poker session').

A Roman temple

°Originally, therefore, certain activities were carried out under the auspices of the gods. 'Auspices', which has the same meaning as 'aegis', has suffered the same °degeneration: nowadays a concert may be held under the auspices of the Royal Dublin Society.

Roman temples were so called because they were often built on hills where auspices had been taken, the word for the tract of sky being observed, *templum*, having been transferred to the building. Furthermore their shape was said to mirror the shape of the tent set up the night before the auspices were taken.

organ
Organon is the Greek word for 'a tool', which was applied to those parts of the body that carried out a particular function — thus the eye is the organ of sight, the nose is the organ of smell, the stomach is the organ of digestion. An organisation is a unit made up of various organs

Roman augury also sometimes involved the examination of the internal organs of birds and other animals for signs. There were various ways of determining whether a sign was good or bad — for instance, anything coming from the left-hand side would be regarded as unlucky or sinister (*sinister* is the Latin word for the left hand in contrast to the favoured right hand — *dexter*, from which we derive *dextrous* meaning 'adroit').

The Romans also resorted to °prophecy and astrology. Their most famous source of prophecy was the Cumaean Sibyl, a prophetess who lived in a cave, whose prophecies

science/scientific derives from the Latin *scire* 'to know' and °denotes any systematically formulated body of knowledge

in written form — the famous Sibylline verses — were long revered by the Romans. Astrology, the study of the stars based on the view that the movements of the stars determined human affairs, was an eastern °influence (*aster, astros* is the Greek word for 'star'; the *logy* suffix derives from *logos* the Greek word for 'word', 'reason', 'account'; astrology is distinguished from *astronomy,* the scientific study of the stars — *nomos* is the Greek word for 'law' and astronomy literally means 'the laws of the stars').

balance of payments a record, usually on a yearly basis, of all transactions involving foreign exchange: (a) °*current transactions* that is, exports and imports (visible and invisible), international transfers (largely °EC fund payments but also °emigrants' remittances), °repatriation of profits by foreign firms, and interest payments on official foreign debt, and (b) °*capital transactions* (official borrowing and movements of °private capital). The term is used, even by °economists, usually to describe the state of *current* transactions. By definition, an overall balance is achieved between current and capital transactions

Ireland cannot °produce everything its citizens demand. It must therefore rely on imports. (*Portare* is the Latin word 'to carry'; *in* — *im* before p — is a Latin prefix meaning 'in' so an import is something carried in to a country; *ex* is a Latin prefix meaning 'out' so an export is something carried out of a country.)

Exports and imports may be visible or invisible. A visible export may take the form, for example, of frozen beef or computers. An invisible export may take the form of tourism because tourists who spend their money in Ireland bring money into the country in the same way as a visible export does; it may also take the form, for example, of the sale of financial services abroad.

If visible imports exceed visible exports, there is a *trade °deficit* (this has occurred in Ireland almost every year since 1920). If visible exports exceed visible imports, there is a *trade surplus* (this has happened in Ireland in the late eighties).

If, as in recent years in the case of Ireland, a country runs a balance of payments deficit on current account, this must be financed by official foreign borrowing, in the absence of private capital inflows. As a result, there can be a build up of foreign debt with adverse effects on living standards (because the interest payments and capital repayments must be made by the °exchequer) and on the value of the currency (because foreign financiers observe the strain on the economy).

Dublin Port. Almost 4,000 ships arrive there each year

bandwagon
the movement towards a °person or set of °ideas gaining °popular support

A bandwagon was a highly decorated wagon carrying a band of musicians used in America especially to draw crowds in a circus parade. In °modern °political parlance, 'to jump (or climb) on the bandwagon' means to throw in one's lot with a politician or political party doing very well in the opinion °polls.

barbarian
an abusive term applied °originally to foreigners but now to any brutish person

The ancient Greeks, though °politically divided into °numerous small city-states, were united by a common °culture, and especially by the Greek language. The languages of other peoples seemed harsh to them — they felt strangers were saying 'Bar! Bar!' all the time. Hence the word barbarian.

The Romans and other °imperialists adopted the word (and 'barbarous' derived from it) because it implied a gratifying cultural superiority and provided a justification for attacks on inferior cultures. Its ugliest offshoot was the °Nazis' concept of *untermenschen* ('subhumans' — *unter* is the German word for 'under', *menschen* is the German word for 'people'); they applied this term to the peoples of eastern Europe whose lands they wanted to rob to provide *Lebensraum* ('living room') for Germans.

bicameral
having two °legislative chambers

Bi is derived from *bis* the Latin word meaning 'twice' (thus a bicycle is a two-wheeler). *Camera* is the Latin word for 'room'. Legislative bodies are either unicameral i.e. having one House, as in Denmark, or bicameral, as in Ireland where we have a Lower House, the °Dáil, and an Upper House, the °Seanad.

Bicameralism has its °origins in the fact that at Westminster the lords spiritual and °temporal (the bishops and the peers) met in one House — the House of Lords — and the commoners in another House — the House of °Commons. With the growth of °democracy, the House of Lords has been left with only the vestiges of power and its purpose has been questioned. Our Seanad is subject to a similar °analysis.

bilateral
between two parties

Bi is derived from *bis* the Latin word meaning 'twice'. *Latus, lateris* is the Latin word for 'side'. The word is frequently used in the °context of foreign affairs. Thus Ireland has a bilateral agreement with Zambia whereby we aid that country by promoting certain agricultural developments there.

Multilateral aid agreements, where there are many parties to the agreements (*multus* means 'many' in Latin) — and which we also have — allow more ambitious aid programmes to be undertaken but they diffuse the sense of responsibility of the donor countries (*donare* is the Latin word 'to give as a gift' from which we also derive 'donation').

In deciding how best to use our aid funds, the Department of Foreign Affairs must weigh up the advantages and disadvantages of these two kinds of agreements in regard to proposed projects.

Unilateral means 'one-sided' (*unus* is 'one' in Latin), for example a unilateral declaration of independence, unilateral disarmament.

blitzkrieg/blitz
a sudden, overwhelming attack

Blitz is the German word for 'lightning' and *krieg* the German for 'war'. The term °originally described the combination of rapid panzer (tank) and air attacks that °characterised the German successes in the opening stages of the second world war. Nowadays an advertising agency may plan a blitz on °television for a client's °product.

bona fide
sincere(ly)

Bonus is the Latin word for 'good'. *Fides* is the Latin word for 'faith' or 'trust'. 'Bona fide' means 'in good faith'. Thus if a dealer were to offer you a new car for £100, you might rightly wonder if it were a bona fide offer.

'Bona fides' means 'good faith' in the sense of genuineness. Thus, 'As °president of the °Plutocratic Party you were perfectly right to question the bona fides of a man who, having spent many decades trying to °organise the °*lumpenproletariat,* now offers his services to the party's °public relations department.'

bourgeoisie
the middle class

Bourgeois is a French word meaning 'townsman' from *bourg* (German *burg*) meaning 'town' or 'city' °e.g. Strasbourg. Townspeople typically lived by trade and so the term *bourgeoisie* came to mean that class who came in the °social scale between the workers (the lower class) and the landowners/°aristocrats (the upper class). Marx used it to describe those who were not °proletarians (wage-earning workers who had no assets apart from their children). The bourgeoisie, according to Marx, were those who owned the means of °production (land, raw °materials and machinery). They exploited the workers and controlled the °state whose °constitution was framed to maintain their control.

history
derives from the Greek *historia* meaning 'what has been learned by inquiry' or the statement of that. 'Histrionic' means 'theatrical' and derives from the Latin word for an actor *histrio, histrionis*

History, according to Marx, was climaxing in a violent struggle between the proletarians and the bourgeoisie — the class struggle — which the proletarians were bound to win because of the laws governing the °economy: the fierce °competitiveness of the °capitalist system would inexorably concentrate the means of production in fewer and fewer hands so that capitalists would progressively eliminate themselves, even if the proletarians did not precipitate the process by a °revolution.

boycott
a non-violent means of coercing someone by combining to cut him or her off from °social and business contacts

In 1880, at the height of the Land League's struggle against landlordism, Captain Boycott, a land agent of Lord Erne, refused to reduce rents by a quarter following a bad harvest. His Mayo tenants were outraged. They °ostracised him: no labourer would work for him, no servant would cook for him, no one would pay him rent. Six policemen had to be assigned to guard him. When he brought in workers from the north to save his crops, a large body of troops had to stand by to guard them. After six months Boycott left his home, Lough Mask House, near Ballinrobe, Co. Mayo, for England with his family.

This form of coercion — called 'boycott' after the °egregious captain — was then applied successfully by the Land League against tenants who made a bid for farms from which the occupants had been evicted.

The departure of the Boycott relief volunteers from Lough Mask House, December 1880

Brechtian

in the manner of the German dramatist Bertolt Brecht (1898–1956)

epic
derives from the Greek *epos* 'a song'. Epics were originally long, narrative poems about a hero or band of heroes. A *saga* is a long prose narrative of the achievements of a family or king, of the kind written in medieval times in Scandinavia (*saga* is Old Norse for 'narrative')

Brecht, like the Irish Nobel prizewinner Samuel Beckett, is a °major figure in °modern drama. He swung away from the naturalism that °dominated European theatre after Ibsen and which sought, through carefully °articulated realistic scenes, to draw the spectator °subjectively into the action. Brecht sought to develop an 'epic theatre' in which the play consisted of a series of loosely connected scenes through which the spectator was invited to consider °objectively the °social and °political complexity of real situations.

In the twenties and thirties Brecht collaborated as librettist with the German composer Kurt Weill (1900–1950). Their best-known work is *The Threepenny Opera*, a modernisation of John Gay's *The Beggar's Opera*; it was turned into a film several times and features the hit-song 'Mack the Knife'.

Brecht, as a °communist (though not a member of the Communist Party), had to flee °Nazi Germany. He returned in 1949 and settled in East Berlin. Some of his plays, °e.g. *The Preventible Rise of Arturo Ui*, attack both Hitlerism and °capitalism. His great period was between 1937 and 1948 when he wrote *The Life of Galileo*, *The Good Woman of Setzuan*, *Mother Courage*, and *The Caucasian Chalk Circle*.

Brussels
the °centre of the °European Community

The headquarters of the °European Council and the °European Commission are both in the Belgian °capital and so 'Brussels' is used in the °media to describe thinking on policy at the highest level in the EC. More particularly, the European Commission has its headquarters in a building in Brussels called the Berlaymont. 'The Berlaymont' is sometimes used to describe thinking on policy at the highest levels of the Commission. The °Court of Justice of the European Community and the °European Investment Bank (EIB) are °located in Luxembourg. The °European °Parliament meets in °plenary sessions in Strasbourg (committees of the parliament meet in Brussels).

The Berlaymont

budget
the financial statement made in the °Dáil at the beginning of each year by the Minister for Finance

Bougette is an old French word meaning 'a bag'. In Britain, where the usage °originated, it is customary for the Chancellor of the °Exchequer to bring his yearly financial proposals in a leather bag to the House of °Commons.

Albert Reynolds, TD, Minister for Finance (1989—)

conventional means 'depending on the agreement of different parties'. *Con* is a Latin particle meaning 'with' and *venire* is the Latin word 'to come' — a convention is an assembly of people or a coming together of minds — an agreement

In Ireland the budgetary process begins in summer each year with the preparation of estimates of expenditure for the next year by each of the °civil service departments, under the close surveillance of the Department of Finance.

Expenditure is of two kinds, °current and °capital. *Current expenditure* is the money the departments spend from day to day on purchases of goods and services or on transfer payments (such as pensions or children's allowances). *Capital expenditure* is the money they spend on investment goods — roads, hospitals, ships, school buildings and the like — and on capital transfers (such as grants and loans to industry). The estimates provide separately for both kinds of expenditure.

The conventional wisdom of financial management °dictates that one should pay one's day to day expenses out of one's current income and that in planning the year's expenditure one should set forth those expenditures clearly. It also dictates that if one must borrow, it is prudent to do so only for capital projects capable of returning at least the cost of repaying the capital sum and the interest payable on it, and that in planning the year's expenditure one should set forth such expenditures clearly too.

The °government gets the money it needs from sales of goods or services but mostly from °taxation and from borrowing at home and abroad. In his budget speech the Minister for Finance reviews the °national °economy and outlines the measures the government intends to take in regard to it in the coming year; he likewise reviews the °social and °cultural services. Then he indicates his proposals for taxation and borrowing.

In recent years Ministers for Finance have sought to improve the budgetary process. The °traditional budget had two °major weaknesses. One was the dispersal of various items of expenditure relating to particular °objectives throughout the Book of Estimates so that it was difficult to see all that the government was doing about a particular problem °e.g. youth employment. The ordering of the estimates into programmes is an attempt to deal with that.

The other weakness was the treatment of certain expenditures on a yearly basis when the assessment of how effective they were needed to be made over a period of years, e.g. industrial development. *Multi-annual budgets,* that is, budgets that project income and expenditure over a number of years (usually three) is an attempt to deal with that weakness. Multi-annual budgets, however, are extremely difficult to prepare in volatile economic conditions (*volare* is the Latin word 'to fly'). Multi-annual budgets are based on °national plans which project over a number of years not only budgetary developments but also developments in various °sectors of the economy.

sector
Like *segment*, 'sector' derives from the Latin word *secare* 'to cut'. The economy may be divided in terms of control: the *private sector* is that part of the economy controlled by private individuals and firms, the *public sector* is that part controlled by the public service. It may also be divided in terms of types of activity, for example the transport sector, the industrial sector, the agricultural sector

A *current budget deficit* occurs when the Minister for Finance provides in the coming year for a greater amount of current expenditure than he expects in income (mainly from taxes). The deficits are met by borrowing (*deficere* is the Latin word 'to fail'), which it is anticipated will be repaid out of growth in the economy. The °total current and capital borrowing by the °exchequer is called the *Exchequer Borrowing Requirement.*

A *mini-budget* is a number of °fiscal changes either to the income or the expenditure components of the budget, or both, e.g. increased tax on petrol, introduced some time after the budget, on a number of occasions in the past, to correct budgetary performance (*mini* is a Latin particle meaning 'small').

C

cabal
a secret faction

orally
Os, oris is the Latin word for 'mouth'. *Auris* is the Latin word for 'ear' — hence 'aural', *Nasus* is the Latin word for 'nose' — hence 'nasal'

Cabala is a Hebrew word meaning 'secret knowledge' and °denotes instruction about the mystical significance of certain combinations of numbers, words and letters which the Jews transmitted orally from father to son. The French used the word *cabale* for 'a group of foreigners'. The word 'cabal' entered English to describe Charles II's group of advisers in the early 1670s — Clifford, Arlington, Buckingham, Ashley, Lauderdale — and was derived from their initials C,A,B,A,L. To this cabal is traced the °origins of the °cabinet.

the cabinet
the government

'Cabinet' is the diminutive of cabin, which derives from the late Latin *capanna*, and means a little or inner room: by transference it means an inner group. The °executive powers of °government are exercised through either a cabinet or a °presidential system. Our government, based on the British model, is a cabinet one. While °*Bunreacht na hÉireann* places the °Taoiseach in full control of the government, it is the government acting collectively as a cabinet that is responsible for its actions to °Dáil Éireann.

(The principle of collective cabinet responsibility was embraced by the cabinet of George III because that °monarch would take individual members of the cabinet aside after a meeting and question them assiduously about who proposed what and who said what, thus exposing individual members of the cabinet to external pressure and undermining group solidarity.)

In the US the heads of the twelve °major executive departments (for example the Secretary of °State) are appointed by the president with the consent of the °Senate. They are known as the cabinet when they act in a body to advise the president.

Some presidents use their cabinets extensively. Others deal with the various members separately. Others rely on groups of personal advisers (the informality of this arrangement has led to such advisers being called 'the kitchen cabinet'). A head of government in a cabinet system who °dominates the cabinet to such an extent that its role becomes °*de facto* advisory rather than executive is said to have a presidential style.

In the European Commission each Commissioner has a small group of advisers, called his or her cabinet, to help him or her with his or her functions. In this °context the word is given a French pronunciation (cabinay) because it derives from the practice in French government. The chief adviser is known as the *chef de cabinet*.

cache
a hidden store (of arms or treasure)

Cacher is the French word 'to hide'.

candidate
one who offers himself or herself for °public °office or at an examination or °election

Candidatus is a Latin word meaning 'dressed in white'. Those who offered themselves for a public office or honour in ancient Rome presented themselves dressed in brilliant white to imply that they were without stain.

capitalism
an °economic system in which the °production of goods and the provision of services is undertaken almost entirely by °private owners — individuals and firms — who from sales in a free market derive profits for themselves, the wages of their workers, the costs of raw materials and machinery, and compensation for the risk-taking involved in their enterprise. Its chief °characteristic is

Capitalis is a Latin word meaning 'relating to the chief (principal) thing', derived from the Latin word for the head *caput, capitis*. 'Capital', meaning the stock (including property and equipment) and/or money used in carrying on a business, comes from a shortening of the expression 'capital stock'.

Capitalism has existed wherever an individual produced some good or service and bartered or sold it. Its most colourful agents were those itinerant traders who through the ages hauled goods from a point of supply to distant points of demand (*iter, itineris* is the Latin word for 'a journey'). Up to °modern times trade was very modest. For example, it has been calculated that in the early part of the fourteenth °century the °total volume of goods coming into France each year on one of the °major trade routes would not fill a modern freight train.

The industrial °revolution transformed the volume of trade and placed capitalists rather than landowners at the centre of °economic activity. It also drew °masses of labourers from the countryside into the towns and cities

that there is no °central °determination of either the °allocation of resources or the rewards for work

Adam Smith

to become wage-earners (°proletarians), and so transformed society. This is the °phenomenon which is referred to by the technical term 'capitalism' which Marx made the °object of his °analysis.

The great Scottish economist and °philosopher, Adam Smith, in *The Wealth of Nations*, published in 1776, examined how the wealth of a country — meaning the wealth available to *everyone* in a country — might be increased. He concluded that capitalism, operating ideally, was a °cornucopia: capitalists increased their own wealth endlessly by producing endlessly, but at the most °competitive prices, what everyone wanted. Society, he felt, should °organise itself in such a way that capitalism would flourish.

Capitalism requires the right to °private property. Since its efficient operation requires the market conditions of free trade, °governments should follow °*laisser faire* policies and limit themselves largely to internal and external security and to the refereeing of market operations (by, for example, preventing °monopolies and restrictive practices). The freedom capitalists required for themselves had in principle to be extended to everyone — everyone had to be free to become a capitalist, and so freedom is seen as a °concomitant of capitalism (hence the expression 'the free capitalist societies').

Industrial capitalism operated in a far from ideal way. The 'dark Satanic mills' (William Blake) produced immense °human misery as well as goods. Soon vehement °critics arose to attack the whole system — none more powerfully or effectively than Karl Marx. Marx laid down the theoretical basis for the great °rival system to capitalism — °communism. With the °Bolshevik revolution in Russia in 1917 and the abolition there of private property, the communist system began to be put to °empirical tests.

Ireland is a small open economy (open to world trade) within the capitalist system. Yet, like most economies in Western Europe, it is also a mixed economy, that is, part of the means of production is in the hands of capitalists and part is controlled by the °state. In addition, the state in a mixed economy takes a large number of indirect measures (regulations and incentives) to direct the economy.

carpet-bagger
a 'blow-in' on the make

After the defeat of the Southern °states in the American °civil war, 1861-65, there were rich °political and commercial pickings for the °victors. The resentful Southerners, seeing numerous Yankee adventurers descending on their cities and towns with their travelling-bags, made of carpet-like °material, dubbed them 'carpet-baggers'. The term is now used of American politicians who run for office outside their home states.

inhabitant
derives from the Latin word *habitare* 'to dwell'. A *habitat* is the natural home of an animal or plant

Yankees or *Yanks* was a term first applied to the inhabitants of the New England states. In the °civil war it was applied to the Northerners generally. Later in °Europe it came to be applied to all Americans (as in 'The Yanks are coming' in the George M. Cohan World War I song). The °origin of the word is uncertain. It probably comes from *Janke*, a diminutive form of the Dutch word *Jan* (John). The Dutch were the first settlers in New England — hence New York was °originally called New Amsterdam.

The Southern °Confederate states were °popularly referred to as 'Dixie'. The origin of the word is uncertain. It possibly derives from the surname 'Dixon' because the line that separated the slave states from the free states was drawn during the years 1763 to 1767 by two surveyors called Charles Mason and Jeremiah Dixon — the famous Mason-Dixon line.

carte blanche
full discretionary power

A French expression meaning literally 'a white card', it is used of a blank paper signed by a person with authority and left to be filled in by the receiver. It gives the receiver a free hand.

Cassandra
someone who expresses gloomy views about the future but is not believed

Cassandra was the daughter of Priam, the king of Troy. One day when she was asleep in the °temple Apollo appeared and promised her the gift of °prophecy if she would make love to him. Cassandra, after accepting the gift, went back on the bargain. Apollo persisted, begging her to give him just one kiss. As she did so he spat into her mouth, thus ensuring no one would ever again believe what she said. So when Cassandra announced at a °critical point in the °Trojan war that the wooden horse left by the Greeks outside the walls of Troy contained armed men no one believed her.

casus belli
something put forward as a justification of war

Casus is the Latin word for 'occasion' (and is to be distinguished from *causa*, the Latin word for 'cause' or 'case'). *Belli* is a form of *bellum*, the Latin word for 'war' and means 'of war'. Leaders intent on war often feel a °political need to justify an attack — before their own people so as to marshal support for the war effort or before the rest of the world so as to °isolate their victim. Thus in September 1939 the Germans arranged for an attack on some of their own installations near the Polish border to provide themselves with a *casus belli*. SS men in Polish Army uniforms carried out the attack, and drugged concentration camp inmates, °cynically code-named 'canned goods', were left dying as 'casualties'. The cause of the war was something quite different.

A *belligerent* is someone who wages war (*gerere* is the Latin word 'to wage'). It is also used to describe the characteristics of such a person.

A *bellicose* person is also aggressive but usually in speech (*bellicosus* is a Latin word meaning 'war-like').

casualty
derives from *cadere* the Latin word 'to fall' — casualties are the dead and injured in a war or accident; we use 'fatalities' for the dead alone

character(istics)
derives from the Greek word *kharaktēr* meaning 'a stamp' — hence the meanings ranging from 'letter' to 'the set of qualities and habits that differentiates one person from another'

catastrophe
a sudden calamity

Kata is a Greek word meaning 'down'. *Strophē* is a Greek word meaning 'turning'. A catastrophe is 'a down-turning (of the wheel of °fortune)'. In Greek tragedy the catastrophe was the crucial turning-point in the plot.

A *cataclysm* is a violent upheaval that is worse than a catastrophe (*kataclusmos*, literally meaning 'downpour', is the word used in the Greek version of the °Bible for the Flood; *diluvium* is the Latin word for 'flood' and *ante* is a Latin word meaning 'before' — *antediluvian* therefore means 'before the Flood' or 'very old-fashioned' as in 'The °office procedures were antediluvian: every Friday afternoon the supervisor stood at his writing desk while the °clerks queued to receive their wages').

A *disaster* is a calamity (*dis* is a Latin prefix meaning

The Cataclysm (Gustave Doré)

'bad'; *astrum* is the Latin word for 'star' — a disaster is an action carried out under an unlucky star; *dys* is the corresponding Greek prefix to the Latin *dis* and the word *dysfunctional*, often used in the °analysis of systems, pertains to the impaired or abnormal functioning of an °organ or system).

A *tragedy* is an unhappy story or turn of events usually involving death. *Tragōidia* is a Greek word meaning 'goat-song' or 'goat-ode'. Drama °originated in ancient Greece when groups of men joined together in a chorus to sing poetry; they wore goat-skins, possibly with the head on top (a feature later formalised in the °*persona* or actor's mask). Drama was born when one member of the chorus stepped forward and began to argue against the story being told by the chorus. He was called 'the protagonist' (*prōtos* is 'first' in Greek, *agōnistēs* is a Greek word for 'combatant' — hence the °modern meaning of protagonist as 'champion' or '°advocate'). Later a second member of the chorus stepped forward to argue with the protagonist. He was known as the 'antagonist' (*anti* is a Greek word meaning 'against' — hence the modern meaning of antagonist as 'opponent'). Later other °actors entered into the dialogue. The chorus eventually disappeared.

Tragedy

The earliest dramas presented °grave and solemn stories — they were tragedies. The tragedy was brought on by an act of °hubris leading to a °crisis which ended in a catastrophe. Tragedies aimed at having a *cathartic* effect. *Catharsis* is a Greek word meaning a 'cleansing' or 'purification'. The °philosopher Aristotle in his *Poetics* defines tragedy as follows:

> Tragedy is a representation of an action that deserves serious attention, that is complete in itself, that is large in range. It uses language enriched by a variety of artistic devices appropriate to the various parts of the play. It is presented in terms of action not narration. By means of pity and fear it brings about the purgation (*catharsis*) of those emotions.

Comedy

As a modern °psychological term, 'catharsis' is used to describe the purging of the psyche that occurs when, through psychoanalysis, repressed thoughts and emotions are brought to the surface of the consciousness.

In contrast to a tragedy, a *comedy* is pleasant and humorous (*kōmos* is a Greek word for 'revel').

caucus
an inner group (either formal or informal) that seeks to determine how a larger °political group or party will act

The ending *-us* would suggest a Latin °origin but the word was coined in America. One explanation of its °etymology is as follows. A short time before the °Revolution there, the caulkers of Boston (caulkers were men who waterproofed boats and ships; caulk is pronounced 'cawk') had a dispute with some British soldiers in which a number of °civilians were killed. Meetings were later held at the caulkers' house (caulk-house) to decide on what further action should be taken against the soldiers.

In the US 'caucus' describes a meeting of party leaders and activists; caucuses are sometimes used for the selection of party °candidates. In Canada 'caucus' is used to describe a whole °parliamentary party, for example the °Liberal caucus, rather than an inner group.

('°Parliamentary party' describes those members of a political party who are members of parliament. Thus the parliamentary Labour Party denotes those members of the Labour Party who are °TDs, °Senators and MEPs — members of the °European Parliament.)

El Caudillo
The leader

Franco

Juan Carlos I

El is the masculine form of 'the' in Spanish — thus El Greco ('The Greek') is a description, not a name, of the great painter. *Caudillo* is the Spanish word for 'leader' derived from the Latin word *capitellum*, the diminutive form of *caput, capitis* 'a head'. In September 1936 General Francisco Franco was appointed head of the unified command of the armed forces of °Nationalist Spain and hailed as 'Generalissimo'. The other generals in the °*junta* that appointed him were not all agreed that in addition he should have °civilian powers. The draft °decree finally accepted by the generals spoke of him as '°Head of Government of the Spanish °state' but the published decree spoke of him as assuming 'all the powers of the Spanish state'. Franco immediately presented himself as °head of state.

The blueshirted °fascist falangists, who admired the German °dictator, Der Führer (Leader) Adolf Hitler, and the Italian dictator, Il Duce (Leader) Benito Mussolini, assented to the appointment and hailed Franco as *El Caudillo*. To maintain the support of the °monarchists who wished to see a king restored as head of state, the wily general maintained a certain °ambiguity as to whether he was head of government or head of state, and if either, for how long. When the Spanish civil war ended, Franco continued to serve as El Caudillo.

In 1947 Spain °legally became a monarchy but it was not until 1969 that Franco named Juan Carlos as his successor as head of state. It was a further six years before Franco died (1975). When Juan Carlos I was installed as King of Spain in 1975, he reintroduced °democracy.

caveat emptor
let the buyer beware

Caveat is a form of the Latin word *cavere* 'to beware'. *Emptor* is the Latin word for 'buyer'. *Caveat emptor* is the °traditional seller's charter. However, °modern consumer protection °legislation has placed an onus (*onus* is 'burden' in Latin) on the seller to carry a higher degree of responsibility than before for enabling the buyer to evaluate the goods or service offered for sale. A caveat is a warning. In the expression 'I would like to enter (or put in) a caveat', a lawyer formally indicates that no step should be taken in a particular matter without giving him or her due notice.

cenotaph
a monument to a °person whose body lies elsewhere

The Cenotaph, Whitehall, London

Kenos, transliterated *cenos*, is the Greek word for 'empty'. *Taphos* is the Greek word for 'tomb'.

A *sarcophagus* is a stone coffin, usually an elaborately carved one. The most famous sarcophagus of °modern times is probably that of Napoleon in Les Invalides in Paris. (*Sarx, sarcos* is the Greek word for 'flesh', *phagein* is the Greek word 'to eat'. The Greeks made coffins of a limestone thought to consume the flesh of corpses.)

A *mausoleum* is a magnificent tomb. Mausolos was a wealthy fourth °century BC Greek °tyrant who set out to build a tomb for himself in Halicarnassus that would be (as it did become) a wonder of the world. The expense of building the mausoleum was so great that a

Lenin and Stalin on display in Moscow. Stalin's body was removed within a short period

Greek °philosopher, on seeing it, exclaimed 'How much money turned into stones!' The *-eum* Latin suffix °indicates place — compare °museum. Considerable remains of the tomb are displayed in the British °Museum. The most famous modern mausoleum is probably the Lenin Mausoleum in Red Square in Moscow where Lenin's embalmed body is displayed.

census
an °official counting of the °population under various °statistical headings

Censere is a Latin word 'to estimate' or 'to tax'. A census, with the registers of people and property derived from it, was °originally an aid to °taxation. A census aims at a complete enumeration of the population. The first successful census of population in Ireland was taken in 1841.

The °major instrument used in taking the census is the census form filled out by each householder. The °Central Statistics Office, which conducts the census, usually issues a preliminary report within four to six months of the census date. Over the following years various volumes appear on °topics such as population (by area, sex and conjugal condition), industries, housing.

conjugal
means 'relating to marriage' from the Latin *con* meaning 'with' and *jugum* 'a yoke'—as the Romans saw it a married couple was yoked together

The results of the census are of great value to officials in the °public service who must plan the provision of services. A planning team may contain a *demographer*. Demography is concerned with the study of population statistics (*dēmos* is the Greek word for 'people' and *graphein* is the Greek word 'to write').

The most famous census in history was that conducted by the Romans in Palestine which brought Joseph and Mary to °Bethlehem.

The two officials at Rome who carried out a census were called 'censors'. Because they had the power to exclude unworthy °persons from the list of citizens, it seemed natural that over the course of time they should be given the duties of ensuring that the public and °private lives of every citizen conformed to the *mos maiorum* — the °traditional standards. The office of censor became the most revered and the most dreaded in the Roman °state. It is from this aspect of their functions that we derive our ideas of 'censor' and 'censorship'.

ceteris paribus
other things being equal

Ceteris is a form of the Latin word *ceteri* meaning 'other'. *Paribus* is a form of the Latin word *par, paris* meaning 'equal'. The expression is used to °isolate the condition which will decide an issue when other conditions are even. Thus, 'The appointment of a member of the board of a °state-sponsored body is a function of the minister to whose Department the body reports. Where a number of well-qualified people is available, the minister will appoint, *ceteris paribus*, a supporter of the °government'.

Et cetera (*etc*) means 'and so on' (*et* is a Latin word meaning 'and' and *cetera* is a form of the word meaning 'other things').

When people or things are equal, they may be said to be 'on a par' or 'comparable' (the prefix *com* is derived from the Latin word *cum* meaning 'with'). When they are not equal, there is a *disparity* between them (*dis* is a Latin prefix that negatives a word). Industrial disputes sometimes hinge on whether one group of workers should get *parity* with another (i.e. the same wages and conditions).

The expression *primus inter pares* 'first among equals' is used by many Christians to °denote the position of Peter among the Apostles and therefore of the Pope among bishops. By extension it is applied to anyone in a group of equals to whom the others accord a °moral authority. (*Primus* means 'first' in Latin, *inter* is a Latin word meaning 'among'.) However, Catholics maintain that the Pope's position is one of primacy in authority as well as in honour. The expression was used °originally to describe the Emperor Augustus's position in the state after he had restored peace to the Roman Empire (to maintain the formality that he had restored the °Republic).

charisma
the quality that makes a °person or the °office he or she holds impressive to others

Charisma is the Greek word for 'grace' or 'gift'. It was used in the early Church to denote the spiritual gifts of the Holy Spirit, such as the gifts of tongues, °prophecy, healing. In °modern times the charismatic movement, a largely non-denominational religious movement, is based on a belief in those gifts. In °secular usage, the word is often associated with magnetic leaders such as John F. Kennedy, Charles de Gaulle, Martin Luther King.

chauvinist
a °person who is excessively °patriotic

Nicholas Chauvin was a simple-minded French soldier who had served in Napoleon's army. Content with his modest °military honours and small pension, he retained an unshakeable pride in the defeated Emperor and the glory of French arms. In °modern times the term 'male chauvinist' is applied to men who resist the claims of women to equality with men.

In Britain in the 1880s the term 'jingoism' came into use to describe the same attitude as chauvinism. It was derived from the phrase 'by Jingo' in a °popular song supporting aggressive moves by Britain against Russia:

We don't want to fight, but, by Jingo, if we do,
We've got the ships, we've got the men, and got the money too.

chron-
anachronism, chronic, chronicle, chronology, synchronise — these are all words whose common element *chron* derives from *chronos*, the Greek word for 'time'

An *anachronism* is something out of harmony with the time referred to (*ana* is a Greek word meaning 'backwards'). Thus, 'Hugh O'Neill could easily have beaten the English at Kinsale if he had used tanks'.

Chronic means lingering, or inveterate, for example 'chronic asthma'.

A *chronicle* is a narrative of events as they occur. Thus, 'Case-studies are a valuable teaching resource. Each one provides not only a chronicle of a real-life problem but also a close °analysis of why things happened the way they did'.

A *chronology* is a table of events with dates. Thus, 'Counsel for the defence suggested there must be something wrong in the chronology prepared by the Gardaí. The defendant could not have entered the premises at 8.30 p.m., grabbed what was in the till and then taken the last train to Wexford. The last train for Wexford left the station at 8.00 p.m.'.

To *synchronise* is to occur at the same time or to make to occur at the same time (*sun* is a Greek word meaning 'with'). The word occurs frequently in thrillers and war movies: 'Let's synchronise our watches'.

Tempus, temporis is the Latin word for 'time' from which we derive:

tempo — the rapidity of movement in music
temporal — relating to the things of this life

temporary — lasting only for a time
temporise — avoid committing oneself, play for time
contemporary — relating to the same time, often misused to mean 'modern', 'present-day'.

-cide
deicide, fratricide, genocide, homicide, infanticide, matricide, parricide, patricide, regicide, suicide, tyrannicide — these are all words whose common suffix *-cide* comes from the Latin word *caedere* 'to kill'. Each word may refer to the °person who has killed or to the act of killing. Thus a homicide may refer to a murder or a murderer

Deicide means the killing of a god, a charge formerly made by Christians against the Jews (*deus, dei* means 'god' in Latin; from it we also derive 'deity', 'deify' and 'deist'; a deist believes in the existence of God but not in revelation — Holy Scripture — while a theist, derived from the Greek word for God *theos*, believes in the existence of God with or without a belief in revelation).

Fratricide means the killing of one's brother, the crime of Cain (*frater, fratris* means 'brother' in Latin).

Genocide means the killing of a race (*genos* means 'race' in Greek). Thus, 'There is reason to believe the Tudors were pursuing a policy of genocide in Ireland.'

Homicide means the killing of a man or woman (*homo, hominis* means 'human being' in Latin).

Infanticide means the killing of a new-born child, the crime of Herod (*infans, infantis* is the Latin word for 'a new-born child'; *in* is a Latin prefix that negatives a word, *fans* is a Latin word meaning 'speaking': an infant is a child that does not yet speak).

Matricide means the killing of one's own mother (*mater, matris* is the word for 'mother' in Latin).

Parricide, derived from the Latin word *parricida,* means the killing of one's own father or other near relative or someone whose person is held sacred; it may also apply to someone guilty of treason against the fatherland. (The *parr* element would seem to be related to the Latin *pater* meaning 'father' but this is not certain. *Patria* is the Latin word for 'fatherland').

Patricide means the killing of one's own father specifically (*pater, patris* is the Latin word for 'father').

Regicide means the killing of a king (*rex, regis* is the Latin word for 'king').

Suicide means the killing of oneself (*sui* is a form of *se* the Latin word for 'self').

Tyrannicide means the killing of a tyrant (*turannos* is the Greek word for 'tyrant').

The murder of Abel (Gustave Doré)

civil service
the departments and °offices directly controlled by members of the °government and the offices attached to the other °constitutional °organs of °state

Civis is the Latin word for 'citizen' from which we also derive 'civic'. In °political science the civil service was distinguished from the military service (*miles, militis* is the Latin word for 'a soldier'). While the °origins of the civil service are traced to those court servants and °clerks who helped kings with their civil, °i.e. non-military, business, the term 'civil service' originated with the East India Company (which was eventually succeeded by the °Raj) to allow it distinguish its civil servants from its military servants. The term was given °currency in Britain by Macaulay, though as late as the 1870s ministers and officials in Britain tended to refer to '°public offices' or

Sean Cromien, Secretary, Department of Finance (1987—)

'public establishments' rather than to the 'civil service'.

The civil service consists of the departments of state (Finance, Health, °Education etc.) and the offices attached to them (the Revenue Commissioners, the Office of Public Works °etc.), and the offices of the °President, °Dáil and °Seanad, and the courts. The people working in the civil service are called 'civil servants'. The civil service departments control the rest of the public service. There are about 35,000 civil servants. The Secretary of the Department of Finance is regarded as head of the civil service.

coalition
a °temporary union of diverse parties to achieve a common aim e.g. °government

Coalescere, from which 'coalition' is derived, is a Latin word meaning 'to grow together' — a coalition is a growing together. Since its accession to power in 1932, the °Fianna Fáil party has consistently been the largest party in the °state and the only party capable of forming a government on its own. On five occasions the other parties have combined to form coalition governments: 1948-51 (under John A. Costello as °Taoiseach), 1954-57 (under John A. Costello as Taoiseach), 1973-77 (under Liam Cosgrave as Taoiseach), 1981-82 (under Garret FitzGerald as Taoiseach) and 1982-87 (under Garret FitzGerald as Taoiseach).

Following the general °election of 1989, °Fianna Fáil, having failed to gain an overall °majority, formed a coalition government with the Progressive °Democrats (under Charles J. Haughey as Taoiseach).

codicil
a supplementary clause (or clauses) to a will

Codicillus is the diminutive form of *codex, codicis* the Latin word for 'a °manuscript volume' (from which we get the word 'code' by a transference of the name of the °medium — the manuscript volume — to the matter it often carried — °laws or regulations). A codicil alters a will in certain particulars. To be effective it must be signed and witnessed just as a will must. In Irish °public affairs, the word occurs most notably in connection with the will of Sir Hugh Lane.

Hugh Lane, born in Ballybrack House, Co. Cork in 1875, was the son of a °clergyman and a nephew of Lady Gregory. He went to London where he became an

Hugh Lane

Lady Gregory

A detail from *Les Parapluies*

°art connoisseur (from the Old French *connoitre*, °modern *connaitre*, 'to know' which in turn derives from the Latin word *cognoscere*). He made a °fortune dealing in art and built up a magnificent collection of his own.

Through his aunt, he became caught up in the great artistic revival in Dublin. He gave many valuable works to the °National Gallery of Ireland. He also proposed to give thirty-nine modern continental works of art, which included °masterpieces of Impressionism such as *Les Parapluies* ('The Umbrellas') by Renoir, to Dublin, if the Corporation provided a suitable gallery for them. Incensed at the procrastination of the city fathers, he eventually had the collection placed on loan in the National Gallery in London. (To procrastinate is 'to put off doing something until some future time' from the Latin *pro* 'onward' and *crastinus* 'of tomorrow'). A will he made in 1913 left those pictures to London.

In April 1915 he went on business to America. He was drowned on his return journey on 7 May 1915 when the *Lusitania* was sunk by a German submarine off the Cork coast almost within sight of his birthplace (*sub* is a Latin word meaning 'under', *mare* is a Latin word for 'the sea' — a submarine is a vessel that moves under the sea). He was last seen helping women and children into the boats. He was forty years old.

Before he went to America, he had drawn up a codicil to his will in which he bequeathed the pictures he had placed in London to the city of Dublin on condition it provided a suitable building for them within five years of his death. The codicil, signed by him but unwitnessed, was found after his death locked in his desk at the National Gallery of Ireland.

A great Anglo-Irish controversy ensued: Ireland's °moral claim to the pictures was clear; equally clear was Britain's °legal claim. The affair ended satisfactorily in an agreement in 1959 whereby about half the collection is held in the °Municipal Gallery of Modern Art in Dublin and the rest is held in the National Gallery in London, and an exchange is made roughly every seven years.

cohort
a large group of people

actuary
— an expert in statistics who calculates insurance risks and premiums (*actuarius* is the Latin word for 'a bookkeeper')

Cohors, cohortis is the Latin word for a big formation of Roman soldiers. (It was one tenth of a legion.) The word still appears in writing about °military affairs but it is more commonly used nowadays by °statisticians, °sociologists, °economists and actuaries, for whom a cohort is an age cohort — any group of people born in a single year.

In the °Republic the 1988 cohort numbered 54,300, of whom 27,939 were boys and 26,361 were girls. The word is also applied to broader time spans. Thus a five-year cohort refers to those born within a five-year period.

communism
a body of ideas which envisages the abolition of °private property, its replacement by °communal ownership and the establishment of a classless society where there are neither rulers nor ruled

Communis is a Latin word meaning 'common'. In its root sense the term 'communist' may be applied to any society that holds all property in common °e.g. the early Church. As a °modern °political term 'communism' emerged in the middle of the nineteenth °century. Marx and Engels used it to describe their °manifesto: they saw communism as a working-class movement and °socialism as a middle-class movement (as, in effect, a projection of °liberalism beyond the political and into the social and °economic areas of life). In 1918, following the Russian °Revolution, the Russian Social-°Democratic Labour Party (the °Bolsheviks) changed its name to the Communist Party of the °Soviet Union. Subsequently the term 'communist' came to distinguish revolutionary socialists from democratic socialists. Like socialism, communism lays stress on the group rather than the individual. It might be described as an extreme form of socialism. However, Karl Marx (1818-83), the great German Jewish °prophet of modern communism — his system is called Marxism after him — distinguished communism from socialism, which he defined as the °penultimate stage in the progress towards communism.

Marx

Socialism envisages a °state that owns and distributes equitably the communal wealth. Marx envisaged communism as arriving with the disappearance of the °state ('the withering away of the state'). Under communism everyone would achieve full °human °emancipation.

Marx, of course, was only one among a number of

analysis
derives from the Greek *ana* here meaning 'again' and *lusis* 'a setting free' — to analyse something is to break it up, physically or mentally, into its elements. *Synthesis*, the opposite of analysis, derives from the Greek *sun* meaning 'with' and *thesis* 'a placing'. To synthesize is to bring various elements together to form a whole. 'Synthetic' describes something °artificial. *Catalysis* is a chemical interaction caused between two substances by the presence of a third which undergoes no change. The unchanging substance is called a catalyst. *Catalyst* is often used of someone whose presence allows understanding, agreement or other interactions to occur in a group. 'Catalysis' derives from the Greek *kata* 'down', and *lusis*

vehicle
— 'a conveyance' from the Latin word *vehere* 'to carry'

thinkers who throughout °history have constructed °utopias. What distinguishes Marx's ideal society is that he worked out a brilliant model, based on his particular form of economic, social and political analysis, which made the realisation of communism inevitable. (Marx, therefore, denied that his system was utopian; it was, he insisted, the only °scientific one.)

Moreover, great numbers of people throughout the world have, until recently, found his thinking either so compelling that they accepted communism as an inspiring programme for life or so °popular that they used it as a vehicle for a revolution to further their ambitions.

Marx believed you could explain everything about a society by analysing the way economic forces °influence and shape its social, religious, °legal, political, and °cultural aspects. Social change, he maintained, entails change both at the level of consciousness and at the economic level. (He encouraged the development of workers' study groups to develop true understanding and to generate in them a desire for change.)

When he looked at °contemporary society he saw that the changes in °production and exchange wrought by °capitalism were momentous. Factory production was dividing society into two classes — the °proletarian °masses living in poverty and the °bourgeoisie, the owners of the means of production, living in °affluence. Because goods were exchanged (i.e. sold) in a free market there was intense °competition. Entrepreneurs (from the French word for 'businessmen') would inevitably seek a °competitive edge by exploiting their workers (helped by the law which at the time forbade combinations of workers, °i.e. trade unions) or by using labour-saving machines (which would depress wages further by making more workers pursue less work). As a result, a deadly class struggle would ensue. The means of production, in the dog-eat-dog conditions of the market, would be steadily concentrated in fewer and fewer hands. Periodic recessions would convulse society further. Finally, the proletarians would rise up and 'expropriate the expropriators' (*proprietas* is a Latin word for 'property', *ex* is a Latin word meaning 'from' or 'away' — to expropriate is to take property away from, to dispossess).

Ironically, the proletariat, from their experience of working in factories, would be socialised, that is, they would become very conscious of the value of working together. They would seize the means of production, produce goods to meet the needs of society rather than the market, and in the first instance arrange for equitable distribution through a state °apparatus. In this way they would achieve socialism. After some experience of socialism, Marx believed that everyone would work together voluntarily for the common good. There would be no need for a state with all its laws and procedures designed to control people. The state would wither away under the glow of a red sun.

irony/ironically — the expression of one's meaning by the use of terms with an opposite meaning, or the fact that an action or condition is the opposite to what one would have expected. 'Irony' derives from the Latin *ironia* which in turn is derived from the Greek *eirōneia*, the practice of an *eirōn*, a dissembler. It is in this °original sense that we use the expression 'Socratic irony'. Socrates loved to pretend he was ignorant because that allowed him to question people closely and fundamentally and so either confute them or lead them to understandings other than the ones they had setting out

Marx elaborated his system in his monumental (2,500 pages) work *Das Kapital* (*Capital*), written in the British °Museum over a period of eighteen years when he lived with his family in great poverty in London. So towering was his genius that no one nowadays can think about °history or economics or society without using Marx's categories: he caused a °paradigm shift.

Lenin

Marx was not, however, a successful revolutionary. He was dead thirty-four years before a revolution inspired by his ideas was achieved by Lenin and his Bolsheviks in industrially backward Russia. Lenin had to make certain adjustments to Marxism (hence the expression 'Marxist-Leninist') to deal with the actual conditions he faced. Later communist revolutions in other countries e.g. China, Cuba, have led to further adjustments to Marxism. As for capitalism, it has shown itself to be far more resilient and subtle than Marx's analysis allowed.

compos mentis
of sound mind

Compos is a Latin word meaning 'in possession of'. *Mens, mentis* is the Latin word for 'mind' from which we derive 'mental' and 'demented'. The expression is usually found in °legal °contexts. For example, relatives may wish the courts to decide whether dear Uncle Ned was *compos mentis* or *non compos mentis* (*non* is the

Latin word for 'not') when he left all his money to buy napkins for cows.

conservatism
a body of °political beliefs which stresses the importance of maintaining the traditional values and °institutions, opposes °radical political change, and favours gradual and peaceful reform as the means of coping with necessary change

Con is derived from the Latin word *cum* meaning 'with'. *Servare* is the Latin word 'to keep'. To conserve is to keep intact. Conservatives are °characterised by a disposition to maintain the °status quo and resist change. In this broad sense we may refer to 'a conservative person', 'a conservative church', 'the conservative wing of the Chinese °communist party'. Because °modern life is marked by great °economic, °social, °cultural and °technological change, 'conservative' tends to have °pejorative °connotations. Change °*per se* is not exclusively either good or bad. It is illogical, therefore, to use the term 'conservative' in an invariably pejorative sense.

Radical is the opposite of conservative. The radical believes that °human advance can be guaranteed by fundamental change in social structures and processes. The conservative believes human nature remains the same throughout °history and that every social system is threatened by the selfishness, conceit and deceitfulness of the individual. Politically, the conservative and the radical are diametrically opposed. The radical seeks °major changes in order to guarantee a better future. The conservative recoils from the dangers inherent in sudden large-scale social change; moreover, he or she believes there is no guarantee of a better future. The °massive support enjoyed by the Conservative Party in Britain suggests that great numbers of people there find the conservative perspective the more realistic one.

tradition(al)
— the process by which beliefs and customs are passed on from one generation to another (*tradere* is the Latin word 'to hand on'; to *extradite* is to hand someone over for trial or punishment to a foreign government — *ex* is a Latin word meaning 'from' or 'direct from', e.g., ex works)

However, conservatism is often regarded as simply a cluster of beliefs, attitudes and practices promoted by the privileged to maintain their own positions. The masses are seen to be lulled into acquiescence by equality before the law (a major condition for peace in society) and the comforts of social stability. A traditional °paternalistic culture bonds them to the great °national institutions, typically, as in Britain, to crown, country and church, and to the °local institutions that individuals are born into and that sustain them throughout their lives — the family, the °local authorities, the local church, the local constabulary.

The °classic conservative model of society as °organic is provided by Plutarch in the fable of the belly (repeated by Shakespeare in *Coriolanus*). The poor people of Rome, squeezed ruthlessly by the moneylenders and finding no solace from the °Senate which supported the °interests of the rich, refused to defend Rome against the Sabines and marched *en masse* to a hill three miles outside the city. The frightened Senate sent emissaries to persuade the people to come back. Their chief spokesman, Menenius Agrippa, ended his appeal with a fable.

Once upon a time, he said, all the parts of the body revolted against the belly. 'You just sit there enjoying yourself', they snorted, 'while the rest of us sweat and slave to keep your gross appetite satisfied!' But the belly simply laughed at them for their naiveté. 'You see', the belly said, 'it's true I receive all the body's nourishment but I send it out again and distribute it to every organ thus giving each the strength to play its part in achieving the common good'. Menenius pointed the moral: 'The Senate, my fellow-countrymen, plays the same part as the belly: it studies the various proposals for °state action and decides what to do, and the fruits of those decisions are shared by you all'. The people were eventually convinced and returned to work for their city.

medieval means 'pertaining to the Middle Ages' (°c. 5th to 15th century) and derives from *medius* the Latin word for 'middle' and *aevum* the Latin word for 'age'. People are said to be 'coeval' if they were born on the same date. *Era* is a series of years reckoned from a particular point e.g. the Napoleonic era, the era of the mini-skirt (*aera* is a Latin word meaning 'number'). An *epoch* is a time so remarkable that it marks the beginning of an era in history — the launch of the first sputnik was an epoch-making event (*epokhē* is a Greek word meaning 'stoppage'). An *aeon* is a vast period in the history of the universe (*aeon* is a Latin word derived from the Greek *aiōn*)

Modern °European conservatism was °articulated initially in the struggle that developed in the later seventeenth °century between the °aristocracy and the °bourgeoisie. The aristocratic party — the landowners and their dependent tenant farmers and farm labourers, supported by the °clergy — struggled to maintain the traditional medieval system. The bourgeoisie — industrialists, merchants, shopkeepers, tradesmen and bankers with their dependent lower classes of °clerks and labourers — sought to destroy the privileges of the aristocracy and do away with °feudal restraints on °production and trade.

°Liberalism, based on the writings of the English °philosopher John Locke (1632–1704) and developed by the French philosophers of the eighteenth century, with its stress on the equality and °freedom of the individual, was the °natural °ideology of the bourgeoisie. Liberalism became the °dominant ideology of the nineteenth century: '°right wing' and '°reactionary' became pejorative terms liberals applied to conservatives.

In the twentieth century conservatives have defined their position further in the struggle against °socialism. They oppose °centralised planning of the economy and the nationalisation of industry. They favour free enterprise and the disciplines of a free market. They favour less °government rather than more government. They seek to curtail the °welfare state and to place on individuals much of the °onus of providing for the contingencies of life.

contingencies — 'chance happenings', literally 'things that touch with you' from the Latin particle *con* meaning 'with' and *tingere/tangere* the Latin word 'to touch'. A contingency plan is one concerned to deal with contingencies

No political party in Ireland calls itself conservative. The Conservative Party in Britain, therefore, is the one most familiar to us. It developed from the Tory Party of the late seventeenth, eighteenth and early nineteenth centuries ('tories' was a name derived from the Gaelic *toraí* meaning 'pursuer' or 'raider' for those dispossessed Irish Catholic landowners who took to the hills and woods and raided the new Cromwellian settlers; it was later transferred to the group in England which refused to concur in the exclusion of James II from the throne).

The Tories supported divine right, °hereditary succession, and the royal °prerogative; above all, they supported the Anglican Church — hence the observation of Agnes Maude Royden that the Anglican Church is 'the Tory party at prayer'. They broke with James II, therefore, because he was seen to favour Catholicism. The Tories, who represented the landowners, were opposed by the Whigs, who represented the moneyed interests of the towns and cities ('Whig' is probably derived from 'whiggamore', the word for a Scottish rebel of the seventeenth century). The Whigs sought to subordinate the power of the king to the will of °parliament — hence they were led in the direction of °electoral reform.

Burke

British conservatives look towards Edmund Burke (1729-97), the Irish °orator and statesman, as the thinker who provided the first — and °classical — exposition of conservatism in his speeches and writings. It was Burke's °dictum 'We must reform in order to preserve' that rescued conservatism from the sterility of opposing all change.

Following the Whig Reform Act of 1832 which began the transformation of the electoral system, the Tories called themselves the Conservative Party. The Conservatives split over the repeal of the Corn Laws in 1846. The Peelites supported repeal and, in an alliance with the Whigs, formed the Liberal party. The Conservatives, in turn, were joined in 1886 by those Whig and Radical elements in Gladstone's Liberal Party who objected to Home Rule for Ireland. That alliance called itself the Conservative and Unionist Party.

After World War I support for the great Liberal Party collapsed and the Conservatives stood as the major opponent of the socialist Labour party.

constitution
the fundamental or basic °law of a country

Constituere is a Latin word 'to make to stand'. A constitution is a basic law upon which all other laws and all the °institutions of the °state rest. A constitution may be usefully thought of as a contract between the people and their rulers. It states what powers the rulers may exercise and establishes the institutions through which they shall do so; it defines the relationship between those institutions; and it states, if it is a °democratic constitution, the basic duties the citizens must perform to enjoy the benefits of democratic °government. A constitution acts as a control by the citizens on the possible abuse of power by those who govern. It also serves as the source of the authority of those who govern.

Modern Irish constitutional °history begins with the Constitution of °Dáil Éireann, 1919. This was superseded by the Constitution of the Irish Free State, 1922, which in turn was superseded by *Bunreacht na hÉireann,* 1937 (*bunreacht* means 'fundamental law' in Irish). *Bunreacht na hÉireann* consists of a preamble and fifty articles.

modern
derives from the Latin word *modernus* meaning 'pertaining to just now' which is itself derived from the Latin word *modo* meaning 'just now'; however, scholars also use the word to describe one of the three great periods into which, broadly speaking, human experience can be divided — ancient, °medieval and modern; in that context 'modern' may denote anything relating to the sixteenth/seventeenth century onwards

Our constitution was much °influenced by the American constitution, particularly in regard to the powers given to the Supreme Court to interpret the implications of the constitution. Typically, a citizen who feels a particular piece of °legislation affecting him or her is contrary to the constitution applies to the courts to have the matter settled. Since the early nineteen sixties the Irish courts have played an active part in elucidating the implications of *Bunreacht na hÉireann*.

The terms of the constitution can be changed only by legislation approved by °referendum.

conurbation
the process by which neighbouring villages, towns and cities, through continuous growth, join together and form a °physical, but not a °political, entity; or the result of that process

Urbs, urbis is the Latin word for city, *con* is derived from *cum* a Latin word meaning 'with'; conurbation, then, means 'forming a city with'. About a fifth of the people of the United States live in the conurbation that stretches from Boston to Washington, DC. About a third of the °population of the °Republic lives in the conurbation that stretches along the east coast from Drogheda to Wicklow.

cornucopia
a superabundance

Cornu is a Latin word for 'horn' and *copia* is a Latin word meaning 'plenty'. *Cornucopiae* or *cornu copiae*,

In this dark painting 'Cronus devouring his children', Goya evokes (literally 'calls forth' — from the Latin *e* for 'out' or 'forth' and *vocare* 'to call') the °atavistic horror of cannibalism (cannibalism derives from the Spanish *Canibal* which itself derives from °*Carib* °via *Caribal*)

transliterated 'cornucopia' in English, means 'horn of plenty'. Zeus was the chief of the Greek gods. (In °primitive times he was the sky god — that's why, when it began to rain, the Greeks would say bleakly 'Zeus huei'—'Zeus is pissing'.) When Zeus was an °infant, his mother hid him away from his father Cronus (Cronus, to avoid a °prophecy that he would be usurped by one of his own children, was wont to eat his new-born offspring). A princess called Amalthea fed Zeus with goat's milk. Zeus was so grateful that he broke off one of the goat's horns and gave it to her, vowing that whoever owned it would always have an abundance of everything he or she desired. Incidentally, the °aegis also came from this goat.

Leader writers in our newspapers will occasionally regret that the °government does not possess a cornucopia and that, therefore, whatever benefits it gives out it must pay for from taxes.

cosmopolitan
a citizen of the world

Cosmos is the Greek word for '°universe'. *Polis* is the Greek word for 'city-state' and *politēs* means 'citizen of a city-state'. The cosmopolitan is not bound by his or her °nationality: his or her °interests extend to the whole world. °Modern °technology is fostering cosmopolitanism by turning the world into a global village (*globus* is the Latin word for 'a ball' or 'sphere'; *sphaira* from which we derive 'sphere' is the Greek word for 'a globe').

coup d'état
a sudden usurpation of °state authority and power, usually by the army or elements of it

Coup is a French word meaning 'blow' or 'stroke', *d'état* means 'of the state' in French. A *coup d'état* is now used almost invariably of the actions of a group (frequently army officers) who bring about a change of °government by force or who attempt to do so.

-cracy
aristocracy, autocracy, bureaucracy, democracy, gerontocracy, phallocracy, plutocracy, technocracy,

Aristocracy is rule by a privileged class (*aristos* means 'best' or 'noble' in Greek). In ancient Greece when the cities became prosperous, the rich families — they called themselves the *aristoi*, the Best People — took over control from the city king, whose role as a war-leader was °critical in the bad times, through the device of annually °elected °presidents. The *aristoi* referred contemptuously to the °mass of the people as *hoi polloi*

thalassocracy, theocracy — the ending *-cracy* comes from the Greek *cratia* meaning 'power'

Nicholas II, Czar of Russia, with his son Alexis who was never to succeed him

'the many'.

Autocracy is literally 'self-rule'; the word 'autocrat' means one who rules in his own interest (*autos* means 'self' in Greek). Among the long list of proud titles renounced by Nicholas II, the last °Czar of Russia, on his abdication in 1917 was 'Autocrat of all the Russias'.

Bureaucracy is rule by °public °officials (*bureau* means 'office' in French) or, more usually, the slow and often unnecessarily complicated procedures — the red tape — thought to °characterise the work of public bodies. The °sociologist Max Weber (1864–1920), observing that any continuing, large scale, complex operation required a bureaucracy for its efficient °administration, identified the following features of a bureaucracy: it was °hierarchical, °impersonal, continuous and expert.

Democracy is rule by the people (*dēmos* means 'people' in Greek).

Gerontocracy is rule by old men (*gerōn, gerontos* is 'old man' in Greek). Spartan °government had a gerontocratic feature — a *gerousia* consisting of twenty-eight elders, all at least sixty years old, and two kings. Plato's last work, *The Laws,* envisages a 'nocturnal council' of old men, all passion spent, working tirelessly for the good of the °state. In the 1970s and early 1980s most of the Russian leaders, survivors from the °revolutionary period, were old men and so the Russian government was often described as 'gerontocratic'. The same held true of the Chinese rulers in and beyond the same period.

Phallocracy is a word coined by °feminists to °denote the °predominance of men in government and public affairs simply because they are men (*phallus* is a Latin word derived from *phallos* the Greek word for *penis*, the Latin word for the male organ; *phallic*, as in 'phallic symbol', is derived from *phallos*).

Plutocracy is rule by rich people (*plutos* means 'rich' in Greek).

A *technocracy* is government by technical experts (*technē* is the Greek word for 'craft'). °Modern societies, increasingly dependent on the development of technology, tend to be technocratic because more and more decisions tend to be made by technical experts.

empire
derives from the Latin word *imperium* meaning 'rule' from which we also derive *imperial* and *imperious*

A *thalassocracy* is a seapower (*thalassa* is the Greek word for 'sea'). The Athenian °Empire, the °historic Venetian °Republic, the seventeenth century Dutch and the eighteenth and nineteenth °century British empires, all of which exercised power through the prowess of their sailors, are sometimes referred to as thalassocracies.

Theocracy is literally rule by God (*theos* means 'god' in Greek). The word is applied to rule by men who claim to speak for God or who claim divine authority for their actions and decisions. A society ruled by a religious leader, such as Iran under the Ayatollah Khomeini, might be described as theocratic. More loosely, the term is applied to a state in which the °doctrines of a particular religion pervade law and government. Thus, Ireland in the fifties has been described as theocratic.

credo
a statement of basic beliefs

Credo is a Latin word meaning 'I believe'. In order to preserve its unity the early Church drew up a statement of the basic beliefs every Christian was expected to subscribe to. The first word of the statement in Latin is *Credo*. 'Credo' is now used to describe any formal statement of beliefs. Thus, 'The equality of men and women, the necessity for a rigorously °progressive °taxation system, and the need to replace multi-seat constituencies with single-seat constituencies — these were elements of his °political credo'.

Creed, meaning a particular religion, is also derived from *credo*.

Credible means 'worthy of belief' — for example, a credible story.

Credulous means 'given to believing on insufficient grounds' — a naive person is credulous.

A person's *credentials* are statements or actions which establish a reason for trusting him or her.

'Credit' in all its senses also derives from *credere*.

crisis
a decisive point, a turning-point, a time of danger

The Greek word *krisis* (*crisis* in English) derives from the Greek word *krinein* 'to judge', 'to decide'. Just as a judgement (*krisis*) determines the outcome of a case so that moment which decided the outcome of an action or experience came to be called 'the crisis'.

Before the use of antibiotics fevers typically reached a high point of intensity — a crisis — after which the patient either recovered or died. Some °connotations of the word are derived from that °context.

The words 'critic', 'critical', 'criticism', 'critique' (a measured review) are used by °academics in a °neutral sense because judgement may be favourable or unfavourable. But 'critic', 'critical', and 'criticism' in °popular speech have °negative connotations — thus, 'He was very critical of the standard of service in the hotel'. 'Critical' is also used to mean pertaining to a crisis — thus 'The situation was critical. He had no food or fuel — and winter was setting in.'

criterion
a standard by which something is judged

Critēs is the Greek word for 'a judge' derived from the word *krinein* 'to judge'. In a °democracy each citizen must decide in a general °election whether to support the °government or not. The work of government is complex. To decide how effectively a government has worked one needs to apply a number of criteria (plural form of criterion) to measure its performance on the °economy, on °welfare, on °culture, on security, on foreign affairs, and so on. To apply the criteria one must know what the government has done in those areas, what resources it had, what difficulties it faced. For this knowledge the citizen relies largely on the °mass °media. Having made these assessments the citizen must make a summative judgement (*summare* is the Latin word 'to add up') and cast his or her °vote. The quality of government depends greatly on the criteria applied bv those whom the government know to be most °influential. In a democracy that ought to mean the electorate.

crusade
an aggressive campaign against some evil real or imaginary

Crux, *crucis* is the Latin word for 'cross'. The crusades were a series of holy wars conducted between 1096 AD and 1270 AD by the Christian kings and nobility of °Europe °ostensibly to free the holy places in Palestine from the Moslems. The Christian warriors wore the cross.

A Moslem holy war is called a *jihad.*

crypto-
secret

Kruptos (transliterated *cryptos*) is the Greek word for 'hidden'. Combined with the name of a group in the form *crypto-*, it °denotes a secret sympathiser, °e.g. crypto-°communist, crypto-°fascist.

The °Spartans had a secret °institution, called the *krupteia*, experience of working with which was included in the training of young men in Sparta. The *krupteia* carried out the duties of both police and spies. It was the duty of young Spartans in the *krupteia* to spy out potential troublemakers among the °subject race, the Helots, whom they then proceeded to murder secretly. To justify this conduct, the Spartan officials called ephors, on entering office, always declared unconditional war on the Helots.

Cryptic means 'secret', 'mysterious'.

***cui bono*?**
to whose benefit?

Cui is a form of *quis*, the Latin word meaning 'who'. *Bono* is a form of *bonus,* a Latin word meaning 'good'. *Cui bono?* literally means 'to whom for a good?' The phrase occurs first in Cicero's writing. *Cui bono?* is a test applied by the worldly wise to help them understand what would otherwise seem daft. Thus, if a councillor proposes that the council should buy °umbrellas to issue to tourists during the summer one could find, by asking who benefits, that the councillor is the first cousin of an umbrella manufacturer!

cum laude
with praise

Cum is a Latin word meaning 'with'. *Laus, laudis* is the Latin word for 'praise' (hence, for example, 'laudatory remarks'). The expression is used in relation to °university degrees which may be conferred in rising levels *cum laude, magna cum laude* (with great praise — *magnus* is the Latin word for 'great') or *summa cum laude* (with the highest praise — *summus* is the Latin word for 'highest', from which we also derive 'summit').

curriculum
a course of studies

Curriculum is a Latin word meaning 'course' or 'race' derived from the word *currere* 'to run' (from which we also derive 'current'). The curriculum is the course of studies for a school or other °educational °institution.

The Department of Education, through a body called the °National Council for Curriculum and Assessment, draws up the curricula (plural form) to be followed in national and post-primary schools.

A *syllabus* (plural syllabi or syllabuses), from a misprint made in 1470 of the Greek word *sittyba* 'a book label', outlines the content of each °subject on a curriculum just as a book label outlined the contents of a book.

A *curriculum vitae* outlines the salient features of one's life and usually accompanies a job application (*vitae* is a form of *vita*, the Latin word for 'life', meaning 'of life').

cynic
someone who °characteristically takes a °mordantly pessimistic view of other people's motives and actions

Kunikos (which transliterates into English as 'cynical') is a Greek word meaning 'dog-like'. The word was first applied to a °philosopher called Diogenes, who was born in Sinope, a Greek °colony on the Black Sea — the *Pontus Euxeinos* or Euxine. One of his aims was to expose the falseness of °current °conventions. So he acted unconventionally. He lived the life of a tramp, sleeping in a tub, and begging food; he performed his bodily functions with a breath-taking lack of ceremony — hence his nickname.

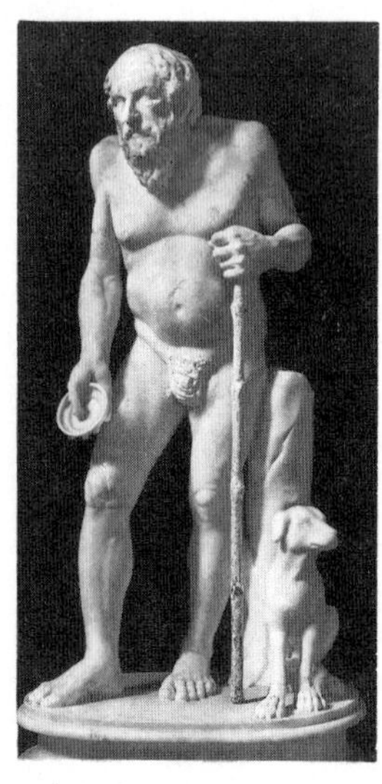

Diogenes

Diogenes was a wit and a showman. When Alexander the Great visited him he asked him to name his wish and he would grant it. Diogenes replied 'I wish you would stand out of my sunlight'. On hearing this Alexander turned to his aides and said 'Were I not Alexander, I would wish to be Diogenes'. On another occasion Diogenes went out in broad daylight with a lighted lamp 'in search of one honest man'.

Diogenes and his followers — the Cynics — were distinguished more by their way of life than by a worked-out system of thought. They aimed to be self-sufficient. They considered asceticism (from the Greek *askēsis* meaning 'training' or 'exercise') to be necessary for °moral °excellence because it develops resistance to the pressures of pleasure and pain. The Cynics preached the °universal brotherhood of man. Indeed Diogenes made a famous claim to be 'a citizen of the world' — a

°cosmopolitan. That was an unthinkable idea up to then in the Greek city-states whose stability and cohesion depended on their being tightly exclusive communities. So Diogenes might be described as the first °anarchist.

Nowadays we use the word 'cynicism' in a °pejorative sense to °indicate the attitude of someone who sarcastically doubts the sincerity or good intentions of other people. However, we should resist attempts by people who seek to brand true statements, pithily expressed but unpalatable to them, as cynical (*palatum* is the Latin word for 'the roof of the mouth'; something palatable may be swallowed with relish by either the mouth or the mind).

D

Dáil Éireann
the Irish House of Representatives

An old Irish word with °historical and literary °connotations, *dáil* means 'assembly'. It was introduced into Irish °politics in 1919 to describe the assembly in the Mansion House, Dublin of the representatives of the Irish people returned in the general °election of December 1918. Though Dáil Éireann, like the British House of °Commons, is called the Lower House, it °dominates the law-making process.

The Dáil currently has 166 members called Teachtaí Dála (TDs) — *teachta* is an Irish word for 'representative'. The °constitution provides that the °total number of members of Dáil Éireann shall not be fixed at less than one member for each thirty thousand of the °population, or at more than one member for each twenty thousand of the population. °Currently members are returned by forty-one constituencies, thirteen of which return three members each, thirteen return four each and the remaining fifteen return five each.

The entrance to Leinster House, where the Dáil and Seanad meet. The Greeks developed three °classical kinds of column (from the Latin *columna*) — Doric, Ionic and Corinthian — most readily identified from their °capitals. The columns supporting the pediment here are Corinthian, identified by the acanthus leaves on the capital. The Doric column, the oldest and severest style, has little decoration on its capital. The Ionic column has spiral forms (volutes) on its capital

Every citizen who has reached the age of twenty-one is eligible for membership of the Dáil (and °Seanad) except the °President of Ireland, the Comptroller and Auditor General, a judge, a member of the defence or police forces on full pay, a °civil servant or a member of the board of a °state-sponsored body.

For Dáil elections every citizen who has reached the age of eighteen and is not disqualified by °law has the right under °*Bunreacht na hÉireann* to be placed on the register of °voters in the constituency in which he or she resided on the 15 September before the publication of the register. Resident British citizens also have this right (under the Ninth Amendment of the Constitution Act, 1984). Electoral registers are published each year. Voting is by secret °ballot. The voting system, as specified in the constitution, is proportional representation by means of the single transferable vote. Five years is fixed by law as the °maximum term of the Dáil (under *Bunreacht na hÉireann* it is limited to seven years). The average term is less than three years.

The Dáil usually sits on about a hundred days throughout the year. Under the constitution the sole power of making laws for the °state is vested in the °Oireachtas; the Third Amendment of the Constitution °Act, 1972, however, in effect conferred law-making powers on the °European Community in regard to those matters covered by the Treaties that established the EC. °Government policy and °administration may be examined and °criticised in both the Dáil and the Seanad, but under the constitution the government is responsible to the Dáil alone. In the law-making process the °primacy of the Dáil is clearly established. Thus in relation to Money Bills the Seanad may make recommendations (not amendments) and if it does, must do so within twenty-one days; moreover, on all Bills the Dáil has power to override the Seanad (by deeming the Seanad to have passed them).

The first Dáil

The chairman of Dáil Éireann, a member chosen by the rest of the House, is called the Ceann Comhairle (*ceann* is an Irish word for 'head', *comhairle* is an Irish word for 'council'). The Ceann Comhairle chairs debates but does not take part in them, and presides over the proceedings of the Dáil. If the Dáil is equally divided on a vote the Ceann Comhairle casts his or her vote — by °convention in favour of the °*status quo*. On the dissolution of the Dáil the Ceann Comhairle is automatically re-elected a TD if he or she so wishes.

decentralise
to undo the concentration of power in a single centre

Centrum is the Latin word for 'centre' — it was °originally the stationary foot of a compass around which the other foot revolved to describe a circle. The Latin prefix *de* negatives a word.

The development of industry led to the growth of towns and cities at the expense of the countryside. Capital cities in particular benefited (*caput*, *capitis* is the Latin word for 'head' from which we derive 'capital' as well as 'decapitation'). In addition, the development of communications led to the drawing of °political power from the countryside, towns and cities to the capital. So in Dublin, as in other capitals, we find a °bureaucracy making all sorts of decisions. As the decision-making system gets clogged, decisions are not taken or not implemented. People get irritated, and call for decentralisation. °Governments have responded by removing parts of Departments from Dublin and placing them in towns, °e.g. part of the Department of °Education is °located in Athlone.

The dispersal of Departments or parts of them around the country looks like decentralisation; and it pleases the host towns because it brings extra business to them. But a Departmental office in Athlone, exercising power in regard to a particular function over the whole country, is no less centralised than if it were located in Dublin. To decentralise you need to take powers from central Departments and give them to lesser bodies such as regional or °local authorities. The litmus test of decentralisation is the question: have powers been devolved or not?

de jure
by °law (legal right)

De is a Latin word meaning 'by' or 'from'. *Jure* is a form of the Latin word *jus*, *juris* meaning 'law'. The expression is often used in contrast to *de facto* meaning 'in reality' (*facto* is a form of the Latin word *facere* 'to do' meaning 'a thing done', 'a reality'). For example, the °Constitution of Ireland in Article 2 states that 'The °national territory consists of the whole island of Ireland',

and thus makes a *de jure* claim to Northern Ireland. However, it recognises the *de facto* position by going on to state in Article 3:

> Pending the re-integration of the national territory and without prejudice to the right of the °Parliament and °government established by this Constitution to exercise jurisdiction over the whole of that territory, the laws enacted by that Parliament shall have the like area and extent of application as the laws of Saorstát Éireann and the like extra-territorial effect.

delegate
representative

De is a Latin particle meaning 'away'. *Legare* is the Latin word 'to send with a commission'. *Legatus* was °originally a Roman general's lieutenant — *Labieno legato* ('with Labienus as his lieutenant') is a recurrent phrase in Caesar's *Gallic War*. The word also came to be used of Rome's ambassadors. It persists in 'legation' (a diplomatic mission) and 'Papal legate' (a Pope's representative). In common usage 'delegate' and 'representative' are treated as °synonymous but °political scientists distinguish them: a delegate is assigned to act on behalf of a group in a manner specified by it °i.e. in accordance with the °mandate given to him or her (thus the delegate of a trade union branch to the union's congress °votes as instructed by the branch); a representative acts on behalf of a group but his or her actions are not °predetermined — he or she is expected to use his or her own judgement (a °TD has that kind of discretion).

It was the great °parliamentarian, Edmund Burke, who first made the distinction when he insisted that he was the representative of the °electors of his constituency, Bristol, not their delegate: 'Your representative owes you, not his industry only, but his judgement; and he betrays, instead of serving you, if he sacrifices it to your opinion.'

A *plenipotentiary* is a representative who acts with full authority (*plenus* is the Latin word for 'full' from which we get 'plenty', 'plenitude', 'plenary', 'plenum'; *potentia* is the Latin word for 'power').

Delphic
pertaining to °prophecy, particularly of an °ambiguous kind

One of the most famous shrines in ancient Greece was that of the handsome, athletic god Apollo at Delphi. Here great and humble people alike sought advice about the future. They would first make sacrifice, pay offerings and go through rituals aimed at creating awe and reverence. Then they would be brought to a vestibule where a priestess sat upon a tripod (a three-legged stool, from the Greek words *treis*, *tria* meaning 'three' and *pous*, *podos* meaning 'foot') which stood astride the supposed navel (the centre) of the world, while round about curled the mildly hallucinogenic fumes of burning laurel leaves. Falling into a kind of fit or trance, she would utter wild and swirling words. Before you left, the priests would hand you the substance of her remarks written out in verse.

A Grecian tripod

Very often the advice turned out °excellently (the priests after all knew more than anybody else about what was going on because they met people from all over Greece and indeed from outside Greece). If it proved to be wrong, the priests could usually point out that the oracle's words meant something quite different, if you had had the sense to see that.

A famous example of this ambiguity concerned Croesus, the fabulously wealthy king of Lydia. When he asked the oracle whether he should make war on the growing power of Persia, he was told that if he did, he would destroy a mighty °empire. Thus heartened, he attacked Persia and was defeated. The oracle explained later that Croesus *had* destroyed a great empire — his own. The oracle's most profound general exhortations were carved into the stone of the °temple at Delphi: 'Know thyself!' and 'Nothing too much!'

Modern °governments and businesses spend a good deal of money trying to foretell events. One forecasting technique they use is called the Delphi method. It involves inviting a number of prominent people in a particular area of activity, °e.g. tourism, to write down what they think is going to happen, and formulating a forecast by judicious °synthesis of their views (judicious means 'according to sound judgement' from *judex, judicis,* the Latin word for 'judge').

demagogue
a popular leader

Huey Long

Dēmos is the Greek word for 'people'. *Agein* is the Greek word 'to lead'. A number of demagogues in ancient Athens, notably Cleon the tanner, gave the word its °pejorative °connotation of facile crowd manipulation (*facilis* is a Latin word meaning 'easy'). A populist (from the Latin word *populus* meaning 'people') is someone who believes that the common people and their concerns should °predominate in °government. Leading populists often turn out to be demagogues.

Huey Long (1893-1935) was one of the most famous demagogues thrown up by the American Depression. He became °Governor of Louisiana. Difficult to °classify because of his °contradictory policies, he was variously described as °dictatorial, °liberal, °fascist, °leftist, °democratic, idealistic, corrupt. He himself liked to pretend he was too different to be classified. On one occasion as he dozed on a bed, a group of journalists in the room fell to °analysing him. Huey suddenly roused himself and brought the discussion to an end, saying: 'Oh hell! say that I'm °*sui generis* and let it go at that.'

democracy
'...°government of the people, by the people, and for the people'
— Abraham Lincoln

When the government — the °Taoiseach and his team of ministers — issue instructions, these are carried out because the government has authority. If you were to ask the government where they got their authority from, they would say 'the people'. They would explain that they were °elected to the °Dail by the people according to procedures laid down by the people in the °constitution; that the members of the Dail, in accordance with the constitution, had elected the Taoiseach to head the government; that he in turn had selected his team of ministers and had them approved by the Dáil — again in accordance with the constitution.

They would assert that, as long as they act in accordance with the constitution, they have the authority to govern.

A °state such as Ireland where the government derives its authority from the people is a democracy — a word meaning 'rule by the people' derived from the two Greek words *dēmos* 'people' and *kratein* 'to rule'.

In the past, few governments were democratic. Rulers derived their power from immemorial custom (the way it 'always' was), from the actual power and wealth they commanded or from religious laws. The forms of government usually found were °monarchies (kingships) or °autocracies or °oligarchies or °theocracies. Democracies flourished only occasionally, for example in ancient Athens, and even there with a very limited °franchise.

In °modern times the American and French °revolutions undermined immemorial custom as a source of authority by providing a °contemporary °alternative — the people. The French revolutionaries, moreover, also weakened religion as a plausible source of governmental authority. They executed a king who claimed authority not only from immemorial custom but also from God (through the principle of the divine right of kings, namely, that a king's authority derived from God). Thus the people alone remain as the obvious source of authority. Without the people's endorsement of some set of beliefs which bind the °state together, would-be rulers must resort to force. Naturally most governments go out of their way to claim they are democratic rather than °tyrannical.

Daniel O'Connell addressing a monster meeting. The Liberator has a claim as strong as that of the American statesman Andrew Jackson (1767–1845) to be the founder of modern mass democracy

'Democracy' is not an exact term because people use it in different senses. In the Greek city-states the citizens came together in one place and °voted on °public issues.

They made their decisions by a °majority. Such democracy is called *direct democracy*. Modern states are believed to be too big and complex to make direct democracy possible (though in Switzerland the people are consulted on proposed °legislation several times a year; moreover computers may facilitate such consultation everywhere). Instead of deciding issues for themselves people elect representatives to act on their behalf. Such indirect democracy is called *representative democracy*.

freedom
Negative freedom is the condition brought about by °minimum inference by government in the lives of the citizens (°liberals and °conservatives espouse that view of freedom). Positive freedom is the condition brought about by a government which acts to create the authentic conditions for °human growth and development (°socialists espouse that view of freedom)

The ideas of freedom (positive or negative) and equality have become core °values of democracy. Since democracies are based on majority rule, freedom (in either sense) and equality can often be at risk. Indeed, many democracies in ancient times quickly °degenerated to mob rule. To promote political freedom and equality, therefore, most democracies guarantee basic rights to all citizens in their constitutions. (It is common experience, however, that the citizens must press their government to honour the guarantee.) Such democracies are called *constitutional democracies*.

Many people, for example °socialists, believe the actual degree of freedom and equality enjoyed by a citizen is related to such factors as his or her income and °education. They feel, therefore, that democracies should go further and aim to bring about a society where every citizen is broadly equal to his or her fellows °economically and socially. States which have laws to bring about political, economic and social freedom and equality are known as *social democracies*.

apparatus
— 'the equipment for doing something' from the Latin word *apparare* 'to make ready'. *Apparat*, derived from 'apparatus', is a Russian word for the communist party machine in Russia; an *apparatchik* is a member of the *apparat*

The °communist countries maintain they pursue the 'real' democracy of economic and social equality; their °critics point out that 'the °dictatorship of the °proletariat' (effectively the dictatorship of the leaders of the Communist Party) precludes democracy because it denies the citizens the right to democratic activity. The communist critique of western systems of government is that under cover of democracy the °masses are economically and socially exploited. Against that the defenders of western democracy adduce the vast apparatus of the °welfare system.

Ireland is a representative democracy constitutionally.

It also has many laws aimed at taking some wealth from the well-off through °taxation to provide for the less well-off; and it has many citizens who would describe themselves as °social democrats. However, it also has many citizens who believe that within the scope provided by the constitution each citizen should be as free as possible to use his or her energy, skills and enterprise in the pursuit of wealth and happiness. Such people are generally opposed to extensive government interference in social and economic affairs. In the spectrum of political allegiance their views would be regarded as °right wing or conservative.

energy is a transliteration of the Greek word *energeia* which is derived from *en* meaning 'in' and *ergon* meaning 'work'. *Ergonomics* is the study of the worker in the workplace with a view to creating conditions in which he or she can work most efficiently. *Ergatocracy* is 'rule by workers' (*ergatēs* is the Greek for 'worker'). *Metallurgy* 'the art of working metals' derives from the Greek words *metallon* 'metal' and *ourgia* 'working'

Because 'democracy' means so many different things people sometimes get involved in protracted and confusing argument about whether a particular state is democratic or not. The fact is that some governments elected by a majority of the people act in an extremely authoritarian manner. It is much more °productive to think of democracy as a quality that exists to varying degrees in different countries at different times.

Thinking of democracy in this way, one can readily appreciate why people tend to acquiesce in authoritarian government in time of war or deep economic recession, that is, when °physical or economic °survival is at stake, when simple and speedy decisions are required. At other times, when there is the opportunity for reflection and consultation, one tends to find greater participation in decisions — or at least the demand for it. One also appreciates that the degree of democracy in a state depends fundamentally on the commitment of the citizens to freedom and justice for one and all.

People who have power usually wish to be free of any supervision of their use of it: decisions they make may be revealed as foolish or unfair. Or worse. Because they derive their power from a popular constitution they invariably proclaim the virtues of democracy. However, if they wish to limit the quality of democracy they have many means of doing so. They may create a sense of °crisis and thereby a demand for strong non-participative government. They may restrict the flow of information

John Philpot Curran

or cloud it with misinformation. They may buy the support of powerful °interest groups by allowing them privileges. Given human nature, it is realistic to suppose that all rulers, however well-intentioned, will fail to meet the democratic ideal.

The quality of democracy at any particular time must largely depend on the interest the people take in how rulers use the powers they, the people, have °delegated to them. As John Philpot Curran (1755–1817), the Irish lawyer and politician, who was father of Robert Emmet's sweetheart, Sarah Curran, declared: 'The condition upon which God hath given liberty to man is eternal vigilance'.

denote
°indicate what is being spoken of

Denotare is a Latin word 'to indicate by a sign'. A distinction is made between what a word denotes and what it connotes. The denotation of a word is the thing, idea or concept referred to. Thus the word 'rat' denotes any of the larger animals of the genus *Mus*. The connotations of a word are the family of meanings, literal or °metaphorical, associated with its use. Thus the word 'rat' connotes such meanings as four-legged, tailed, living, dirty, sneaky, disloyal. (*Connotare* is a Latin word meaning 'to indicate with' or 'in addition'.)

dénouement
the °final resolution of a play or other complicated situation

Dénouer is the French word 'to unknot' derived from *de*, a Latin particle that negatives a word, and a Latin word *nodare* 'to knot'. To refer to 'the final dénouement' is °tautologous.

de novo
afresh

De is a Latin word meaning 'from' or 'by'. *Novo* is a form of the Latin word *novus* meaning 'new'. The expression °denotes a fresh start: 'Let us forget about what happened in the past and build up our relationship *de novo*'.

determinism
a belief that the movement of everything in the °universe is fixed in advance

Terminus is the Latin word for 'destination'. *Determinare* means 'to set the destination in advance', 'to ordain'. When °modern men and women renewed the °scientific exploration of why things in the world act the way they do, they unfolded a whole range of causes and effects; and as they began to see everything fitting into a system they conceived the world as a kind of machine, a predetermined instrument like a clock. They then began to apply the idea to °human society — their study of the °economic system suggested economic determinism, their study of the way people were ranked in society suggested °social determinism.

Marx expounded a form of economic and social determinism to explain how the forces of °production (the way people meet their °material needs), the stages of °history and the °evolution of °social consciousness (°law, religion, °morality) develop. But he also spoke of the conscious direction of these events by men, though, he averred, we cannot overleap 'the natural phases of °evolution'. Men can read the signs wrongly, and indeed Marx did so himself. Still his °analysis has helped us understand how economic factors mould our °personal, social and °political lives.

deus ex machina
a °totally unexpected intervention that resolves a difficult situation

Deus is the Latin word for 'a god', *ex* is a Latin word meaning 'from', *machina* is a Latin word for 'machine'.

Drama was invented by the Greeks, imitated by the Romans, and passed on to us. Not all ancient playwrights were as great as the Greek °tragedians, Aeschylus and Sophocles. Many allowed their plots to become so complicated that only the arrival on stage of a god, conveyed through the air by a machine, could resolve the situation. Many a °modern playwright or film director has relied on a *deus ex machina* in the form of a rich aunt or the US Cavalry.

dictator
a non-°monarchical absolute ruler

Dicere is the Latin word 'to say' from which 'dictator' is °ultimately derived. A dictator declares what is to be done. In times of great °crisis the Romans would appoint a dictator for a six-month period to assume all the powers of the °state. A despot (from the Greek word *despotēs* meaning 'master') may be a dictator or an absolute monarch such as the °Czar of Russia was. A *benevolent despot* is one who rules paternalistically (*pater* is the Latin word for 'father') — with care for the interests of his °subjects, as opposed to a *tyrant* (from the Greek word *tyrannos* also meaning 'master') — an absolute, non-°dynastic ruler who cares only for his own interests.

A *diktat* (a German word meaning 'something dictated') is a brutal order or harsh statement that must be accepted without discussion.

The appointment of Fabius as dictator. Note the *fasces* carried by his entourage ('entourage' means 'followers' or 'attendants' from the French word *entourer* 'to surround')

didactic
intended to instruct

Didaskein is the Greek word 'to teach'. An *autodidact* is someone who is self-taught (*autos* is the Greek word for 'self').

doctrinaire
pertaining to someone who applies principles rigidly without making allowances for circumstances

Doctrina is the Latin word for 'doctrine' — literally 'knowledge imparted by teaching' — derived from the word *docere* 'to teach'. To indoctrinate is to teach a set of doctrines until they are completely accepted by the °person being indoctrinated. To use advanced and intensive °psychological techniques to indoctrinate is to brainwash. Thus during the Korean War (1951-53) the North Koreans brainwashed captured American soldiers so that they °publicly and voluntarily repudiated their homeland and its °values.

Doctrines may be religious, °political, °scientific etc. A set of doctrines may form an °*ideology*. An ideologist (or ideologue) who insists on applying doctrine irrespective of practical considerations would be described as doctrinaire. Those in °government in Britain during the period of the Irish Famine were doctrinaire °*laisser faire* °economists and refused to intervene in the economy to avert the consequences of the potato blight. They believed that the provision of free or cheap food would make it impossible to bring into being an effective market which, they thought, was the only long-term solution to the shortage.

laisser faire
'to let happen' — these two French words mean 'to allow' and 'to do' respectively; an alternative form *laissez faire* is also used

draconian
a description for an exceptionally harsh °law or °government measure

Draco was an Athenian law-giver — his was the first written Athenian °code (621 BC) — who imposed the death penalty for a breach of any of his laws and so his name became a by-word for severity. A later Greek described this code as 'writ in blood'.

dynasty
a succession of hereditary rulers

Dunamis is a Greek word for 'power' from which dynasty is derived (as well as 'dynamite', 'dynamic' and 'dynamo'). Dynastic rule provides for orderly succession, normally from father to eldest son, and therefore °political stability. (Hereditary derives from the Latin word *heres, heredis* 'an heir'.) But it provides no proof against incompetent rulers. The Brehon law of *derbfine*, whereby succession proceeded from °election among the royal family embracing the male members for four generations, provided for choice of successor, but it was a frequent source of disorder caused by disappointed °candidates.

'Dynasty' may be used nowadays in relation to a family which over a number of generations has won political office at the polls — a political dynasty — or which over a number of generations has maintained itself in the front ranks of business — a commercial dynasty.

E

eclectic
building a °philosophy of life by selecting and gathering together elements that please you from other philosophies of life

Eclegein is the Greek word 'to select'.

economy
the system by which goods and services are °produced and °allocated among consumers

Oikos is a Greek word meaning 'house' and *nomos* is a Greek word meaning 'a law'. The Greek word *oikonomia* (transliterated into Latin as *oeconomia* and into English as *economy*) °originally described the ruling or management of a household. The word may now be applied to the management of the °material resources of an individual, a community, a °locality ('the local economy'), a region ('the Mid-West economy'), a country ('the °national economy'); it may be applied °globally ('the international economy', 'the world economy'). When the °media refer to 'the economy', they usually mean the national economy. Since thrift is one of the great virtues pursued in household management, the word *economical* means in common usage 'thrifty' or 'efficient'.

Economics is the °scientific study of the economy. It is divided into °macroeconomics and °microeconomics. Economics has been called 'the dismal science' (Thomas Carlyle in *Latter Day Pamphlets*) because it was seen as seeking to cope with Malthus's view that °humanity was condemned to a losing battle between °population growth and scarce resources. *Economists* are experts in economics.

National economies are of three kinds. In *free market economies*, the °government plays very little part in the production, exchange and consumption of goods and services. In *command economies*, the °central government, through a planning system, allocates resources. In *mixed economies*, market forces play a large part but the government intervenes extensively. Ireland is a mixed economy.

Gross Domestic Product (GDP) measures the output of the factors of production located in the domestic economy regardless of who owns them (*domestic* derives from the Latin word *domus* 'a house'; it may refer to the home of an individual and contrast, like the word '°private', with '°public'; it may also refer to the national home, and in that sense contrast, like the word 'national', with 'foreign'). In essence the GDP is the °total value of a country's annual output of goods and services. *Gross National Product* (GNP) is GDP adjusted for income flowing out to non-residents and flowing in to residents. It identifies the output, income and expenditure of Irish residents in a year in Ireland.

GDP and GNP are often used as benchmarks against which to measure certain activities. Thus in Ireland in 1987 public °sector expenditure (the total spending controlled by the °public service) was just over fifty per cent of GDP.

When goods and services are produced and not declared for tax purposes, they will not be counted in the GNP. This unrecorded production of goods and services constitutes *the black economy*.

education
the long process whereby people develop the attitudes, knowledge and skills that their society feels they should have in order to function °productively in society; however, a °perennial opposing view of education defines it as a process of °moral and intellectual development of °persons towards truth, goodness and beauty

Educare is a Latin word meaning 'to rear' or 'to develop' (and is to be distinguished from the word *educere* 'to lead out'). Education is distinguished from training which is concerned simply to transfer skills and competencies (and is usually a relatively short process).

Education is °characterised by the approach taken by educators in either of two ways: a *liberal* education is one in which knowledge is pursued for its own sake ('liberal' derives from the Latin word *liber* meaning 'free' — a liberal education was the kind people in °medieval times thought to be appropriate to a freeman — a gentleman rather than a craftsman or servant); a *utilitarian* education is one that is pursued for the sake of practical advantages ('utilitarian' derives from the Latin word *utilis* meaning 'useful').

In Ireland education is characterised by the level of its participants in one of three ways: °primary, post-primary (secondary, vocational, community,

for their own sakes rather than for the sake of society

comprehensive) and third-level (°university, regional °technical college, etc.).

°*Bunreacht na hÉireann* commits the °state to provide for (and therefore not necessarily itself to provide) free primary education for all.

e.g.
for example

E.g. is an abbreviation of the Latin expression *exempli gratia. Gratia* means 'for the sake of', *exempli* means 'an example'. The MGM motto *ars gratia artis* means 'art for the sake of art' (*ars, artis* is the Latin word for 'art'). *Artificial* literally means 'made by art' (the *ficial* ending derives from the Latin word *facere* 'to make'). The German word *ersatz* means 'a replacement' and is sometimes used in English to mean artificial in a decidedly °pejorative sense. For during World War II, the Germans, cut off from external supplies of certain °materials, °produced a wide range of ersatz goods, such as rubber, coffee, tea, sugar, which did not always satisfy the consumers' expectations.

egoism
the °moral disposition to be concerned solely with one's own interests

Ego means 'I' in Latin. *Egotism* means 'self-conceit', 'selfishness'. Leaders may be egotistic or egocentric ('self-centred'). In Freudian °psychology the ego is the self-consciousness (as opposed to the *id*, the sum °total of the automatic, instinctual responses to pleasure and pain — *id* is the Latin word for 'it'). 'Ego' is now used in °popular speech for 'self-image' as in 'His ego took a bruising on the quiz show. They asked him what two and two was and he said twenty-two'.

Alter ego means 'one's other self' (*alter* is the Latin word for 'other' from which we derive 'alternative'). It is used of friends so close that in any given situation one can be relied upon to act in the same way as the other would.

Doppelgänger is a German word meaning 'one's double' (literally 'one's double goer') manifesting in a natural way as a °physical lookalike or in a °sinister way as a wraith. The use of a *doppelgänger* is a common device in German fiction.

Éire
Ireland

The ancient Irish worshipped a goddess of sovereignty whose various names — Fódhla, Banba, Éire — were often applied to the country itself. Éire came to be most commonly used.

Under the °constitution enacted in 1922 by the °Dáil, the °state was described as the Irish Free State (in Irish *Saorstát Éireann*).

°*Bunreacht na hÉireann,* the Constitution of Ireland enacted by the people in 1937, states in article 4 'The name of the State is Éire, or in the English language, Ireland'.

John Scottus Ériugena as depicted on the Irish five pound note

In the °Republic of Ireland Act, 1948, the Dáil provided that 'the description of the State shall be the Republic of Ireland'. Note the distinction between 'name' and 'description'. The usage preferred by the government is the constitutional one. Thus the °President is the President of Ireland (*Uachtarán na hÉireann*) and the government is the Government of Ireland (*Rialtas na hÉireann*).

Ériu is an old form of Éire; Ériugena means 'born in Ireland' — compare '°indigenous'. John Scottus Ériugena (c.800-877) was the greatest figure among the °philosophers of his age. A °Neoplatonist and Greek scholar, he headed the school at the court of Charles the Bald of France.

He was also famous for his wit. Once when he was among those dining with the king, he being at one end of the table, the king at the other, the king could not resist making an outrageous pun at John Scottus Ériugena's expense: 'Can anyone tell me', said the king, 'the difference between an Irishman [*Scotus* in Latin] and a pig [*sottus*]?' John Scottus shot back: 'The table'.

The term 'Ériugena' distinguishes the Irishman from Duns Scotus (c. 1270-1308), a famous Franciscan philosopher who was born in Scotland (and from whose name the word 'dunce' is derived).

élitist
favouring a select group for °social and particularly °political privileges; it has the

Élite is a French word meaning 'chosen' derived from the Latin word *eligere* 'to select' (from which we also get 'elect', 'election', 'electoral' 'electorate'). An élite is a °minority within a group which exercises preponderant °influence over the group (*pre* is a Latin particle here

°connotation of applying standards which can be attained only by the few

meaning 'surpassingly'; *ponderare* is the Latin word 'to weigh').

A *ruling élite* is that °minority in a °state which holds most of the °public °offices. People may enter the élite through such advantages as their birth and the social connections thereby established, the schools they go to, their ability or the positions their wealth wins for them.

Probably most people regard élites as snobbish and anti-°egalitarian — 'élitism' and 'élitist' are usually °pejorative terms; others regard élites either as the °natural °product of man's tendency to associate with people of like tastes and talents or as a means of asserting standards of °excellence in a society (not necessarily standards of moral excellence but standards of excellence in whatever activities a society places value on: thus an élite army corps is so identified not because it is exceptionally good °morally but because it is exceptionally good at killing).

empirical
pertaining to knowledge derived from experience

Empeirikos is a Greek word meaning 'from experience'. To experience is to °articulate for oneself the meaning of a real life situation whether it be an action, a relationship (such as marriage), a walk in the mountains, a kiss. Here, for example in the experience of a kiss or falling in love, what is stressed is the newness of experience, that is, it reshapes our thoughts and feelings in such a way that we see the world anew, as it were. That element is true of all genuine experience even if it is not always manifest to us. In that sense experiencing is °synonomous with knowing and learning.

Experience, like knowledge, can be true or false, though we tend to regard experience as always true. The experienced person is one who, through living and acting in a particular area of human life, and reflecting on it, has acquired understanding and knowledge of that area, and is capable of articulating it to others. The experienced person is usually regarded as a wise person. However, it is worth recalling what was said of the Bourbons when Charles X abdicated and fled Paris in 1830: 'They experienced everything and learned nothing'.

Locke

The word 'empiricist' has a special meaning in the °history of °philosophy and the attempt to explain knowledge. The empiricists believed that what we know are the impressions or sense data that objects leave on our senses, and that consequently we have no direct knowledge of the external world (*data* is the plural form of *datum*, a Latin word literally meaning 'a thing given'). We can only know the external world, therefore, through inference from these impressions or sense data. What we know about the world is nothing more than complexes of these impressions or sense data. Thus 'table' is a word we use to refer to a complex of impressions like hardness, colour, shape, size °etc. It does not refer to the real table at all. In other words, our sensations, instead of being knowledge of the real thing, are barriers between us and things.

Hume

Statements of fact, then, are inferences, from our impressions, to the real world. Empiricists consequently have always had a problem with the connection between thought (language) and reality. This is called the problem of verification, of how, if we know only our impressions, do we establish the truth of what are called factual propositions (*verus* is the Latin word for 'true'; to verify is to establish the truth about something). The empiricist account of knowledge locks the knower inside himself or herself. Solipsism, that is, self-enclosedness, leads to the problem of how we know other persons or things. (*Solipsism* derives from the Latin words *solus* 'alone' and *ipse* 'self'; a *solecism* is a grammatical error and is derived from a Greek word *soloikismos* meaning 'speaking like the citizens of Soloi', that is, incorrectly; Soloi was a °colony of Athens; the Athenians, °sophisticated and chic, were inclined to sneer at their ruder countrymen; Athens was in a district called Attica; 'Attic' meaning 'from Attica' was used as a synonym for 'the finest'.)

Berkeley

Among the greatest empiricist philosophers were the British thinkers John Locke (1631–1704) and David Hume (1711-76). The Irish thinker George Berkeley (1685–1753), Bishop of Cloyne, after whom the °University of California at Berkeley is called, has °traditionally been ranked among the empiricists. However, note that in *The Irish Mind* Harry Bracken argues that °modern research suggests Berkeley should be °classified not with the British empiricists but with the Cartesians, the followers of the French mathematician and philosopher, René Descartes (1596–1650), the founder of modern rationalist philosophy, who enunciated the famous principle *cogito ergo sum* ('I think — therefore I am'). A good deal of °current British philosophy is a refined version of empirical thinking.

encyclical
a circular letter sent by the Pope to all Catholic bishops dealing authoritatively but not necessarily infallibly with religious and °social issues; the term is used in other Christian Churches too

Kyklos is the Greek word for 'circle': an encyclical is sent round in a circle among the faithful. Probably the most famous encyclical of °modern times is Pope Paul VI's *Humanae Vitae* (issued in 1968) which condemns °artificial forms of birth control (encyclicals, usually written in Latin, take their titles from their first few words — *humanae vitae* means 'of human life' in Latin).

ephemeral
lasting for a short time

Epi (*eph* before a vowel or a word beginning with h) is a Greek word meaning 'upon' or 'at'. *Hēmera* is the Greek word for 'day'. In Greek °tragedy the gods — the °immortals — often address men as *ephēmeroi* — 'beings of a day'. A writer's *juvenilia* (writings done in his or her youth, from *juvenis* the Latin word for 'young' from which we also derive 'juvenile') are usually ephemeral. Newspapers and periodicals are referred to as 'ephemera' (the plural of the Greek word *ephēmeron*, 'a thing of no lasting value'). *Hēmera* lurks in the title of Boccaccio's *Decameron*, a book made up of stories, like Chaucer's *The Canterbury Tales*, told on successive days (in the case of the *Decameron* ten days — *deka* is the Greek word for 'ten').

eponymous
pertaining to someone who gives his or her name to something, °e.g. a place, people, book, play, film

Epi is a Greek word meaning 'upon' or 'at'. *Onoma* is the Greek word for 'name'. Thus we might say that the great Celtic god Lugh is the eponymous god of Louth (*Co. Lughaidh*), Lugnaquilla, and the month of August in Irish (*mí Lúnasa*); that at the end of *Hamlet* the eponymous hero dies of a wound from a poisoned sword; that Pallas Athene, who sprang fully-armed from the head of Zeus, is the eponymous goddess of Athens.

the establishment
those who control, or °influence those who control, a country

The modern usage of the word is traced back to *The Spectator* of September 1955 where Henry Fairlie wrote in his regular column: 'By the "Establishment" I do not mean only the °centres of °official power though they are certainly a part of it—but rather the whole matrix of official and °social relations within which power is exercised' (*matrix* means 'womb' and derives from *mater* the Latin word for 'mother'; by extension 'matrix' means that within which something is embedded). 'Establishment', derived from the Latin word *stare* 'to stand', means 'setting up on a firm foundation'. The people who maintain a °state would include °politicians, senior °public servants, newspaper owners, leaders of trade unions and other °major °interest groups. The establishment is an informal concept and therefore one cannot define precisely who belongs to it. It has a °conservative °connotation and those who belong to it would contrast with °radicals, °iconoclasts, °revolutionaries (depending on how conservative the society is). The term may also be applied to any °organised segment of society — for example the medical establishment, the cycling establishment.

ethnic
pertaining to race

Ethnos is the Greek word for 'a people'. The flood of °emigration that followed the Great Famine (an exodus often referred to as the Irish diaspora, because it was similar to the scattering of the Jewish people following their unsuccessful revolt in Palestine against the Romans in the first and second °centuries AD — the Jewish diaspora) has resulted in the existence of large numbers of people (perhaps as many as sixty million) of Irish ethnic °origin in Britain, the US, Canada and Australia. *Diaspora* is derived from the Greek words *dia* meaning 'through' or 'across' and *spora* meaning 'scattering'. *Ethnology* is the study of the various peoples that make up the °human race (*logos* is the Greek word for 'a word', 'reason', 'account').

The Romans capture the °Temple of Jerusalem, 70 AD

eu-
eugenics, eulogy, euphemism, euphony, euphoria, euthanasia — these are all words whose common prefix *eu-* means 'well' in Greek

Eugenics means the °science of °producing fine offspring, applied particularly in livestock breeding, especially horse breeding. It became notorious when °Nazi Germany applied it as a policy for the breeding of °humans (*genikos* means 'concerning stock or race' in Greek).

A *eulogy* is a speech or article in praise of someone (*logos* means 'word', 'reason', 'account', in Greek); it tends to be formal, often delivered at a funeral. (An *encomium*, from the Greek *enkōmion*, is also a speech in praise of someone — usually a living person — and so is a *panegyric*, from the Greek *panēgurikos* meaning '[a speech] fit for a °national assembly' — *pan* is the Greek for 'all' *aguris* is the Greek for 'assembly'.)

A *euphemism* is a mild expression for something harsh or distasteful. Thus a speaker would be euphemistic if he or she were to °characterise a raving °lunatic as 'somewhat odd' (*phēmē* is the Greek for 'speech').

Euphony is a pleasing sound (*phōnē* is 'voice' or 'sound' in Greek).

Euphoria is a °state of great delight (*phoria* is 'feeling' in Greek).

Euthanasia is the act of bringing about an easeful death, notorious for its being a policy of Nazi Germany towards old unproductive people, the °physically and °mentally handicapped, and the sexually deviant (*thanatos* is 'death' in Greek).

European Community the association of twelve Western European countries based on the Treaty of Rome (25 March 1957)

Europe is Greek in °origin. It may mean 'broad-face' (*eur-opē*), a °synonym for the full moon, and a title of the Moon-goddess Demeter. It may also mean 'good for willows' (*eu-ropē*) and therefore 'well-watered'. *Community*, derived from the Latin *communis* meaning 'common', °denotes a group bound together by common interests. The EC is not a °state, but it may be an embryonic state (*embryonic* derives from the Greek *embryon* 'a swelling in [a mother]' and therefore pertains to a seedling).

Robert Schuman, the French statesman who is regarded as the father of the European Community. Each year, 9 May is celebrated as Schuman Day throughout the EC

The origins of the European Community (EC) are usually traced to the Paris Treaty of 1951 which established the European Coal and Steel Community. In 1957 the Rome Treaties established the European °Economic Community (EEC) and the European °Atomic °Energy Community (EURATOM). The °institutions serving the three Communities were merged in 1967. A Single European °Act (SEA) was agreed at the European Council meeting in Luxembourg in December 1985. It modified and extended the EEC Treaty. The SEA came into effect on 1 July 1987.

The basic aim of the Communities is to promote peace and prosperity by establishing economic and °political unity between the countries of Western Europe, particularly between France and Germany. The original six members (Belgium, the °Federal Republic of Germany, France, Italy, Luxembourg and the Netherlands) were joined by the United Kingdom, Ireland and Denmark in 1973, by Greece in 1981, and by Spain and Portugal in 1986.

The EC has abolished customs duties in trade between member states, has a common external tariff and a Common Agricultural Policy (CAP). Workers from member states are free to work anywhere in the Community and citizens have the right to settle in any

member state they like. The European °Monetary System (EMS) helps Community trade by keeping the values of the °currencies of the member states relatively stable, and the Community's free °competition policies have removed abuses. The Community enters into external trade agreements on behalf of its member states, has special funds to promote regional and °social development, develops Community industrial policy, and provides aid for developing countries, notably through the provisions of the Lomé °Convention which it has signed with more than sixty African, °Caribbean and Pacific (ACP) countries.

Notwithstanding the progress towards °integration which has been made to date, many barriers — °technical, °physical and °fiscal — remain within the Community. Furthermore, these so-called non-tariff barriers represent a considerable cost to the Community in terms of prices, growth and °employment. In 1985, the European Commission under its °President, Jacques Delors, drew up a °White Paper which listed the measures — some 300 in all — required to eliminate these barriers and thus complete the internal market. The °objective of adopting all these measures by 31 December 1992 was subsequently enshrined in the Single European Act.

The signing of the Rome Treaties, 25 March 1957, in the Palazzo Farnese

Political co-operation between the member states was introduced formally in the Single European Act. The member states collaborate in the development of a common approach to foreign policy. Notable examples of political co-operation are a common Community position at the Western Economic °Summits, at the United Nations and on specific °topics such as the Middle East.

Jack Lynch, TD, °Taoiseach (right) and Dr Patrick J. Hillery, Minister for Foreign Affairs, sign the Treaty of Accession to the European Community on behalf of Ireland in Brussels, 22 January 1972

There are two sorts of Community °law: °primary law (the Treaties) and secondary law (the °Acts of the institutions). Both are binding on °national °governments and take precedence over national law. For this reason, Ireland was obliged to amend its °constitution by °referendum before assuming the obligations of membership.

Secondary law is the product of the Community's °legislative process. In the case of °major policies, draft proposals for action are put foward by the Commission and considered for adoption by the Council of Ministers with the advice or opinion of the European °Parliament and of the Economic and Social Committee. Given a Council decision, the Commission is usually responsible for its implementation and enforcement. The Commission also has the power to legislate without reference to the other institutions on day-to-day management issues. Points of law, interpretation of the Treaties °etc., are decided by the Court of Justice of the European Communities. The implementation of secondary legislation by the government in Ireland is overseen by the °Oireachtas Joint Committee on Secondary Legislation. In addition, the government submits a twice-yearly report to the Oireachtas on developments in the European Communities.

The European Council is a meeting of Community °heads of state or government. Under the Single European Act, they meet at least twice a year. They deal with political affairs and the °strategic policy decisions.

The EC Council of Ministers consists of a ministerial representative of each member state. The ministers attending are those who carry the appropriate national responsibility for the matter in hand (Foreign Affairs, Agriculture, Finance, etc.), but the premier council is, generally speaking, that of Foreign Ministers. The presidency of the Council is held for six months by each state in turn.

Jacques Delors, °President of the EC Commission and architect of the Single European Act ('architect' derives from the Greek *archos* 'chief' and *tektōn* 'a builder')

The Commission of the European Communities, which has a four-year °mandate, consists of seventeen members, two from each large country and one from each of the smaller countries. Commissioners take an oath to uphold the Community and forswear national allegiances. They act as a collegiate body. The Commission's primary role is the initiation of Community legislation. In carrying out its responsibility, the Commission can call on the services of a largely Brussels-based secretariat °organised into departments known as Directorates General and with a total staff of around 11,000. The senior EC officials in Brussels are colloquially referred to as 'Eurocrats' (on °analogy with '°bureaucrats').

The European Parliament consists of 518 members °elected for a five-year term. The last elections took place in 1989. Parliament is required to be consulted on many issues, and is in effect consulted on all matters of importance to the Community. Parliament's opinion is often °influential in the drafting of Community legislation. It has power, within certain limits, to alter the annual Community °budget; and parliament finally adopts the budget and grants a discharge to the Commission and the other Community institutions on the satisfactory implementation of past budgets. Parliament can also give an opinion on its own initiative.

Members of Parliament may table °oral and/or written questions, with or without debate, to the Commission, the Council and the Foreign Ministers acting in political co-operation. This is an important power, and it is used to bring to light many aspects of Community business. Parliament's main work is done in its eighteen specialist committees, and committee reports are debated and adopted by the Parliament in °plenary session.

The Court of Justice, consisting of twelve judges plus a presiding judge, is the final arbiter of Community law. It decides on alleged Treaty infringements which may be referred to it and in certain cases may provide Community institutions and national courts with definitive interpretations of Community law.

The Economic and Social Committee is the most important of the many advisory committees in the Community structure. It has 189 members, drawn from the twelve member states, and represents employers, workers and various and general °interests. The Committee provides opinions on Commission proposals, and can also put forward opinions on its own initiative.

P. J. Hillery

Richard Burke

Michael O'Kennedy

Peter Sutherland

Ray MacSharry

The European Investment Bank (EIB) is the Community's long-term financial institution. It borrows on the financial markets and lends on a non-profit basis for investment projects promoting regional development, industrial modernisation and trans-national Community projects. The EIB also provides EC development finance in many °third world countries.

The Court of Auditors fulfils for the Community institutions the role of a comptroller and auditor-general.

The Irishmen who have served as EC Commissioners are: Dr P. J. Hillery (1973–76), Richard Burke (1977–81; 1982–85), Michael O'Kennedy (1981–82); Peter Sutherland (1985–89), Ray MacSharry (1989–).

ex cathedra
with absolute authority

Ex is a Latin word meaning 'from'. *Kathedra* means 'chair' in Greek. The *cathedra* (the Latin transliteration of *kathedra*) was the chair or pulpit from which a lecture was given and therefore it came to mean the place from which authoritative statements were made. The °doctrine of Papal Infallibility states that when a pope speaks *ex cathedra* (from the chair of Peter) on matters of faith or °morals, to be held by all the faithful, he is speaking infallibly ('not liable to error' — *in* is a Latin prefix that negatives a word, *fallere* is the Latin word 'to deceive' from which we also derive 'fallacy' and 'fallacious').

A *cathedral* is a church where a bishop has his seat.

exchequer
the °national treasury

Scaccarium is the Latin word for 'chessboard' from which we get the word 'chequered'. In °medieval times the Court of Exchequer in England was charged with looking after the king's revenues and was so called because a chequered cloth was laid on the table of the court. Its various columns were assigned to thousands, hundreds, scores and tens of pounds, and to shillings and to pence; with the use of various types of counters, it provided a simple accounting display unit for a virtually innumerate society (*numerus* is the Latin word for 'a number', *in* is a Latin negative particle).

The Chancellor of the Exchequer in Britain is the equivalent of our Minister for Finance. The British finance department is known as The Treasury.

The word 'exchequer' occurs in Ireland where the source of funding of °government services is being discussed. Governments either charge directly for the services they provide — the issue of passports, for example — or bear the cost of the service 'out of the exchequer' — from taxes or borrowing.

It occurs in the title of the quarterly statement by the Department of Finance — The Exchequer Returns — which outlines how government tax revenue and expenditure is proceeding. This document is of great interest to °economists and financial °institutions (which make loans to government) and to individual investors.

It also occurs in the terms Exchequer Account, °Exchequer Borrowing Requirement, Exchequer Bill and Exchequer Stock. The Exchequer Account is the principal account of the government. All tax receipts are eventually lodged to this account and payments in respect of government expenditure are made from it. The account is maintained at the Central Bank. A °budget °deficit gives rise to an Exchequer Borrowing Requirement. In order to supplement Exchequer receipts, the government resorts to °domestic and foreign borrowing, both short-term and long-term. One form of domestic short-term borrowing is effected through the issue of Exchequer bills. These bills, which can have a maturity range of one month, three months and six months, are issued weekly, by tender to banks and other financial institutions. The bills are issued at a discount (£100's worth at maturity for say £97 at issue). Exchequer bills are bearer instruments, which means that there is no register of ownership. They are transferred by endorsement, that is, by signing on their reverse side. Exchequer bills are attractive to the banks and other financial institutions because they allow them to earn income on cash they cannot afford to tie up in long-term investment (because of the cash-flow requirements of their own °organisations). Longer term domestic borrowing is effected through the issue of government gilts or stocks. These gilts may have a maturity up to twenty years and are issued as the need arises. On occasions, government gilts have been given the name Exchequer stocks.

ex officio
by reason of one's office

E (*ex* before a vowel) is a Latin word meaning 'from'. *Officio* is a form of *officium* meaning 'public position' in Latin — hence 'office', 'official', 'officious'. The expression is used in relation to membership of certain °institutions or committees and °denotes that a certain °person is a member by reason of the office he or she holds. Thus the °Taoiseach, the °Tánaiste, the Chief Justice, the °President of the High Court, the °Ceann Comhairle, the chairman of °Seanad Éireann and the Attorney General are all *ex officio* members of the Council of °State (the body that advises the President in the exercise of certain of his or her functions).

ex parte
from one side only

Ex is a Latin word meaning 'from'. *Pars, partis* means 'part' in Latin. *Ex parte* is an expression which means giving only one side of a matter, being partial or one-sided. In law, *ex parte* describes an application by one side in a °judicial proceeding without formal notice having been given to the other side of the intention to make the application.

Because the courts are bound to follow the rules of °natural justice one of which is that a °person has a right to be heard in his own defence (the rule in Latin is *audi alteram partem* — hear the other side), a court will not, on an application made *ex parte,* °determine finally any contested issue between persons. Orders made *ex parte* generally relate to preliminary or procedural matters arising before proceedings are commenced, for example an application for leave to serve a summons on a person resident outside the jurisdiction of the °state or to substitute service of a document by post for personal service.

The other great rule of natural justice is that the judge should be impartial (the rule in Latin is *nemo judex in causa sua* — no one may be a judge in his own case, that is, where his or her own interest is involved).

extempore
without preparation, on the spur of the moment

Ex is a Latin word meaning 'from'. *Tempus, temporis* means 'time' in Latin. The expression is used of °public speaking. Someone who successfully speaks extempore is admired because the feat is so difficult.

F

Fabianism
the °strategy of the Fabian Society, founded by British °socialists in 1884, to seek social and °political change peacefully and gradually rather than through °revolution

Fabian is derived from the Latin name *Fabius*. When the Carthaginian general, Hannibal, crossed the Alps with his elephants and invaded Italy, he trounced the Roman armies sent against him. The Romans then appointed Q. Fabius Maximus as °dictator. He stubbornly refused to hazard his troops in a pitched battle with Hannibal. He resorted to skirmishes and guerrilla °tactics to contain the Carthaginians. Indeed his impatient Roman °critics nicknamed him *Cunctator* ('The Delayer'). The policy, however, worked. Hannibal's strength was gradually dissipated and he left Italy in 203 BC without having attained his °objectives.

fait accompli
an accomplished fact

Fait is the French word meaning 'a fact'. *Accomplir* is the French word 'to do' or 'to accomplish'. Thus, 'By the time his warning got through to the °government the rebel takeover of the °television station was a *fait accompli*'.

fanatic
someone who is excessively enthusiastic about a leader, a movement or even an activity — a fan

Fanum is a Latin word for 'temple'. Fanatics were °originally religious enthusiasts — they were *fanaticus* i.e. inspired by a deity of some kind. The word 'profane' derives from *fanum* and *pro* a Latin prefix meaning 'before' — a profane thing is something that is before, i.e. outside, the temple. In its weak sense 'profane' is equivalent to '°secular', in its strong sense it means 'blasphemous'.

fascism
the aggressive, °dictatorial, totalitarian, °nationalistic, °right wing movements associated especially with Hitler and Mussolini

The *fasces* were a bundle of rods tied around an axe which was carried before a Roman consul as a °symbol of his authority. Mussolini (1883–1945), who dreamt of restoring Italy to greatness, harked back to Roman times and used the *fasces* as a symbol for his movement: the bound bundle of rods represented the strength a society derived from uniting around an authoritarian °political leader (the axe). The other °dictators and extreme right wing leaders who appeared in other countries later, for example Hitler in Germany, Mosley in Britain, Quisling

The fasces

in Norway, Franco in Spain, were also called fascists. Fascism was a heady mix of °nationalism, °socialism, °pseudo-scientific theories of race, mass °psychology, violence, discipline.

It appealed to ordinary people frightened by widespread °unemployment and world recession because it gave hope, it gave a glimpse of glory, and for some time it improved the °physical conditions of the °masses.

Fascism found its most powerful expression in Germany where it was called national socialism (in German 'national sozialismus'), hence 'Nazi', but German socialists and °communists rejected it. Being anti-communist, it attracted support from the °conservatives and right wing elements (the German conservatives thought they could control the Nazis with the help of the army and its °traditionalist officers). It was anti-°democratic and °illiberal (it did not tolerate any ideas other than those of the leader). It was totalitarian — it demanded a total commitment to the °state on the part of the citizens, this being seen as an essential condition for their own °welfare (*totus* means 'all' in Latin).

Though the °original fascists have disappeared, the term is still sometimes loosely used to abuse anyone opposed to °left wing or liberal positions.

Mussolini

fate
destiny

Fata is a form of the Latin word *fari* 'to speak' meaning 'the things that have been spoken [about a person by an oracle]', and therefore his or her destiny. The *Fata* were °personified as the three goddesses of fate. The Greeks named them as Clotho who assigns each man and woman his or her lot at birth, to be born rich or poor, healthy or weak, Lachesis who spins the thread of life, and Atropos who cuts it at the end 'with th'abhorred shears' (as Milton says in *Lycidas*).

The idea that a °person's life and death are determined at the moment of birth fascinated and depressed the Greeks and gave them one of their greatest literary themes. Thus Oedipus, destined to kill his father and marry his mother, does so in spite of the extraordinary

The Three Fates in St Stephen's Green, Dublin, presented by the °Federal Republic of Germany to the Irish people in gratitude for help received after World War II

efforts of his parents and himself to escape that fate; and in Homer's *Iliad* Achilles knows that if he stays on at Troy he will die young but become famous whereas if he returns home he will live to a ripe old age but die obscure. (He stays on and is killed by a Trojan arrow which strikes the only °vulnerable part of him, his right heel; for when he was born his mother, the goddess Thetis, in order to make him °immortal, had dipped every bit of him in the river Styx except the heel by which she held him — a fateful oversight.)

Trojan
— pertaining to the city of Troy (also called Ilium). Paris, the son of Priam, king of Troy, fell in love with Helen, the beautiful wife of the Greek prince Menelaus, and carried her off to Troy. The Greeks gathered a great fleet and pursued the lovers. Thus Helen's became 'the face that launched a thousand ships' (Christopher Marlowe, 1564–1593, in *Dr Faustus*)

If their belief in fate is strong, people tend to become *fatalistic*, that is, passive. 'Whatever will be, will be' is how the °popular song expresses it; 'There's a divinity that shapes our ends/Rough-hew them how we will' is how Shakespeare in *Hamlet* expresses it. Fate is associated with death, the most awesome feature of one's destiny; and so we describe an accident in which someone is killed as 'fatal'.

federation
a union of a number of °states or associations

Foedus, foederis is the Latin word for 'a treaty'. When a number of states that wish to retain their identity to some degree come together for a long-term common purpose and subscribe to a treaty or °constitution providing for a °central authority, they may be described as either a confederation or a federation. They are distinguished by the fact that the central authority of a confederation is far weaker than that of a federation. In a confederation the central authority acts only indirectly on the citizens through the °governments of the component states. In a federation the central authority (the federal government) acts directly on the citizens in regard to matters ascribed to it in the constitution, while the governments of the states act directly on the citizens in regard to matters ascribed to them. The United States of America, whose Latin motto *E pluribus unum* means 'From many one', is the paramount exemplar of a federation. It has a written constitution which provides for a central government — the federal government — and state governments for each of the fifty states. The federal and state governments have all got a separate °legislature, °executive and judiciary. The

The logo of the United States ('logo' is short for 'logotype' — *logos* is 'word' in Greek, *typos* is 'stamp' or 'impression' in Greek — and is used to describe the design of the words or symbol, or combination of both, by which an organisation seeks to be instantly recognised)

federal government acts directly on the citizens in specified matters.

In °modern times states have tended to form federations rather than confederations. Thus Switzerland describes itself as a confederation (Confederation Helvetica — hence CH on Swiss car-plates, *Helvetia* being the Latin word for 'Switzerland') but since 1848 it has been a federation. The German Federal Republic, the USSR, Canada, Australia and India are also federations. States with a single government like our own are known as unitary states (*unus* is the Latin word for 'one'). A unitary state usually has °local or regional authorities but these are °totally subordinate to the °national government. A federal solution to the problem of Northern Ireland is sometimes proposed, that is, that the government of Ireland might be shared by a federal government, representative of the whole country, and two (or more) state governments.

fellow traveller
someone who goes along with the °official °communist line while denying he or she is a communist

The term came into vogue in the 1930s in Britain to describe people intellectually sympathetic to the Russian °communists. George Bernard Shaw, the Irish-born °Fabian who returned enthusiastically from his visits to Russia, was accused of being a fellow traveller. So were many Americans during the course of Senator Joe McCarthy's notorious anti-communist campaign in the US in the 1950s.

feminism
a movement aimed at promoting the rights of women

Femina is a Latin word meaning 'woman'. The suffragists at the beginning of the twentieth °century campaigned to secure equal °political rights for women (*suffragium* is the Latin word for 'vote') — the right to °vote and the right to stand for °election. Feminism today is concerned to attain °economic and °social equality too for women. It had its °origins in the °radical °politics of the 1960s when various °minorities, for example the blacks in America, sought to liberate themselves from °legal discrimination and deleterious °stereotyping (*dēlētērios* is a Greek word meaning 'hurtful').

Women began to appreciate the economic and social disabilities from which they suffered. They began to campaign to liberate themselves — hence Women's Lib.

Countess Markievicz, 1908. A Sinn Féin activist, she was elected MP for Dublin in 1918, the first woman to be elected to the House of Commons. She did not take her seat at Westminster but became a minister in the °cabinet of the first Dáil

Consciousness-raising (CR) groups and courses in assertiveness helped women °psychologically in sustaining their campaign. Subsequently some advances have been made in marriage and °employment law (in Ireland the important Employment Equality Agency was established in 1977 to promote equal employment opportunities for men and women) and stereotyping is being tackled in the schools through, among other measures, the elimination of sexism in texts. The hard °sociological reality, however, is that the vast °majority of positions in the middle and top ranks of business and °public administration are held by men. Moreover, there are still parts of the country where 'herself' thinks it best to say nothing.

Emily Davison throwing herself under the King's horse at the Derby 1913. Her death greatly intensified the women's suffragist campaign

Fianna Fáil
the name of Ireland's largest °political party

The Fianna were a group of heroes led by Finn Mac Cumhaill, whose exploits are recounted in the Fenian Cycle of legends ('Fenian' is derived from 'Fianna'). They were believed to be a standing army in the service of the High King Cormac Mac Airt, who flourished in the third °century AD. *Fál* is an Irish word meaning 'destiny'. The Lia Fáil (the Stone of Destiny) is a famous stone on the Hill of Tara in Co. Meath on which the °pagan High Kings stood at their °inauguration.

Fianna Fáil is usually translated 'Soldiers of Destiny'. The name was adopted by the new °republican party founded by Eamon de Valera and his followers in the Scala Theatre, Dublin in May 1926 after their break with the °militant republicans of the Anti-Treaty movement. The party contested the two general °elections held in June and September 1927, gaining forty-four seats in the first and fifty-seven in the second — almost as many as the ruling Cumann na nGaedheal party. On 10 August 1927 de Valera and the Fianna Fáil deputies abandoned their policy of abstention from the °Dáil and took their seats for the first time.

However, deputies were required by the °Constitution of the Irish Free °State to take an oath of allegiance to the British °monarch before they could take their seats — a thing repugnant to republicans. De Valera cut this °Gordian knot: he removed the °Bible on the table beside the register of those taking the oath, declared he was taking no oath and signed the register. The entry of Fianna Fáil into the Dáil ensured thereafter the constitutional and °democratic character of Irish °politics.

In the general election of 1932 Fianna Fáil won seventy-two seats and emerged as the biggest party in the Dáil. In March 1932 de Valera, with the support of Labour, formed a °government. The peaceful transfer of power from William T. Cosgrave's Cumann na nGaedheal °administration to de Valera's new administration was a crucial moment in Ireland's democratic experience. Fianna Fáil went on to become the °dominant force in °modern Irish politics.

fiat
a magisterial command

Fiat is a form of the Latin word *fieri* and means 'let it be done!'. It derives from God's magisterial command in *Genesis*, the first book of the °Bible: 'Fiat lux!' ('Let there be light!'); *magister* is the Latin word for 'master' from which 'magisterial' derives. Thus, 'On Monday, Reagan told the United °Nations that the United °States would continue to fight for °democracy in Nicaragua, as it would all over the world, including in South Africa. The °sentiment was admirable, but democracy can seldom be imposed by American fiat'. (*The Sunday Times,* 27 September 1987)

sentiment means 'feeling'. *Sentimentalists* are people governed more by feelings than reason (*sentire* is the Latin word 'to feel')

Fiat, the Italian car-makers, derive their name not from the Latin word but from the initial letters of their name in Italian: Fabbrica Italiana Automobili Torino (The Italian °Automobile Factory, Turin).

Fiat lux! (Gustave Doré)

fifth columnist
a secret supporter of the enemy operating from within

The Spanish °civil war broke out in July 1936. In October of that year the °nationalists under General Mola were poised to seize Madrid. When asked by a group of foreign journalists which of his four columns would take the city, Mola replied that it would be that 'fifth column' of secret nationalist supporters already within the °capital. Madrid held out until the end of the war in March 1939.

filibuster
to obstruct °legislation by making interminable speeches during a debate

An American °political term, filibuster comes from the French *filibustier,* a corruption of the English word 'freebooter', meaning 'a piratical adventurer'. Filibusters were common practice in the US °Senate where, until comparatively recently, debate was unlimited. It was a favourite °tactic in the 1960s by which Senators from the South thwarted the attempts of the °majority to introduce °civil rights legislation. Since 1975 a filibuster can be ended by a °vote of three-fifths of the full Senate.

Fine Gael
the name of the second largest °political party in the °state

W.T. Cosgrave

Fine is an Irish word for 'extended family'. *Gael* is the Irish word for the Celtic-speaking race that was °predominant in Ireland from the Iron Age (several °centuries BC) to the fall of Gaelic Ireland in the seventeenth century. 'Fine Gael' like '°Fianna Fáil' signals that the party seeks to be a broadly based °nationalist party.

In January 1933 de Valera called a snap general °election and won an overall °majority in the °Dáil. A second electoral defeat within a year was a °traumatic experience for the Cumann na nGaedheal party (founded in 1923 by the pro-Treatyites). The idea took hold that a united opposition party should be formed by a merger of Cumann na nGaedheal, the °Centre Party, and the Blueshirt movement (headed by General Eoin O'Duffy and called the National Guard, previously the Army Comrades' Association).

Following the °government's banning in 1933 of the quasi-°fascist National Guard on the grounds that it was a threat to °democratic °institutions, a new party called Fine Gael (United Ireland) was formed from those elements (*quasi* is a Latin word meaning 'as if'; used as a prefix it means 'to some degree'). The °charismatic but politically inept O'Duffy was appointed leader of the party. After a year O'Duffy resigned and William T. Cosgrave succeeded him.

The association with the Blueshirts was to be an embarrassment for Fine Gael for some time. The party has on five occasions successfully challenged Fianna Fáil as the °natural party of government by forming °coalition governments. It has not, so far, succeeded to government on its own.

fiscal rectitude
the management of the °public finances in a strictly prudent manner

Fiscus is a Latin word for 'money chest'. It °originally signified a wicker-basket such as the Romans used to store and carry about large sums of money. In °imperial times it came to be applied to the Emperor's — and therefore the °state — treasury. Fiscal, derived from *fiscus*, refers to the public purse — the °exchequer. *Rectitudo, rectitudinis* is a Latin word for 'straightness' or 'rightness'.

In °modern times Irish °governments like most other governments took on the task of delivering an enormous range of services to their citizens. They charged for a small number of these but provided most of them 'free'. The money for the 'free' services came from the taxes paid by the citizens. Borrowing from financial °institutions at home and abroad was °traditionally accepted as the proper way to finance °capital projects.

Governments found it difficult °politically to resist demands for more and more 'free' services. °Taxation increased sharply as a result. The citizens began to resist increases in taxation but continued to demand more 'free' services.

Governments sought to satisfy these °contradictory demands by borrowing °massively to meet current as well as capital requirements ('current' means 'running' or 'belonging to the period of time now passing' and derives from the Latin word *currere* 'to run' — the ancients thought of the passage of time in terms of a running river). The °national debt, which must be repaid out of taxation, soared. Fiscal rectitude is a term used to °denote the °regime of cutbacks in public services and high taxation being applied by the Irish — and other — governments to rectify the public finances.

focus
the °central point, the point upon which attention centres

Focus is the Latin word for 'hearth'. The fireplace is a °natural centre in any home but the hearth was sacred to the Romans because it was dedicated to their household gods — the Lares and Penates. The focus of the Roman °state — the altar of the goddess Vesta in the Roman °Forum — contained the °eternal flame, tended by the Vestal Virgins. If the fire went out it was considered °ominous for the state and the Vestal responsible was whipped.

forensic
pertaining to the courts of °law

Forensis is a Latin word meaning 'relating to the forum' (where the Romans held their courts of law).

Forensic evidence is °physical evidence that has been

subjected to °scientific analysis, such as fingerprints, fibres, guns.

A *forensic expert* is someone who °produces forensic evidence (like the °state pathologist).

Forensic medicine is that scientific study of the human body which allows the development of forensic evidence on such issues as cause and time of death, contact with certain substances, fingerprints.

forum
a place where, or °medium in which, discussion may take place

Forum is a Latin word meaning 'market-place'. Every Roman town had its forum where citizens met not only to buy and sell but also to talk about °public affairs and to listen to addresses from lawyers engaged in °law cases or from °politicians campaigning. In Rome the latter spoke from the *rostra*. A *rostrum* (singular form) was the beak of a ship.

In the first Punic War (264-241 BC) the Romans went to sea for the first time and defeated the Carthaginians, one of the great °thalassocracies of ancient times. They were so proud of this that they set up the *rostra* from the captured ships in the forum in Rome to adorn the platforms for the speakers there. Subsequently the platform itself came to be called a rostrum.

Our use of the term 'forum' allows us to say something like '°Television is not a good forum for serious, °philosophical discussion'.

The rostrum of a Roman ship consisted of a beam to which were attached sharp and pointed irons or the head of a ram and the like. It projected just above the keel of a warship and was used to sink another ship by ramming and breaking in its sides. In this drawing the rostrum has three sharp irons. The beam of wood attached to the mast and used to spread out the square sail to catch the wind was called the *antenna* (plural 'antennae' or 'antennas') — hence our use of that word as a °synonym for an aerial, which receives or emits radio signals, and as a description of the feelers on insects

fortune
whatever comes by chance

Fortuna was an Italian goddess identified in °classical times with 'chance' or 'luck'. In the °original cult she signified fertility, increase, plenty, so 'fortune' tended to mean most commonly 'good fortune'. It also came to mean the result of good fortune — prosperity or wealth. The rather godless Julius °Caesar attributed many of his successes to the working of Fortuna; Napoleon, when asked to approve the promotion of an officer to field rank, always put the question: 'Is he lucky?'; and throughout °history the reputation of some generals for being lucky and others for being unlucky has in itself been a factor in the outcome of battles.

The Roman °orator Cicero, in his famous speech *Pro Lege Manilia*, considered a general or leader needed four qualities — knowledge (*scientia*), professional ability (*virtus*), prestige (*auctoritas*) and good luck (*fortuna*).

For the Greeks, luck was a °central force in °human affairs. They believed they could control it by craft or °technique — hence their adage 'luck loves craft'. °Machiavelli also regarded the ability to control fortune as a sign of the great statesman.

the fourth estate
the °mass media

Estate is derived from the Latin word *stare* 'to stand'. An estate is an order of people upon which the power of the °state stands or was deemed to stand. In Britain there are three estates of the realm — the lords spiritual, the lords °temporal and the °commons. It was the Irish °orator, Edmund Burke, who coined the phrase 'the fourth estate'. Speaking in the House of Commons, he observed that there were three estates in °parliament, but — referring to the newspaper reporters' gallery — 'Yonder sits the Fourth Estate, more important than them all'.

There were three estates in pre-°revolutionary France, too. They met as three houses: the nobles, the °clergy and the representatives of the people. The Third Estate (the representatives of the people) took the first formal step in the Revolution. For, when King Louis XV1 summoned the Estates General to meet in Versailles in 1789, an immediate and crucial issue was whether or not they should meet as one deliberative body or separately in three Houses. If they met separately, the two higher orders could concert to °veto the decisions of the Third Estate. If they met together, the numerical superiority of the Third Estate (it had the same number of representatives as the other two estates combined) would give it °predominance.

The Third Estate refused to meet formally until the issue was resolved. Eventually, a number of the clergy broke rank and joined with the Third Estate. The Third Estate thereupon declared itself to be the °National Assembly.

the Furies
spirits of punishment, called Erinyes by the Greeks, who avenged wrongs done to kindred, especially murder within the family or clan

In Greek °myth Orestes was the son of Agamemnon and Clytemnestra. When Clytemnestra and her lover Aegisthus murdered Agamemnon, Orestes, who was only ten at the time, was spirited away by his nurse to avoid being killed himself. When he became a man he visited the °Delphic Oracle to enquire whether or not he should avenge his father's death. He was told that if he neglected to do so he would become an outcast from society. So he secretly returned to Mycenae, bent on killing Aegisthus and his own mother.

He gained entry to the palace and succeeded in despatching Aegisthus with his sword. When he rounded on his mother, Clytemnestra tried to soften his heart by baring her breast and appealing to his filial feeling (*filius* is the Latin word for 'son'). Orestes, however, beheaded her with a stroke of his sword and she fell beside the body of her lover.

That night the fearful Erinyes appeared, swinging their scourges, and attacked the °matricide. Orestes set out for Delphi but they pursued him there. When he went into exile they continued to torment him, so much so that he went mad. They persisted, even though he performed many cleansing rituals and offered the °holocaust of a black ram to the gods. Finally, he came to Athens. There, in a trial in which the god Apollo defended him and the eldest of the Erinyes led for the prosecution, he was acquitted. The Erinyes gave up their pursuit of him.

Styx
In Greek myth, the ghosts of the dead descended to the underworld and made their way to the Styx where they paid Charon to ferry them across. If they were good, they were sent to the delightful Elysian Fields; if they were evil, they were sent down deeper into Tartarus for punishment; if they were neither good nor evil, they were sent to the Asphodel Meadows to join the throngs of torpid, aimless dead

The °philosopher Heraclitus (c.500 BC) said of the Furies that even if the Sun were to leave his course they would find him out. According to some they represented the ghost of a slain °person while to others they were actual curses which had become personified. Anyhow, they were as real to the Greeks as the banshee is to Irish people. Their abode was in Erebus beyond the river Styx in °Hades (the lower world called after the heartless god who ruled there) and so their power to punish reached beyond the grave. To avoid giving them offence they were often called the Eumenides ('The Gracious Ones') just as the treacherous Black Sea was °euphemistically called the 'Pontus Euxeinos' ('The Sea Friendly to Strangers') so as not to ruffle the god of that dreaded waterway.

G

-gamy
bigamy, monogamy, polygamy — these are words whose common ending *-gamy* derives from the Greek word *gamos* meaning 'marriage'

Bigamy means having two wives or husbands at the same time (*bi* derives from *bis* the Latin word for 'twice').

Monogamy means having one wife or husband (*monos* means 'alone' in Greek).

Polygamy means having more than one husband or wife at the same time (*polus* means 'many' in Greek). There are two forms of polygamy — polyandry and polygyny. *Polyandry* means having more than one husband (*anēr, andros* means 'man' or 'husband' in Greek). *Polygyny* means having more than one wife (*gynē* is the Greek word for 'woman' or 'wife' from which we also derive 'gynaecology').

geo-
geocentred, geodesic, geography, geology, geometry, geopolitics — these are all words whose common prefix *geo-* derives from *gē* the Greek word for 'earth'

Geocentred is applied to the thinking of those °cosmologists who believed that the °universe is °centred on the earth (whereas the earth is heliocentric — centred on the sun — and the sun is a peripheral star of the Milky Way; *hēlios* is the Greek for 'sun', from which we also derive 'helium' the light gas that abounds in the sun's atmosphere).

Geodesic means concerned with measuring the surface of the earth (*daisis* is the Greek word for 'division').

Geography is the study of the earth's surface and atmosphere (*graphein* is the Greek word 'to write').

Geology is the study of the earth's °physical composition (*logos* means 'word', 'reason', 'account' in Greek).

Geometry is the branch of mathematics concerned with the properties and relations of lines, surfaces and solids in space, so called because it was developed as an aid for man's measurement of the earth (*metria* is the Greek word for 'measuring' from which we also derive 'metre').

Geopolitics is the art or study of politics conceived as being largely °determined by the peculiar features of the territory occupied by °states, such as lack of access to the sea (*politikos* is the Greek word for 'relating to the affairs of the state').

Two other words derived from *gē* in quite common use are *apogee* and *perigee*. The movement of the planets in relation to the earth is elliptical. When a planet is at its furthest point from the earth it is said to be at its apogee (*apo* is a Greek word meaning 'far from'). When it is at its nearest point it is said to be at its *perigee* (*peri* is a Greek word meaning 'near'). *Apogee* is also used in a transferred sense to mean 'the highest point' or °zenith.

gerrymander
when ruling °politicians draw or re-draw °electoral districts in such a way as to favour their supporters and so distort the outcome of elections, they are said to gerrymander

In 1812 when Elbridge Gerry was °Governor of Massachusetts, the °state °legislature divided Essex County into two districts with boundaries so drawn as to give the °maximum advantage to the ruling °Republican Party. Normally, boundaries follow °natural features such as rivers and mountains but in this case they frequently reached out oddly to include certain °isolated homesteads. Looking at a map of one of the districts, someone said 'Hey, that looks like a salamander!' (a kind of lizard). Someone else rejoined: 'I'll tell you what it is — it's a *gerry*mander!'

ghetto
a run-down, impoverished part of a city whose °inhabitants are forced to live there either because of their poverty or race

Borghetto is an Italian word meaning 'little borough' (*borgo* is 'borough') from which some say the word derives. Others say it comes from *getto*, the name of the foundry in Venice where a ghetto was established in the sixteenth °century. It was °originally used in reference to the area of a European city to which Jews were confined. It is now used of any poor district of a city, such as Harlem in New York.

glasnost
the °Soviet policy of 'openness'

Glasnost is the Russian word for 'openness'. It °characterises the style of °government of Mikhail Gorbachev — an openness to ideas, including the revision of °modern Russian °history; greater °freedom, including the release of at least some non-conformists from prison — °political prisoners, dissidents, refuseniks; greater freedom of expression in the °media; greater freedom of movement between the Soviet Union and the

Gorbachev

rest of the world, including the °emigration of Soviet Jews to Israel. A °concomitant policy, *perestroika* ('restructuring'), seeks reforms of the °economy that would °produce the kind of consumer wealth that characterises the western, non-°communist countries.

Glasnost and *perestroika* seek to change the °arthritic °bureaucracy that developed under the °gerontocracy of Leonid Brezhnev (1906-82), Yuri Andropov (1914-84), and Konstantin Chernenko (1911-85).

G-men
°government-men — armed °federal (that is, employed by the US government rather than a °state government) detectives who in the 1930s combated violent crime under the leadership of J. Edgar Hoover

In September 1933 George Kelly — °Public Enemy Number One, commonly known as Machine-gun Kelly from his favourite piece of protection — was captured by federal agents in Memphis, Tennessee. He had been on a spending spree in Mexico with his wife Kate after pulling off a successful job, and both of them were relaxing in bed in a rented bungalow. Suddenly law officers burst into the room. Kelly reached for his machine-gun but realising that double-barrelled shot-guns were trained not only on him but also on Kate, he surrendered. 'Don't shoot, G-men!' he yelled, thus coining what became an American colloquialism widely known from its use in gangster movies.

Gordian knot
a °person is said to cut the Gordian knot if, when faced with an intricate and difficult problem or task, he or she solves it by decisive force or by evading the conditions

Just over three hundred years BC, when Alexander the Great was conquering Asia, he came to the city of Gordium. There he was told of a °local curiosity — a chariot in the palace of the former kings which was bound to its yoke by a knot of cornel-bark that no man had ever been able to undo.

The day before he left the city, Alexander went up to the palace and there, surrounded by his friends, tried to loosen the knot. No matter how much he pulled, the knot remained stubbornly tight. He began to fret because if he failed, he would lose face with his men. So, drawing his sword, he slashed the knot in half and claimed, correctly, that the knot was loosened, if not untied.

Götterdämmerung
the twilight of the gods

Götter is the plural of *gott* the German word for 'god' *Dämmerung* means 'twilight' (strictly, the half-light before either dusk or dawn). In the Scandinavian *Nibelungen* °saga, Valhalla (the Hall of the Slain) was the great hall where Wotan and the other gods and goddesses sat with the slain heroes carried thither by the Valkyrie. In the end Valhalla is consumed by fire and the power of the gods fades. Richard Wagner based his *Ring* cycle of °operas on that saga: the last of the operas, *Götterdämmerung*, ends in the death of the hero, Siegfried, and the destruction of Valhalla by fire.

Adolf Hitler, in his heyday as °dictator of Germany, was received with great ceremony each year when he visited Bayreuth in Bavaria to see Wagner's operas performed in the Festhalle there. The destruction of Germany at the end of World War II and Hitler's own death in the bunker in Berlin as the Russian armies closed in are sometimes described by historians as the *Götterdämmerung*.

government
the group of people who exercise the °executive power of the °state

Kubernein is the Greek word 'to steer'. The °government steer the ship of state. In business the chief °executive and his management team have the executive (implementing) power; the board has the policy-making power. In °political contexts the government has the executive power: °parliament has the policy-making (°legislative) power.

°*Bunreacht na hÉireann* provides that the government shall consist of not less than seven and not more than fifteen members. The °Taoiseach is the head of the government. He and his deputy, the °Tánaiste, and the Minister for Finance must be members of °Dáil Éireann. The other members must be either °TDs or °Senators, and no more than two of them may be Senators. Each government minister heads up one or more of the Departments of °State. The government, however, meet and act as a collective body known as the °cabinet and are collectively responsible to Dáil Éireann for their °administration of the °public service. The members of government in office at the date of a dissolution of Dáil Éireann continue to hold office until their successors have been appointed.

The Latin equivalent of *kubernein* is *gubernare*, from which we derive 'governor'. A helmsman in Latin is *gubernator* — from it we derive 'gubernatorial' as in the gubernatorial °elections in the US, °i.e. the elections for State Governors.

A helmsman in Greek, *kubernētēs,* transliterates into *cybernētēs*. *Cybernetics* is the study of automatic communication and control in functions of living bodies and in mechanical electronic systems such as computers — in simple terms the study of self-steering systems.

-graph
autograph, biography, calligraphy, cardiograph, cartography, encephalograph, epigraph, graphic, graphology, hagiography, heliograph, mammograph, monograph, photograph, seismograph, telegraph, topography

Autograph means a °person's signature (*autos* means 'self' in Greek).

Biography means an account of a person's life (*bios* means 'life' in Greek). An *autobiography* is a person's account of his or her own life (*autos* means 'self' in Greek).

Calligraphy is beautiful handwriting (*kallos* means 'beauty' in Greek). The example of calligraphy (below) is from a copy of the Koran in the Chester Beatty Library.

— these are all words whose common component *graph* comes from the Greek word *graphein* 'to write'

Robert Emmet (1778–1803): 'When my country takes her place among the nations of the earth, then and not till then let my epitaph be written'. (Speech from the dock)

Oscar Wilde (1854–1900), born in Dublin, an epigrammatist of genius: 'No woman should ever be quite accurate about her age. It looks so calculating'. *(The Importance of Being Earnest)*

A *cardiograph* is a record of a heart scan (*cardia* means 'heart' in Greek).

Cartography means map-drawing (*carte* is the French word for 'chart').

An encephalograph is a record of a brain scan (*enkephalon* is 'brain' in Greek).

An *epigraph* is an inscription on stone, a motto, or a pithy statement that may appear at the beginning of a book or of each chapter of a book (*epi* is a Greek word meaning 'on'). *Epitaph* is an inscription on a tomb (*taphos* is the Greek word for 'tomb'). An *epigram* is a self-contained witty statement, for example Oscar Wilde's definition of a °cynic in *Lady Windermere's Fan* as 'A man who knows the price of everything and the value of nothing' (*gramma* is a Greek word for 'writing' or 'letter').

Graphic may be used to describe the arts of writing, printing, drawing, painting, etching, engraving. It is also used in the general sense of 'vivid'.

Graphology is the study of handwriting (*logos* is the Greek word for 'word', 'reason', 'account'). Thus, 'The graphologist who studied the ransom note concluded it was written by a one-legged sailor with a hacking cough'.

A *hagiography* is the biography of a saint. In °secular usage, it may refer to a gushing, °uncritical biography of a °public figure (*hagios* is the Greek word for 'holy').

Heliography is a means of transmitting messages by reflecting sunlight on mirrors (*hēlios* means 'sun' in Greek).

A *mammograph* is the record of a breast scan (*mamma* is 'breast' in Latin).

A *monograph* is a treatise on a single °subject or class of subjects (*monos* means 'alone' in Greek).

A *photograph* is a picture taken by a camera (*phōs, phōtos* is 'light' in Greek).

A *seismograph* is an instrument for measuring (usually on the Richter scale) earthquakes (*seismos* is 'shaking' in Greek).

A *telegraph* is an °apparatus for sending messages or signals over long distances by electricity (*tēle* is a Greek word meaning 'afar').

Topography is the description of a limited °geographical area or, by transference, the features of such an area (*topos* is 'place' in Greek from which we also derive 'topic' because *ta topica* were the places marked by headings where Greek scholars located references in books; 'topic' came to be transferred to the reference itself).

guillotine
a machine for inflicting °capital punishment by decapitation

Joseph Ignace Guillotin, a French doctor, was one of the 1,139 °delegates (270 from the nobility, 291 from the clergy, and 578 from the Third Estate) to the °fateful meeting of the °Estates General in Versailles in 1789. He successfully promoted a law which required that all death sentences be carried out by means of a machine. The intention was to make the privilege of °decapitation available to everyone (and not to nobles only) and the process of execution as painless as possible. The guillotine

came into use in 1792 and became one of the enduring °symbols of the °Revolution.

Nowadays the word usually arises in a °parliamentary °context. It is an important function of the °government to manage the progress of its °legislative programme through the °Dáil and °Seanad. If the government is promoting a particularly urgent piece of legislation, it may 'apply the guillotine', that is, it may name a time by which debate on the Bill must cease and the vote be taken. The procedure was introduced into the House of °Commons in 1882 by the British Prime Minister, W.E. Gladstone, to deal with the obstructionist (°filibustering) °tactics of Parnell.

The word also occurs nowadays in printing. A guillotine was used to cut this book into its design shape.

habeas corpus
an order made by a higher court in response to a complaint that someone is being unlawfully detained

Habeas is a form of *habere* the Latin word 'to have' meaning 'let you have!' *Corpus, corporis* is the Latin word for 'body' or '°person' from which we derive 'corporate', 'corporation', 'corporeal' and 'corpulent'. The phrase means 'Let you produce the person'. The °official in whose custody the person is held is ordered to °produce the person in court on a named date and certify the grounds on which he or she is being detained. If the court is not satisfied that the person is being held in accordance with the °law, it may order the person's immediate release.

Habeas corpus sets a definite term to the period a person may be held in prison without a formal charge in court. Article 40 of the °constitution, under which an order of habeas corpus is made, lays down stringent rules to protect the °freedom of the individual.

head of state
the chief citizen who represents the °state

The head of state is either a °president or a °monarch. In some states, e.g. the US, the head of state — the president — is also head of °government. In others the offices of head of state and head of government are separate. Thus in Ireland, the °Taoiseach is head of government and the President is head of state. In monarchies, such as the UK, it is usual for the monarch and the head of government to be separate officers.

hegemony
leadership of a group of independent °states through having effective °influence or power over them

Hēgēmōn is the Greek word for 'leader' from which hegemony is derived. The map of °classical Greece presented a patchwork of small independent °states such as Athens, Sparta, Corinth, Boeotia. In the face of external threats they needed to unite. So it was under the hegemony of Sparta that they thwarted the designs of the Persian King Xerxes to conquer Greece. When there was no external threat, they fell to warring among themselves. A protracted war (the famous Peloponnesian War, described by Thucydides in one of the most brilliant pieces of °historiography ever penned) conducted by two sets of allies, one under the hegemony of Sparta, the other under the hegemony of Athens, ended in the defeat of Athens. But the Peloponnesian states were so exhausted that they quickly fell under the hegemony of King Philip of Macedon.

In the °modern world the western states are under the hegemony of the US and the eastern bloc countries are —or were — under the hegemony of the USSR. The non-aligned states do not acknowledge the hegemony of either superpower. 'Hegemony' is also applied to the leadership of one °dominant °social class over others.

hetero-
heterodox, heterogeneous and heterosexual — these are all words whose common prefix *hetero-* means 'other' or 'different' in Greek

Heterodox is the opposite of *orthodox* and means having a different (and therefore wrong!) opinion. (*Doxa* is 'opinion' in Greek. *Orthos* is 'straight' or 'right' in Greek.) Bishop William Warburton (1698–1779) caught the distinction between the terms nicely in a remark to Lord Sandwich: 'Orthodoxy is my doxy; heterodoxy is another man's doxy'.

Heterogeneous is the opposite of *homogeneous* and means 'diverse in character' (*genos* means 'kind' in Greek, *homos* means 'same' in Greek).

Heterosexual is the opposite of *homosexual* and means 'attracted to the opposite sex' (*sexus* is 'sex' in Latin). A woman homosexual is sometimes called a *lesbian.* Lesbos is a Greek island. Its most famous °inhabitant was an inspired °erotic, lyric poetess, Sappho (*circa* 600 BC), who was accused of being homosexual. Lesbian speech and style is sometimes called 'Sapphic'. (*Circa* is a Latin word meaning 'around' or 'about' frequently shortened to c.)

honoris causa
honorary

Honoris is a form of *honor*, the Latin word for 'honour'. *Causa* means 'for the sake of' in Latin. Each year our °universities seek to honour people who have contributed to the good of the community in an outstanding, often non-°academic, way by conferring degrees on them *honoris causa.*

hubris
overweening pride

Hubris was an important concept in Greek life and literature: it was a preoccupation of °tragedians and °historians. Basically, the Greeks believed that any insolent or wanton °act would inevitably bring destruction to the °person who has committed the act of hubris. Thus they believed the invasion of Greece by the Persian king Xerxes was an act of hubris and therefore bound to fail. We might say Hitler's attack on Russia was an act of hubris.

humanist
someone concerned with human beings and their interests exclusive of any supernatural dimension

Humanus is a Latin word derived from *homo* the Latin for 'human being' — 'human' means 'pertaining to the nature of man'. *Humane* means having the feelings proper to a human being. A *humanist* was °originally a student during the Renaissance period who devoted himself or herself to the study of the ancient °classical texts. These were °pagan so a student of them was seen as pursuing a °secular interest in human nature. Gradually the term 'humanist' came to be applied to anyone who placed human interests and the mind of man above everything else.

hypo-
hypocrisy, hypodermic, hypoteneuse, hypothermia — these are words whose common prefix *hypo-* is a Greek word meaning 'under'

Hypocrisy is a pretending to be better than one really is (*hypocritēs* is the Greek word for 'actor').

Hypodermic is used of a needle for injecting under the skin (*derma* is the Greek word for 'skin'). Since some drug addicts inject themselves with a hypodermic needle the slang term 'to hype' has come into use to mean 'to over-stimulate'; thus to hype a film or a book is to promote it beyond its true worth.

The *hypoteneuse*, from the Greek word *hyperteinein* 'to stretch under', is the line opposite the right angle of a right-angled triangle (which was drawn by the Greeks with the right angle above and the hypoteneuse below).

Hypothermia means subnormal body temperature, a condition that often leads to the death of elderly people in winter (*thermē* means 'heat' in Greek — hence 'therm', 'thermal' and 'thermo-°nuclear').

Hyper is a Greek word meaning 'above' — the opposite of *hypo* — from which we get *hyperbole* 'an extravagant expression' (*ballein* is the Greek word 'to throw'; a hyperbole, then, is an overshooting), *hypermarket* 'a store bigger and more extensive in its range of goods than a supermarket', *hypercritical* 'excessively °critical', *hyper-active* excessively active, and *hypersensitive* 'excessively sensitive'.

hypothesis
a supposition made as a basis for reasoning in the hope of discovering some truth from it

Hypo is a Greek word meaning 'under'. *Thesis* is the Greek word for 'that which stands'. A hypothesis is a foundation for reasoning. The concept is very important in °science which proceeds through subjecting hypotheses (plural of hypothesis) to scientific tests.

A *hypothetical question* is one which sets forth a set of conditions and asks the °person addressed what he or she would do, or how he or she would °react, if the conditions were realised. °Media people frequently put hypothetical questions to °politicians (so as to give their readers, listeners or viewers a fix on the future). Politicians usually respond by simply saying: 'That's a hypothetical question!' (because they don't wish to have their hands tied).

I

iconoclast
one who attacks old cherished ideas or practices

Eikōn is the Greek word for 'image' from which 'icon' is derived. *Klaein* is the Greek word 'to break'. The Byzantine °Empire was °centred on Byzantium (Constantinople, now Istanbul). It lasted from AD 330 when Byzantium was °officially dedicated as the °capital of the Roman Empire to 1453 when the city fell. One of the features of the Christianity that developed there was an extraordinary, possibly superstitious, devotion to icons — holy images, statues, and emblems. In the eighth °century the Emperor Leo III began a °crusade against this practice, that lasted one hundred and twenty years and involved vast destruction.

The iconoclasts were only partly motivated by religious zeal. The devotion to the icons was promoted by the °monasteries. These were steadily extending the amount of property they owned and, since they were exempt from income tax, they were increasingly limiting the Emperor's revenues. The attacks on them reduced their wealth and °influence.

Ireland experienced iconoclasm at the hands of the Puritan Cromwellians (that is one of the reasons so much of the statuary in our old °monastic buildings is defaced). In °secular usage, a mordant revisionist °historian might be described as iconoclastic (*mordere* is the Latin word 'to bite' from which the French word *mordre*, the immediate source of 'mordant', derives). Thus Lytton Strachey, who in his *Eminent Victorians* debunked such revered figures as Florence Nightingale and Cardinal Manning, was an iconoclast.

revisionist
— someone who reviews a settled account of an historical period with the intention of changing people's view of it (*re* is a Latin prefix meaning 'again' and *visere* is an intensive form of *videre* the Latin word 'to look at')

i.e.
that is

I.e. is an abbreviation of the Latin expression *id est*. *Id* means 'that', *est* means 'is'.

imprimatur
°official permission to print; formal assent

Imprimatur is a Latin word meaning 'let it be printed'. Following the development of printing in Europe, the Catholic Church established a formal system of °censorship. Manuscripts ('things written by hand': *manus* is the Latin word for 'hand', *script* derives from the

Latin word *scribere* 'to write'; a *typescript* is a text produced by a typewriter) were submitted to °ecclesiastical censors who, if they found the texts unobjectionable, certified them with the Latin words *nihil obstat* ('nothing hinders') and passed them to a higher authority, such as a bishop, who gave them his imprimatur.

Church censors were not noted for their whimsy. However, in France before the °Revolution a son of the playwright Crèbillon was an official literary censor. One of his evaluations is renowned: 'By order of Monsignor the Chancellor I have read the work by Mr Mahomet entitled *The Koran* and have found in it nothing contrary either to religion or to °morality. Signed: Crèbillon fils'.

In °secular usage, imprimatur means 'sanction'. Thus, 'The minister would never have issued such a statement without the °Taoiseach's imprimatur'.

in camera
in °private

Camera is the Latin word for 'vault' and therefore a private room. The expression *in camera* is used in a °legal °context. Where evidence may unfairly jeopardise the good name or prospects of someone, a judge may decide to hear it *in camera* — in his private chamber or in court with the press and °public excluded. Certain proceedings, such as private family matters, are usually held in camera.

in flagrante delicto
caught in the act

In is the Latin word meaning 'in'. *Flagrante* means 'blazing' in Latin. *Delicto* is a form of *delictum* which means 'crime' in Latin. *In flagrante delicto* literally means 'while the crime is blazing'.

inflation
a process whereby prices rise and money loses its value

Inflare is a Latin word 'to blow into', 'to inflate'. There are three basic reasons for a rise in the prices of goods and services. Firstly, if consumers have a great deal of money and suppliers have a small amount of goods and services, a situation arises in which 'too much money chases too few goods': the suppliers raise their prices. Secondly, if the costs of °production such as wage costs and the cost of oil/°energy rise, producers will put up their prices in order to get back the money to cover the increased costs. Thirdly, if the °government finances any part of its °deficit by borrowing directly from the °Central Bank, it increases the money supply and thereby fuels inflation.

The most common measure of inflation is the *consumer price index*. The °index is constructed by the Central °Statistics Office by taking the cost of a representative sample of goods and services at a particular time (the base year) and measuring at °regular intervals the percentage changes in the cost of the same sample. In the 1970s the rate of inflation in Ireland reached levels of over twenty per cent. In the 1980s the inflation rate fell below three per cent.

The opposite of 'inflation' is 'deflation'—*de* is a Latin prefix meaning 'from'.

infrastructure
the support system underpinning any activity

Infra is a Latin word meaning 'below', *struere* is the Latin word 'to build'. The word occurs in °public affairs mostly in the °context of industrial development. Industry needs a certain infrastructure to function properly. There must, for example, be a transport system to bring in raw materials and bring out finished goods, a water supply (large amounts of water are used in many industrial processes), a telecommunications system, an °energy supply. Many °government agencies, especially the °local authorities, are involved in providing and maintaining the infrastructure required by industry.

Apart from this °physical infrastructure there is the need for a °social infrastructure — a framework of °law and order, an °educational system, a financial system °etc.

in loco parentis
in place of a parent

In is a Latin word meaning 'in'. *Loco* is a form of *locus*, a Latin word meaning 'place'. *Parentis* is a form of *parens*, a Latin word meaning 'parent'. The expression is used in °legal and °educational °contexts. Someone who acts in the place of a parent — say a teacher — is deemed to have the responsibility for, and rights over, a child that a parent has.

(*Locus standi* means 'a right to interfere', literally 'a place on which to stand'. Thus the courts operate completely independently of the °government. Nonetheless it is conceivable that a citizen might appeal to the Minister for Justice to have a decision made against him or her in the courts changed. In such a case the minister would refuse, saying he or she had no *locus standi* in the matter.)

interdict
prohibit

Interdictum is a Latin word meaning ‘a thing forbidden’. Certain Roman judges had the power to settle disputes by either ordering or forbidding something to be done. Their orders to do something were called *decreta* (decrees). Their orders forbidding something were called *interdicta* (interdictions).

In °canon law an area may be placed under interdict, that is, the people living in the area may be forbidden the sacraments. It is a °communal penalty aimed at forcing a Christian community to live up to its religious duties.

interest groups
voluntary associations of people who promote a special interest or cluster of interests which they share, especially through representations to °government

Interest, a form of the Latin word *interesse* ‘to be among’, means ‘a concern’. Interest groups, also called ‘pressure groups’, range from powerful °national associations to small °local °organisations, for example a local tourism body. Notable among the national interest groups are the °Confederation of Irish Industry (CII), concerned to represent industry in matters of trade, °economics, finance, °taxation, planning and development; the °Federation of Irish Employers (FIE), concerned to promote and protect employers’ interests in industrial relations, labour and °social affairs; the Irish Congress of Trade Unions (ICTU), the °central authority for the trade union movement; the Irish Farmers’ Association (IFA), which looks after the interests of all farmers other than dairy farmers; the Irish Creamery Milk Suppliers’ Association (ICMSA), which looks after the interests of dairy farmers.

The °major interest groups have permanent °offices and staffs. They provide research and information services, negotiate on behalf of their members, °lobby ministers and °government departments, provide spokespersons for the °media, and represent their group internationally.

°Political scientists distinguish between *special* interest groups, which are marshalled by a single interest (for example The Connemara Pony Breeders' Association) and *general* interest groups, which are marshalled by a wide spectrum of interests (for example a church).

Interest groups are politically important by reason of either their numerical strength (the number of potential °voters they represent) or their °strategic strength (their ability to obstruct the flow to the community of key goods or services). It is a major task of government to serve the °public interest, that is, the interest of the community as a whole, and to protect it from damage by interest groups.

Iron Curtain
the frontier set up by the °communist bloc countries after World War II

To maintain his °dictatorship Stalin required rigorous control over the movement of people and ideas. The Iron Curtain was one element in his system of control. The term's °origin is uncertain. It was used in the thirties by Hitler's °Propaganda Minister, Dr Joseph Goebbels, and other anti-°Bolshevik German writers. It was °popularised by Winston Churchill (1874-1965) in a speech he made at Fulton, Missouri, the home town of President Harry Truman, in March 1946: 'From Stettin in the Baltic to Trieste in the Adriatic an Iron Curtain has descended upon the Continent'.

Following the victory of Mao Tse Tung and the communists over the Chinese °Nationalists under Chiang Kai-shek in 1949, the tight border control exercised by the Chinese came to be described as the 'Bamboo Curtain'.

Churchill—one of the greatest orators of modern times. *Orator* is Latin for 'a public speaker'. *Rhētor* is its Greek equivalent, so 'oratory' and 'rhetoric' are synonomous (though 'rhetoric' often carries a connotation of being high-flown). A rhetorical question, one that does not expect an answer, is a device used by orators and writers to heighten interest: 'Shall I compare thee to a summer's day?' (Shakespeare, *Sonnets*)

irredentist
someone who advocates the forcible recovery of territories lost by his or her country

Irredenta is an Italian word meaning 'unredeemed', derived from the Latin *redimere* 'to buy back' (from which we also derive 'Redeemer'). Territory may be lost through conquest (as parts of Northern Italy were to the Austrians in the nineteenth °century) or by partition. The Provisional IRA is sometimes described as irredentist. Irredentists are also called *revanchists* (from the French word *revancher* 'to take revenge').

J

judicial review
the power of the Supreme Court to declare whether any °laws, proposed or enacted, or any actions of the °government or other °institutions are against the °constitution or not; or the power of the High Court to exercise supervisory jurisdiction over inferior courts, °tribunals, °public bodies and public °persons

Judex, judicis is a Latin word meaning 'a judge'. Judicial review of °legislation is a °major protection afforded to the citizen against any abuse of power by the government. A law declared by the Supreme Court to be repugnant to the °constitution ceases to exist forthwith ('repugnant' in this context means 'inconsistent with', derived from the Latin *re* 'against' and *pugnare* 'to fight' from which we also derive 'pugnacious'). The Attorney General, who is appointed at the same time as the government, is the government's °legal adviser. He helps the government to meet the exacting demands of the constitution in regard to legislation.

Judicial review of the courts is concerned with the process by which a decision was made and raises issues such as: was there power to make the decision? was the procedure in accordance with °natural and constitutional justice? It is a protection which reinforces that provided by the appeals system of the courts whereby there is a right of appeal to a higher court for a re-hearing (rather than a review).

junta
an °oligarchic ruling group, especially in Latin American countries

Junta is a Spanish word derived from the Latin word *junctus* meaning 'joined' (from which we also derive 'junction', 'injunction', 'conjunction' and 'adjunct'). A junta (also junto) may describe a °cabal or °conspiracy. The typical Latin American junta consisted of representatives of the various armed forces — the army, navy and air force. The Argentinian junta that unsuccessfully engaged in war with Britain over the Falkland Islands (Las Malvinas) in 1982 was deposed and °democratic °government re-installed. The word *junta* was °originally used in Spain and Italy to describe an administrative council.

jury
a group of people sworn to decide the facts of a case heard before them; in criminal cases a jury decides guilt on the basis of facts

Jurare is the Latin word 'to swear' from which 'jury' is derived. °*Bunreacht na hÉireann* provides that if you are charged with a crime you have a right to be tried by a jury (unless the alleged crime is a °minor offence or one being tried by the Special Criminal Court). Some °civil cases may also be tried by a jury but there is no °constitutional right to this. Every citizen aged between eighteen and seventy who is on the °electoral register is both eligible and liable for jury service, with a few exceptions °e.g. a member of the Garda Síochána. A jury has twelve members. They decide the facts. The judge decides the law. In criminal cases the jury no longer needs to be unanimous ('of one mind' from *unus* the Latin word for 'one' and *animus* the Latin word for 'mind').

Kafkaesque
conveying a feeling of being real and unreal at the same time

Franz Kafka (1883–1924) was born in Prague, the son of a rich Jewish Czech merchant. He studied °law and became a °clerk in an insurance office. His real interest was in writing. After a while he threw up his job and settled down in Berlin to write. His bad relations with his father, his unsatisfactory love-life, his poverty — all played on his °hypersensitive nature and broke down his health. He died of pulmonary tuberculosis. In *The Trial*, which was published the year after he died, the famous Kafkaesque feeling is created through an account of the experiences of a man, simply called K., who is given to understand that he is to be arrested on a charge that no one will specify.

Some people describe their experience of dealing with °bureaucracy as Kafkaesque.

kaiser
the German °Emperor

Kaiser is the German version of Caesar. *Czar* (or Tsar) is the Russian version of it. 'Caesar' was °originally the family name of the Julian clan at Rome. Its most famous member was the great °dictator Julius Caesar. The name was assumed by Octavian (the future Augustus) as the adopted son of Julius Caesar. He handed it on to his successors — it was even used by those emperors who did not belong to the Julian clan.

Keynesian
embodying the thinking of the British °economist, John Maynard Keynes (1883–1946)

Keynes (pronounced Kanes) was °centrally concerned with the issue of how the economy might be managed so as to achieve full °employment. He saw the level of °total demand (consumption plus investment) as crucial. If total demand was not great enough, he urged °governments to intervene to increase it. They might do this by direct action, such as building roads, by indirect action, such as giving °entrepreneurs incentives to invest or cutting °taxation to stimulate consumption, or by a

Keynes

combination of both. If total demand were running at too high a level (and creating °inflation, itself a threat to employment), governments should seek to moderate it by restrictive measures. He also saw the government might need to stimulate demand by households for goods and services through the °medium of a °budget °deficit which would increase total demand.

In the mid-1950s, while the rest of the western world was experiencing an economic boom, Ireland suffered from severe recession; the economy was stagnant, unemployment widespread, and °emigration in spate. Yet Ireland was investing large amounts of money — abroad. In 1958 Dr T.K. Whitaker, the then Secretary of the Department of Finance, presented a plan for recovery to the government — the famous *Economic Development*. It reflected Keynesian principle in so far as it provided for greater intervention in the economy by the °state. It placed the economy in a good position to take advantage of an upturn in the international economy. (For a small open economy like Ireland international conditions are crucial.)

Whitaker

From 1972, for about ten years, the government ran a °current budget deficit in addition to borrowing heavily for °capital projects. However, whereas Keynesian principles would suggest that the deficit should be governed by the °state of the economy, throughout the 1970s and early 1980s the deficit steadily increased, irrespective of the fluctuating state of the economy.

If the economy had grown steadily on a surge of international growth, we might have been able to maintain our standard of living while generating enough funds to repay the money borrowed to finance the °Exchequer Borrowing Requirement.

Many economists would now say that Keynes's prescriptions are no longer relevant because the world economy has changed significantly since his time. In the latter half of the eighties the Irish economy has begun to grow again but now the growth owes more to the creation of a climate favourable to business as a result of °fiscal °rectitude, than to Keynesian intervention by the state.

kibbutz(im)
Jewish °communal society/ies in which the means of °production are owned by all, and work and its produce are shared by all

The impoverished Jews of Russia, °ghettoised and forbidden to own land, found °socialism an attractive °ideology. In response to the °pogroms of the late nineteenth °century there began a movement among them which harnessed their yearning for the °traditional pastoral life (*pastor* is the Latin word for 'shepherd') and a commitment to socialist principles: groups of them would return to Palestine and set up co-operative farming settlements.

They were also determined to abandon the °traditional pacifism (*pax, pacis* is the Latin word for 'peace') of the Jews when attacked — they would defend themselves. Defiantly self-sufficient, they worked co-operatively and defended their settlements themselves. (Reinforcing their socialist principles was the fact that the land was so poor it required a collective effort to work it.) The two hundred and seventy or so *kibbutzim* are now a notable element of Israeli social °organisation.

The suffix *-im* is a Hebrew plural form; hence cherub, cherubim and seraph, seraphim. The Arabic equivalent is *in*; hence fellah, fellahin (Egyptian peasant(s)) and bedouin (tent-dwelling nomad Arabs, derived by the French from the Arabic word *badawin* meaning 'dwellers in the desert').

L

the labour force
the °total number of people at work or available for work

Labor, laboris is the Latin word for 'work' (from which we also derive 'laborious', 'elaborate', 'laboratory'). A country's capacity to °produce goods and services depends partly on the numbers in the labour force and on the skills they possess. The labour force comprises employers, employees, self-employed persons, and all those °unemployed. In 1988 our labour force numbered 1,310,000 of whom 1,091,000 were employed and 219,000 were unemployed.

law
rules established by the authority of custom or the °legislature and °promulgated and enforced by the °state for the common good

The third power of °government (after the °legislative and °executive powers) is the judicial or judging power (*judex, judicis* is the Latin word for 'judge'). It is exercised in regard to three kinds of cases — °constitutional, criminal and civil. The Supreme Court decides issues arising from interpretation of the constitution.

In criminal cases (*crimen, criminis* is the Latin word for 'a crime') a man or woman is tried for breaking a law, whether an important or a °minor one. The Director of °Public Prosecutions, after considering the evidence compiled by a Garda, decides whether a suspect should be prosecuted or not. Depending on the nature of the crime, the accused is tried by the District Court, the Circuit Criminal Court, the Central Criminal Court or the Special Criminal Court. The accused may be either convicted or acquitted. If convicted he or she may be given a prison sentence or a fine or both. There is a system of appeals.

In civil cases (*civilis* is a Latin word meaning 'pertaining to a citizen') a person (the plaintiff) brings an action against an individual or body (the defendant), for example a °private company or the state, to seek damages for injuries done, to enforce a contract, or to get an injunction (a court order to ensure the defendant refrains from some action the plaintiff believes would unlawfully injure the plaintiff or his or her interests). Depending on the nature of the case, it is heard in the District Court, the Circuit Court, or the High Court. There is a system of appeals.

The government provides the administrative services the courts require, as well as in certain cases free °legal aid; it also appoints the judges. Solicitors and barristers assist the parties involved in cases.

Jurisprudence is the °science or knowledge of law (*juris* is a form of the Latin word *jus* and means 'of law'; *prudentia* is a Latin word meaning 'knowledge').

left/centre/right
the range of °political thought and °organisations, conceived as moving in an arc from °anarchism at one extreme to right wing °dictatorship at the other

continent (*al*)
derives from the Latin *terra continens* 'continuous land'

When in June 1789 King Louis XVI of France capitulated to the wishes of the Third Estate (the representatives of the people) and ordered the three Estates to meet together in one assembly, the nobles sat on the king's right (the place of honour) and the Third Estate on his left. In subsequent French assemblies and in other continental °parliaments in the nineteenth °century, the °democratic, °liberal representatives took seats on the left of the °president's chair. From this practice developed such terms as left, extreme left, leftist, left wing, left of centre, centre, right of centre, rightist, right wing, extreme right.

The left ranges from °anarchists to °communists, °socialists and °social democrats, the right from °fascists to °conservatives. The °centre seeks to draw support from both left and right. In Ireland there is only °minority °electoral support for the parties of the left (the Labour Party, the Workers' Party and the Democratic Socialist Party between them received less than 15% of the °votes in the 1989 general election). Yet Ireland exhibits one of the °major features of a socialist °economy, namely, that the proportion of the °gross national product handled by agencies of the °state is very high. The parties lean °pragmatically to left or right.

In the °Dáil the government party or parties sit, by °convention, to the left of the Ceann Comhairle.

legislature
the °institutions of °government that make, amend or repeal °laws

Lex, legis is the Latin word for 'law' (from which we also get 'legal' and 'legislation') — the legislature is the law-making body. In Ireland the legislature is the °Oireachtas. It consists of the °President of Ireland, °Dáil Éireann and °Seanad Éireann, although in °popular speech 'Oireachtas' is often used to °denote the Dáil and Seanad only.

leitmotiv
leading theme

Leiten is the German word 'to lead'. *Motiv* is the German word for 'motive' (from the Latin word *movere* 'to move'). A *leitmotiv* was °originally a musical device, a kind of musical tag that identifies a particular °character or idea and that recurs in the orchestra at appropriate moments, often with subtle alteration, for example to suggest a change of mood from joy to foreboding.

Wagner

Perhaps the greatest exponent of its use is Richard Wagner, particularly in the *Ring* where leitmotifs — nearly two hundred in all (for the Rhine gold, Wotan, Siegfried's sword Nothung, °etc.) — are used to bind together the four °operas in the cycle (*Rhinegold, The Valkyrie, Siegfried* and *The Twilight of the Gods* or *Götterdämmerung*). *Leitmotiv* is now applied generally. Thus, 'A leitmotiv of the party's document on finance is the need to reduce foreign borrowing'.

The verbal component *leit* also occurs in *gauleiter*. *Gau* means 'district' in German. *Leiter* means 'leader'. The gau was the regional unit of the °Nazi Party's °organisation. The party °official who headed a gau was called a gauleiter. Because of the demeanour of many of these, 'gauleiter' has come to be applied generally to anyone who wields petty authority in an overbearing manner.

liberalism
a body of °political beliefs which stresses the rights of the individual within the °state (as opposed to the rights of the

Liber is a Latin word meaning 'free'. Liberalism developed in Europe in the late seventeenth °century in opposition to the arbitrary, °despotic rule then prevalent. It sought to limit the powers of °governments over their citizens through such measures as the enactment of written °constitutions and bills of rights, and the extension of the °franchise. It °located the source of authority not

community which is stressed by °socialists) and the development of °economic and political °institutions which favour the free market in °production and distribution

maximise
means to achieve or seek to achieve the maximum — the highest point or greatest amount attainable (from *maximus*, a form of *magnus* the Latin word for 'great'). *Minimum* is the lowest point or least amount attainable (from *minimus*, a form of *parvus* the Latin word for 'small'). A maximalist is someone who holds out for the maximum of his or her demands and rejects compromise — the Bolsheviks were maximalists, and so were the anti-Treatyites. A *minimalist* is someone who seeks, or is prepared to accept, a minimum; in art a minimalist seeks to communicate using the least possible intervention — thus Samuel Beckett is probably the most famous minimalist in modern writing

in custom and °tradition or religious beliefs but in the idea that every man had by nature °inalienable rights.

°Totalitarianism is therefore anathema to liberals (*anathema* means 'accursed' in Greek; the word was used in the early Church as a solemn denunciation of a person or thing — 'Let him/it be anathema!'). It is difficult to define liberalism because it has taken many different forms at different periods in different countries. However, °political liberalism — liberal °democracy — asserts the right of individuals to choose their form of government and to participate in the choice of members of the government and in the conduct of °public affairs. This derives from a view of man as °autonomous, rational and self-interested, and of the °state as properly concerned to maximise freedom by, among other things, adopting °*laissez faire* policies in economic affairs. Liberals, then, seek to build the institutions of government in such a way that the °freedom of the individual is interfered with as little as possible.

They favour °private property and free trade — factors that enable the individual to maintain and extend his or her freedom. Prizing freedom far more than equality, they are not egalitarian (which would require equality of material as well as other benefits) but they do favour equality of opportunity because they would see that as a condition for their understanding of freedom in society (*egalitarian* is derived from the Old French word *égal*, itself derived from the Latin *aequalis* meaning 'equal'). Socialists regard the liberals' endorsement of equality of opportunity as a hollow assurance that the satisfactions of life are open to everyone—like the Ritz Hotel.

For liberals religion and °morality are °private matters and have minimal bearing on the economic and political orders. Liberals, therefore, seek to withdraw religion and morality from the public arena into the arena of the private — they call for the separation of Church and State. The °modern notion of °pluralism flows from this. It asserts that one's moral vision and actions are one's own concern and not that of the state, unless they result in harm to others. Harm is narrowly defined in terms of the right to life and property. Otherwise liberals advocate as much tolerance as possible and a minimalist approach to °legislation especially in the area of morality, which is interpreted in a narrow sense referring mostly to sexual and related matters. The way we produce and distribute wealth, for example, is rarely seen by liberals as a moral issue.

°Critics of the liberal position on morality in public affairs assert that it assumes that large areas of life covered by °law and controlled by institutions are morally neutral. All laws and institutions, they say, have a moral dimension: laws are by their nature °normative, and institutions operate through policies which are also by their nature normative. Thus, by seeking to exclude moral debate from certain areas of life, liberals, their critics say, are really legitimating the application of their own morality and suppressing that of others. (That is why Marx called liberalism an °ideology.)

In the nineteenth century liberals aligned themselves with °nationalist movements with a view to enhancing individual freedoms. Nowadays they favour supranational bodies such as the °European Community and the United °Nations as providing stronger guarantees of freedom than nation-states (*supra* is a Latin word meaning 'above').

lobby
to seek to °influence °legislators to pass laws favourable to one's group interest

Lobia is a late Latin word meaning 'portico'. A lobby is the ante-chamber to a °legislative hall and therefore an apt place to waylay legislators. Nowadays °TDs are lobbied by letter and °telephone as well as by °personal encounter.

In Washington lobbying is a formally recognised function: there are some 11,000 registered lobbyists who are retained by a plethora of °special interest groups, ranging from foreign countries to °local trade associations, to bring pressure to bear on legislators (*plēthōra* is a Greek word meaning 'fullness' used in English for 'an excessively large number'). 'Lobby' by extension may mean a special interest group — thus the gun lobby is those Americans who °organise themselves to prevent any curtailment of the citizen's right to possess fire-arms.

In Britain 'the Westminster lobby correspondents' are a group of journalists who are given briefings by ministers on controversial issues, attributable only to an °anonymous 'reliable source'. (A °comparable group in Ireland are the accredited °political correspondents who share facilities in °Leinster House.)

local government
the system of local authorities which carry out a range of functions delegated to them by the °Oireachtas

Locus is the Latin word for 'place' from which we get 'local' (as well as 'locality', 'location', 'allocate', 'dislocate'). °Historically, the °central °government depended on local authorities to carry out certain of the functions of government in their areas. °Modern °communications allow central government to act directly in areas throughout the country by setting up local offices (as the Department of Social Welfare has done). In addition a number of °state-sponsored bodies, for example the Electricity Supply Board, An Post, Telecom Eireann, may have local offices in an area. Local authorities, then, are by no means the only °public service bodies to be found locally.

The °major units of local government are the twenty-seven county councils (Tipperary is divided into two councils — the North Riding and the South Riding) and the five county boroughs (city councils or °corporations) of Dublin, Cork, Limerick, Waterford and Galway. In addition there are six boroughs, forty-nine °urban district councils and thirty towns with town commissioners.

Frank Feely, Dublin City and County Manager (1979—). The holder of the office is regarded as the doyen of city and county managers ('doyen', feminine form 'doyenne', is derived from the Latin *decanus,* from which we also derive 'dean'; 'doyen' means the senior member of a profession or class; 'deacon' derives from the Greek *diakonos* 'a servant')

Each local authority has an elected council which meets to decide policy. The day-to-day work is carried out by the county manager and his staff. The county management system, based on a US model, was introduced in Cork in 1929. It was first promoted in Ireland by Coroner John J. Horgan (who in 1917 conducted the inquest on those who died in the *Lusitania*). The system was extended to the rest of the country in 1942.

The local authorities are controlled by the Department of the Environment because most of their work is concerned with the °physical environment. Local authorities provide public housing, build and maintain public roads, ensure water supply and sewerage, control

libraries
Liber, libri is a Latin word for 'book' from which 'library' derives. The Romans wrote their books on long strips of paper which they rolled around a stick — they called such a roll a *volumen* (from the Latin word *volvere* 'to roll') — hence our 'volume' and 'voluminous'

the physical development of their areas, protect the environment from all forms of pollution, make available recreation and amenity services (such as libraries, °museums and playgrounds), appoint vocational education committees and also look after a group of relatively °minor functions such as vehicle licensing and the upkeep of courthouses.

lynch law
summary punishment of lawless or suspected °persons by hanging, carried out by unauthorised people

The sheriff who faces down a mob that wants to lynch his jailed but innocent prisoner is a commonplace of western movies. Charles Lynch (1737-96) was a Virginian farmer and °patriot who, during the American War of Independence, headed an °irregular court formed to punish Loyalists.

Machiavellian
a description for a °person who is devious, cunning and unscrupulous

Machiavelli

Niccolo Machiavelli (1469–1527) was born in Florence, the son of a lawyer. When he was twenty-four, the ruling Medici family was driven from the city and Machiavelli got a job with the new °republican government as a °civil servant. When the Medici regained power in 1512, Machiavelli was jailed and tortured.

On his release he retired and wrote books. The most famous of these was called *The °Prince* and it established Machiavelli as the father of °political science — the study of statecraft. How do you make a °state great? Not by being Christian — gentle, just, compassionate — but by being ruthless, aggressive, proud, Machiavelli says. 'A prince who wishes to maintain his power must know how to do wrong, when necessary'. Deceit is a diplomat's best weapon. Whatever is good for the state is good.

The °morality of *The Prince* was so anti-Christian that in time Machiavelli's Christian name was transferred to Satan: 'Old Nick'.

magnum opus
a masterpiece

Magnum is the Latin word for 'great'. *Opus, operis* is the Latin word for 'work'. The words are usually applied to an artist's crowning achievement. *Opus* is also used in numbering musical compositions. *Opera*, the plural form of *opus*, is used as a singular noun in English (following the Italian) — opera — to describe a drama presented in music and song. The word 'masterpiece' derived from a practice of the town craft guilds of the Middle Ages. In order to be admitted to a guild and so become a master, a journeyman had to submit his 'masterpiece' to the guild (a journeyman was a hireling, °originally someone paid by the day — *journée* is the French word for 'day' derived from the Latin word *diurnus* meaning 'daily'). If the guild were satisfied, the journeyman was admitted to membership.

majority
the greater number

Major is a form of *magnus*, the Latin word 'great', and means 'greater'. °Democracy works on the basis of decision by a majority. The principle is often applied to carry a decision for that course of action which the greatest number of people opt for. Such a majority is a *simple majority*. In such cases the greatest number may not be an absolute majority. An *absolute majority* is any number greater than half of the votes. An absolute majority which must reach a specified level, say sixty per cent, is called a *qualified majority*.

In order to rule comfortably a °government usually requires an absolute majority of the seats in the °Dáil. However, for various reasons, a minority government, °i.e. where the government does not have an absolute majority, may provide stable government ('minority' derives from the Latin word *minor* meaning 'lesser').

Rule by majority could °degenerate to authoritarian or even mob rule. To protect individuals and minorities our °constitution, like other °liberal constitutions, provides for the protection of a range of basic °human rights through appeal to the courts.

The word 'majority' is also used in Britain to denote the number of °votes by which a successful °candidate exceeds those of his or her nearest °rival.

The silent majority is an American °political concept which °denotes the supposed °conservative majority of the people in contrast to the vociferous liberals who command the °media (*vox, vocis* is the Latin word for 'voice', *ferre* is the Latin word 'to carry').

mandate
the sanction given by the °electors to the °government to act in accordance with their election °manifesto

Mandare is the Latin word 'to command'; *mandatum* is 'that which has been commanded'. The basic mandate a °democratic government receives from the electorate is to govern in the common interest in accordance with the °constitution. Endorsement of its election manifesto strengthens a government's capacity to take specific actions. However, if governments find that their manifesto or elements of it cannot be implemented, or if they find that actual conditions demand actions contrary to their manifesto, they feel they have the right to continue in °office: they fall back on the basic mandate to govern.

-mania
dipsomania, egomania, kleptomania, megalomania, nymphomania, pyromania — these are all words whose common ending *-mania* means 'madness' in Greek

Mania is a °mental illness characterised by elation and violence. A *maniac* is someone who suffers from mania (such a person may be described as 'manic' or 'maniacal'). The suffix *-mane* denotes an enthusiast rather than a mad person — thus a balletomane is a °fan of ballet.

Dipsomania is the condition of the alcoholic (*dipsa* means 'thirst' in Greek).

Egomania is the condition of someone excessively self-centred (*ego* is the Latin word for 'I').

Kleptomania is the condition of someone who cannot resist the impulse to steal (*kleptein* is the Greek word 'to steal').

Megalomania is the delusion that one is powerful; it is often applied to a passion for big things (*megalo,* like *mega*, is a Greek prefix meaning 'big').

Nymphomania is used to describe the condition of women who are seized by uncontrollable sexual desire (*nymphē* is the Greek word for 'a bride'; in Greek °mythology, a nymph was also one of the female divinities who lived in woods, rivers, mountains °etc.).

nymph
The Greeks called their wood-nymphs *dryads* (*drys* is the Greek for 'oak-tree') —thus Keats in 'Ode to a Nightingale' addressed his subject as 'light-winged Dryad of the trees'. They called their water-nymphs *naiads* (*naein* is the Greek 'to flow') —thus Sir Walter Scott in 'The Lady of the Lake' refers to 'the guardian Naiad of the strand'

Pyromania is the condition of someone who cannot resist starting fires (*pyr* is the Greek word for 'a fire'). *Pyracanth* is a thorny evergreen shrub that fruits in fiery red berries (*akanthos* is the Greek word for 'a thorn'). *Pyrotechnics* is a display of fireworks (*technikos* means 'skilled' in Greek). *Arson*, the unlawful setting fire to another's property, derives from the Latin word *ardere* 'to burn' (from which we also derive 'ardent'). An *incendiary* is someone who maliciously sets fire to property or foments trouble (*incendere* is the Latin word 'to kindle'). *Incandescent* is 'to glow white hot' derived from the Latin word *candere* ' to glow' and *in*, a Latin particle °denoting intensity. To *ignite* is 'to set on fire', derived from the Latin word for a fire *ignis* (from which we also derive 'ignition' and 'igneous'). To *scintillate* is 'to sparkle' (*scintilla* is the Latin word for 'a spark'; used as a noun in English it means a hint or a trace: 'There wasn't a scintilla of evidence to connect him to the crime').

manifesto
a °political party's statement of the policies it will follow if it is °elected to govern

Manifesto is an Italian word meaning 'placard' or 'poster'. A manifesto is now usually a document issued before an election which sets forth the policies a party will follow in relation to such issues as the °economy, °employment, °social °welfare, housing, °education, and °taxation. It is a useful document for party workers canvassing at doors and for briefing the °media.

The most famous manifesto was the °*Communist Manifesto*, written by Karl Marx and Friedrich Engels, and published in 1848: 'Let the ruling classes tremble at a communist °revolution! The °proletarians have nothing to lose but their chains. They have a world to win'.

mass media
newspapers, journals, °television, radio and any other instruments of communication with the °public

Media is the plural form of the Latin word *medium* 'the middle': a medium is literally a thing in the middle — a channel — through which a message is carried from a sender to a receiver. The channels we have for reaching the °population — the mass media — are described as either print (newspapers and magazines) or electronic (radio and television). *Mass* derives from the Latin word *massa* 'a body of matter that can be moulded' which in turn probably derives from the Greek word *massein* 'to knead' (like dough). It came to be applied to the broad bulk of the population.

materialism
the view that nothing exists but matter. (Materialists, therefore, deny the existence of spiritual, i.e. non-material, things such as God)

Materia is the Latin word for 'timber' or 'building materials', and the word 'matter', derived from it, has come to mean the basic constituent of reality. Marx has been described as a materialist °philosopher. By that is meant that he believed man's endeavours to meet the material conditions of existence determined the °character of his °social and °moral relationships. °History is the fruit of that process. Hence the Marxist view of history is called historical materialism.

Occasionally, churchmen °criticise 'the growing materialism of Irish society'. They do not mean by that that more and more Irish people are becoming philosophic materialists. They mean that more and more Irish people are placing the acquisition of wealth (material goods) before all other °values such as justice and charity. They do *not* mean that the acquisition of wealth is itself to be condemned. One should note that, on this use of the word, a poor person may be as materialistic as a rich one; sometimes much more so. Think of 'The Bull' McCabe in John B. Keane's play *The Field.*

maverick
an American expression meaning 'unbranded stock'

A Texas lawyer, Samuel A. Maverick, took possession of a herd of cattle in payment of a debt in 1845. Not being a cattleman, he took little interest in them — he did not even realise the importance of branding them — and loosed them on an island to multiply naturally. Eight years later he had the herd brought to the mainland. Surprisingly, it seemed not to have increased. What had happened was that numerous cowpokes had roped some of the cattle for themselves — the °law of the range allowed anyone to take possession of unbranded cattle. The men who took the cattle came to be called 'maverickers' and unbranded cattle came to be described as 'maverick'. Transferred to people, 'maverick' °connotes someone who is wayward, eccentric — an outsider. Thus a maverick °politician is one who does not belong to any party or who, if he or she does, is conspicuously non-conformist.

Merrion Street
the °centre of °government

The Department of the Taoiseach and the Department of Finance are °located in Government Buildings, Upper Merrion Street, Dublin. The °media often use the term 'Merrion Street' to refer to thinking on policy (rather than party °political) matters at the highest levels of government.

Merrion Street

Dublin Castle. Note that the columns supporting the pediment are Ionic. The cupola crowns an hexagonal tower ('cupola' derives from the Latin *cupula*, a diminutive form of *cupa* 'a cask'; *hex* is Greek for 'six', *gonia* is Greek for 'angle'; *penta* is Greek for 'five', hence *pentagon; hepta* is Greek for 'seven', hence *heptagon*; *octo* is Greek for 'eight', hence *octagon*)

The Department of Education is located in Marlborough Street. 'Marlborough Street' is used to refer to the policy-makers on °education.

The Department of the Environment is mostly located in the Custom House, Dublin. 'The Custom House' is used to refer to the policy-makers on °local government.

The Department of Foreign Affairs is located in Iveagh House, St Stephen's Green, Dublin. 'Iveagh House' is used to refer to the policy-makers on foreign affairs.

The Department of Industry and Commerce is located in Kildare Street. 'Kildare Street' is used to refer to the policy-makers on industry and commerce.

The Revenue Commissioners are located in Dublin Castle. 'The Castle' is used to refer to the Revenue policy-makers.

Áras an Uachtaráin, the residence of the °President of Ireland, is in the Phoenix Park, Dublin; the °Taoiseach 'goes to the Park', on his °election by the °Dáil, to receive his seal of office from the President.

The two Houses of the °Oireachtas, Dáil Éireann and °Seanad Éireann, meet in Leinster House, Dublin. 'Leinster House' is used to refer to the °legislature. 'The House' refers to either the Dáil or Seanad, depending on the context.

metaphysical
pertaining to an area of °philosophy that discusses the questions left unasked by the particular °sciences — the fundamental questions of life and the nature of reality

Meta is a Greek word meaning 'after'. *Physical* derives from *phusis*, transliterated *physis*, the Greek word for 'nature'. *Metaphysical* is opposed to the concreteness of the *physical*. Thus the metaphysical poets of seventeenth °century England (°e.g. Donne, Marvell) are so called because they raised profound questions that nature poets do not. Their verse is sometimes described as cerebral (relating to the brain — *cerebrum* in Latin) as opposed to naturalistic. Incidentally, metaphysics (after physics) is so called because an early editor of the books of the great Greek philosopher, Aristotle, listed his work on these questions after his work on physics.

metropolis
the °capital city of a country or district

Mētēr, mētros is the Greek word for 'mother'. *Polis* is the Greek word for 'city' (strictly 'city-state'). The ancient Greeks were great traders. Cities like Athens and Corinth would occasionally send out groups of their citizens to °colonise other parts of the Mediterranean (from the Latin *medius* meaning 'middle' and *terra* meaning 'earth' — the Mediterranean was the sea in the middle of the known world). These would establish trading ports — like Naples in Italy. A metropolis was °originally the mother city of a Greek colony i.e. the city from which the colonists came.

The metropolitan area of a city is the area controlled by the city council. 'Metropolitan' applied to France in 'metropolitan France' refers to the mother *country* and therefore excludes overseas territories or colonies. A metropolitan in a Christian °hierarchy is the bishop of the chief see of a Church °province — it is a concept derived from the Greek city-colony relationship.

micro
microbe, microcomputer, microcosm, microeconomics, microphone, microscope — these are all words whose common prefix *micro-* comes from the Greek word *micros* meaning 'little'

A *microbe* is a tiny living being (*bios* is 'life' in Greek).

A *microcomputer* is a small computer (*computare* is a Latin word 'to reckon').

A *microcosm* is a representation in miniature of something large. Thus man, with a body made up of interrelated parts and a spirit within it, has been regarded by some °philosophers as a microcosm of the world (*cosmos* is the Greek word for 'universe' — the ordered °universe in contrast to chaos, the °primal, disordered world; order brings beauty and so we call those preparations applied to enhance the beauty of the body 'cosmetics'). A microcosm reflects on a small scale a *macrocosm* (*macros* means 'big' in Greek). Just as the word '°analogy' allows us to extrapolate our understanding of something known into something less known, so microcosm allows us to extrapolate our understanding of something small into something large.

Microeconomics is the study of the °economics of small units, °e.g. shops, factories, in contrast to *macroeconomics* which is concerned with the study of the economics of large aggregates, e.g. °total °production of the economy as a whole (*grex, gregis* is the Latin word for 'a flock';

°*ad* is a Latin word meaning 'to' — an aggregate, °originally 'adgregate', is those things brought together — made to flock together; to *segregate* is 'to group apart' — *se* is a Latin prefix meaning 'apart'; a *congregation* is a large number of individuals who voluntarily flock together — *con* is a Latin particle that means 'with'; a *gregarious* person is a sociable person who likes to be in a flock; an *egregious* person is someone outside the flock — *e* is a Latin word meaning 'out of' — and therefore exceptional, usually in an outrageous way).

A *microphone* is a small °apparatus for amplifying the voice (*phōnē* is the Greek word for 'voice') and contrasts with *megaphone*, a non-powered, conical instrument used to trumpet the voice (*megas* is a Greek word for 'great').

A *microscope* is an instrument for magnifying tiny objects (*skopein* is the Greek word 'to look at'). When scientists first examined water and other liquids under the microscope, they were surprised to find what looked like little rods floating in them. They called these microscopic °organisms *bacteria*, the plural form of the Greek word *bactērion* meaning 'a little stick'. A bacillus (plural bacilli) is an infectious bacterium (the Latin form of *bactērion*). *Bacillus* is the Latin word for 'a little rod'.

modus operandi
manner of working

Modus is the Latin word for 'manner'. *Operandi* is a form of the Latin word *operare* 'to work' and means 'of working'. There are usually many ways of doing a job. The particular scheme chosen by someone might be described as his or her 'modus operandi'. The expression is often used in police circles where criminals may be identified by their M.O. (*modus operandi*). Thus, 'Before he touches anything, he sits down and makes himself a cup of tea ....'

modus vivendi
a means of accommodating to one another

Modus is the Latin word for 'manner'. *Vivendi* is a form of the Latin word *vivere* 'to live' and means 'of living'. When people on bad terms with one another nonetheless succeed in developing procedures that allow them to co-operate, they are said to have worked out a *modus vivendi*. Hostile, but not warring, countries also find that they must work out a *modus vivendi* in order to enjoy the benefits of trade and °cultural exchange.

In the °modern world the two superpowers (*super* is a Latin word meaning 'above' or 'beyond') have worked out a *modus vivendi* that is °characterised by periods of sharp °competition and confrontation followed by periods of *détente* (a French word meaning 'relaxation').

monetarist
someone who believes strict control of money supply ensures optimum °economic performance and price stability

Friedman

optimum
derives from the Latin *optimus* 'best'. Note that 'maximum' and 'optimum' are not identical terms. Thus, the maximum output of a factory is the amount that could be produced if the machinery were kept constantly in operation. The optimum output, broadly speaking, is the greatest amount that can be produced consonant with maintaining the machinery, the morale of the workers,

There was a °temple on the Capitoline hill in Rome dedicated to Juno Moneta (Juno the Reminder). Juno, the °eponymous goddess of the month of June, was the queenly wife of °Jupiter. The protectress of marriage (at Roman marriages the knot in the bride's girdle that the bridegroom had to untie was consecrated to her), she was concerned to remind couples of their vows. Beside the temple there was a mint for striking coins which came to be called the *moneta*. From that word we derive 'money', 'monetary', 'monetarist' and 'mint'.

While °Keynesians argue that °governments should intervene in the economy to ensure that the greatest possible °employment is created consonant with keeping °inflation in check, strict monetarists argue that governments should concentrate on creating conditions in which money flows towards those activities that are most efficiently managed and for whose °products or services there is a real (not an °artificially contrived) demand.

Monetarists believe in free market conditions. Since governments are concerned more with °political than with economic benefits, strict monetarists wish to see governments involved as little as possible in the production of goods and services. They feel, moreover, that governments cannot undertake those tasks efficiently. Monetarists, therefore, favour °privatisation.

The great °prophet of °modern monetarism is the American economist Milton Friedman. He has largely °influenced the economic thinking of recent British °Conservative °ideologues — hence the Thatcherites' obsession at one point with the control of money supply, and their continual concern about inflation (seen by them as a °concomitant of Keynesianism).

and the rate of profit. An *optimist* is someone who takes a hopeful view of the future. A *pessimist* is someone who takes a despondent view of the future (*pessimus* is the Latin for 'worst')

When economists speak of the government's *monetary policy*, they are thinking of its °strategic decisions in relation to interest rates and money supply. When they speak of the government's °*fiscal policy*, they are thinking of its strategic decisions in relation to taxes and public expenditure.

monolithic
like a single massive block of stone

Monos is the Greek word for 'alone'. *Lithos* is the Greek word for 'stone'. The ancient standing stones with ogham inscriptions that are found in various parts of Ireland are monoliths. But the word 'monolithic' is usually applied to large, enduring °organisations that present a single, impassive front to outsiders. Thus, 'The monolithic Russian °state brooks no internal dissent'.

Megalithic pertains to a huge stone, particularly such as is found in prehistoric monuments (*mega* is derived from *megas* the Greek word for 'large'; in °physics and in the decimal system it °denotes 'million' or 'a million times', for example 'megavolt').

monopoly
the exclusive supply of, and therefore trade in, some good or service

Monos is a Greek word for 'alone'. *Polein* is the Greek word 'to sell'. In a free market the price a particular good or service can command is determined by the amount that consumers are willing to pay while buying the °total quantity of the good or service on offer (the market clearing price). A monopolist has no °competitors and therefore can raise the price by restricting supply or simply by °fiat. A trader can create a monopoly by cornering the supply of raw materials or the means of turning it into goods, or both. Groups of traders can form a cartel or oligopoly (*oligos* is a Greek word for 'little' or 'few') to eliminate competition among themselves and hike prices.

Because monopolies may unfairly affect consumers, °governments usually enact °legislation to prevent the creation of monopolies. Indeed one of the directive principles of °social policy embodied in °*Bunreacht na hÉireann* urges that the °state should ensure that 'the operation of free competition shall not be allowed so to develop as to result in the concentration of the ownership or control of essential commodities in a few individuals to the common detriment'. The state has passed legislation relating to mergers and monopolies and has established a Fair Trade Commission.

The state reserves to itself a monopoly in certain commodities. Thus the Electricity Supply Board, a °state-sponsored body, has a monopoly in the sale (though not the °production) of electricity. Enterprises such as the ESB may be referred to as natural monopolies. A monopoly is described as natural where the one large operator achieves efficient production through °economies of scale and where the sharing of the market with another supplier would deny that efficiency to both suppliers.

A *monopsonist* is the opposite of a monopolist. It is a °person who, or °organisation which, is the sole buyer for the goods or services of several sellers (*opsonein* is the Greek word 'to buy'). The grocery trade in Ireland, increasingly concentrated in a small number of supermarket chains, is tending towards monopsony. Monopsony allows the buyer to take unfair advantage of sellers.

morganatic marriage
a marriage between someone of exalted rank and someone of lower rank in which the inferior partner and the children of the marriage have no claims on the title or estate of the person of exalted rank

Morgengabe is an Old German word. It °denoted the gift from the husband to the wife on the morning (*morgen* in German) after the wedding, which represented the only claim she had on him.

Between 1848 and 1916 the Hapsburg °Empire was ruled by the Emperor Franz Joseph. In 1893 the Emperor's only son, Rudolph, committed °suicide with his mistress, Marie Vetsera, at a royal hunting lodge called 'Mayerling' in the Vienna Woods. The line of succession then passed to the Emperor's nephew, Franz Ferdinand. Franz Ferdinand wished to marry Countess Sophia Chotek. Just as in England royal marriages are governed by the Royal Marriages Act, so in the Austro-Hungarian Empire they were governed by the Hapsburg Family °Law.

Under a provision of that law the Countess Sophia, although belonging to the ancient nobility of Bohemia, was ineligible for marriage with a °prince of the Blood Imperial. The Emperor, however, agreed to a morganatic marriage: Franz Ferdinand had solemnly to swear and declare that neither his wife Sophia nor their issue should be entitled to succeed to the Hapsburg throne. Franz Ferdinand was left in no doubt that he was regarded as having contracted a *mésalliance* (a French word meaning 'an unsuitable marriage'; *més-* is a prefix equivalent to the English 'mis-').

On 23 June 1914 Franz Ferdinand and Sophia were °assassinated by a Slav °nationalist, Gavrillo Princip, as they drove in an open car through the streets of Sarajevo, °capital of the Slav provinces of Bosnia-Herzegovina, which had been annexed by the Hapsburgs in 1908. This assassination triggered a chain of events that led directly to World War I.

When the Emperor Franz Joseph died in 1916, he was succeeded by his grand-nephew, Archduke Charles Franz Joseph (1916-18), the last Hapsburg Emperor.

A morganatic marriage was proposed as a solution to the °constitutional °crisis that arose in Britain in 1936 when King Edward VIII declared his intention to marry Mrs Wallis Simpson, an American divorcée. It would have required amendment of the Royal Marriages Act, but was not in any event deemed acceptable to the people. The king abdicated and became the Duke of Windsor. Wallis became his duchess.

multinationals
large companies with °production and marketing operations °located in a number of countries

Multus is the Latin word for 'many'. *Natio, nationis* is the Latin word for 'nation'. Many multinationals deploy °budgets greater than Ireland's national budget. Furthermore they often trade in °strategically important goods such as oil, minerals and other °natural resources. They enjoy great °political °influence, therefore, by reason of their size and the importance of their trade. They can play off one country against another. Their very °character allows them to avoid the full scrutiny of any one °government. Multinational corporations, on the other hand, bring many advantages to a late-industrialising country such as Ireland. They increase output, °exports and °employment (though not enough to silence their °critics) and they provide 'demonstration' effects in the form of showing the latest production °methodology.

municipal
pertaining to a town or city that has the status of a °corporation

A member of a Roman °colony with the right to °vote was called a *municeps* (from the Latin word *munia* meaning '°official duties' and *capere* the Latin word 'to take'). The full gathering of *municipes* (plural form) was called a *municipium. Municipalis* is a Latin word meaning 'pertaining to a *municipium'.* In Ireland corporations with their mayors, aldermen and burgesses are municipalities and as such are part of the °local government system.

museum
a place where artefacts of various kinds are stored and exhibited

inspiration
To inspire is literally 'to breathe into' (from the Latin *in* meaning 'in' and *spirare* 'to breathe') —to influence, especially with exalted ideas or emotions. To conspire is literally 'to breathe together' (*con* is the Latin 'with') — conspirators agree secretly to act together for a purpose

The *Mousai* (the Muses) were the nine daughters of Zeus and Mnemosyne (Memory), each a goddess of one or other of the arts. The Latin *-eum* suffix denotes 'place'. A long poetic °convention has poets appealing to their muse to give them inspiration. The National Museum of Ireland exhibits a wide variety of materials ranging from °neolithic to °modern. In countries other than Ireland and Britain art galleries are often called museums — for example, the Prado Museum in Madrid and the Museum of Modern Art in New York.

The muses and their arts (in brackets) are: Thalia (°comedy), Terpsichore (dance), Clio (°history), Euterpe (lyric poetry), Erato (love poetry), Urania (°astronomy), Calliope (°epic), Melpomene (°tragedy), Polymnia (sacred song).

The Ardagh Chalice— one of the greatest treasures in the National Museum

mutatis mutandis
after making the necessary changes

Mutare is the Latin word 'to change' (from which we also get 'mutable', 'immutable', 'mutant'). The phrase means 'those things having been changed which ought to be changed'. It is a useful expression for a rule-maker who can deploy it in such a way that he or she does not have to repeat °*ad nauseam* a rule that can be applied with small, obvious changes to different categories. Thus, 'The customs °regulations for the °importation of motor cars apply *mutatis mutandis* to spare parts and accessories'.

nationalism
a concept used to embrace the reasons (common territory, °culture, language, religion are the ones usually advanced) why a particular group of people have a particular identity and are called a nation or people

Natio, nationis is the Latin word for 'a people' or 'nation'. The concept of nation is not clearly defined but it is important because nationalism gave rise to the °political °dogma that every nation should have its own °state, and that dogma has been the most °dynamic force in nineteenth and twentieth °century political °history.

'State' derives from *status* a Latin word meaning 'condition' or 'way of existing' or 'well-being' which itself is derived from *stare* the Latin word 'to stand'. Thus we speak of the state of the country, the state of the arts, and such. From this, the word came to refer to the °social and °economic conditions of a group of people. Then in the form *état*, as in *Etats generaux*, in French and 'estate' in English, it came to refer to the large groupings within a kingdom. Dante (1265-1321) contrasts 'a free state' (*stato*) with a °tyranny, and we see the word beginning to refer to the form of °government or to the people governed. The first clear-cut use of 'state' in our sense is in Machiavelli's *The °Prince*—it occurs in the very first sentence. Machiavelli also talked about Italy's being divided into many 'states', signifying different °centres of 'rule over men' and different forms of rule. He also talks of 'matters of state'. For him a state is an °organisation with the capacity to exercise force within a particular territory over its people and against other such states. The first formal theoretical account of 'state' as a °legal structure of force and power and controlled by a government understood as a legally constituted power centre came with Hobbes who equates the Latin *civitas*, 'commonwealth' and 'state'. Though the word did not find general acceptance in this sense in England until the late nineteenth century, it was so used on the Continent in the eighteenth century and from there transferred to the US where the federal government was referred to as 'the state' and the constituent governments as 'the states'.

The defining characteristics of a °modern state 'as a °person of international law', which are set forth in the Montevideo °Convention of 1933, are:

(a) a permanent °population
(b) a defined territory
(c) a government
(d) a capacity to enter into relations with other states.

A state may embrace a whole people and a whole country, like the French state. (A country is a °geographic entity forming part of a °continent which itself may contain regions such as °provinces and counties.) It may embrace a number of countries (or parts of them) and a number of nations. Thus the United Kingdom consists of three countries — England, Scotland, Wales — and Northern Ireland (a part of a country) and of three nations — English, Scottish and Welsh — and a part of a nation — the Irish nation. It may embrace a part of a nation and a part of a country, like our own state.

The word 'statistics', meaning tabulations of figures, also derives from the Latin *status*—statistics originally related solely to those of a state.

natural resources
any attribute of the natural environment which °humans consider to be of value in promoting their °welfare

Natura is the Latin word for 'nature', the °physical reality of the world. *Resource* derives from the Latin word *resurgere* 'to rise up' and °denotes anything to hand that can meet a need. In some discussions the term 'natural resources' is used in a very restricted sense to mean metals, coal, oil and gas. In other discussions it seems to be a very compendious term that even includes people ('our greatest natural resource').

In discussion it is probably useful to divide natural resources into those that are renewable and those that are not. Minerals and fuels such as coal, oil and gas are not renewable. (Coal, oil and gas exhaust themselves in use but most metals can be reused through recycling.) Among the renewable sources are water, soil, forests, fish, wildlife, solar and tidal energy, air. Non-renewable sources are said to be finite. 'Finite' derives from the Latin word *finire* 'to limit' and means 'limited'.

nemesis
retribution

Nemesis was a mysterious Greek goddess °personifying retribution ('punishment as a repayment for evil' derived from the Latin prefix *re* meaning 'back' and the Latin word *tribuere* 'to give' from which we also derive 'tribute', 'attribute', 'contribute' and 'distribute'), directed principally towards °humans who have been presumptuous. The word *nemein* from which nemesis is derived means 'to give someone his or her due'. It can specifically represent divine indignation at undeserved good °fortune. In Greek °tragedy Nemesis is the goddess who brings down all immoderate good fortune, checks the presumption which attends it and is the punisher of ordinary crime. We might say nowadays of the fall of a spectacularly successful speculator 'His nemesis came in the form of a glut of oil on the spot market'.

'Nemesis' by Albrecht Dürer (1471-1528). During the time of the Renaissance, Nemesis, the goddess of vengeance, merged with the capricious °Fortuna, so Dürer depicts his winged goddess as bearing an expensive goblet to reward the good and a reins to control the evil. (*Caper, capricis* is the Latin word for 'a goat'; 'capricious' means 'freakish' or 'changeable' like a goat — hence, also, 'caprice'. 'Capricorn' means 'like a horned goat' — *cornu* is the Latin 'a horn')

neo-
a prefix meaning 'new'

Neos is the Greek word for 'new'. *Neo-* may be combined with any °historical movement or idea, e.g. neo-°classical, neo-°pagan, neo-gothic, to mean a new or °modern form of it.

Neo-colonialism is the process by which a strong country gains or retains °economic control over a weak country by buying and controlling its °natural resources or means of °production (*colonia* is the Latin word for 'colony'). Old-style colonialism was naked °expropriation of the °natives.

the Stone Age
is divided by scholars into three periods — neolithic (the one closest to us), mesolithic (the one in the middle — *mesos* means 'middle' in Greek), and palaeolithic (the one most distant — *palaios* means 'old' in Greek)

Neolithic means 'new (i.e. later) Stone Age' (*lithos* means 'stone' in Greek).

A *neologism* is a newly coined word like 'wordgloss' (*logos* means 'word' in Greek).

Naples derives from its °original Greek name *Neapolis* 'new city' — hence Neapolitan meaning 'pertaining to Naples' (*polis* means 'city', strictly 'city-state', in Greek).

neophyte
a novice; a young, inexperienced practitioner

Neos is the Greek word for 'new'. *Phytos* is a Greek word meaning 'sown' or 'planted'. A *neophyte* was a new convert to Christianity in the early period. The term is now applied generally to mean 'a beginner' or 'novice' (from the Latin word *novus* meaning 'new'). Thus, 'At 44 Mr Giovanni Goria is the youngest Prime Minister of his country [Italy] in the post-war period. He is not a °political neophyte, however, as he has served as Treasury Minister since 1982, and has earned °credit for masterminding °economic progress in that time'. (Editorial, *The Irish Times,* 8 August 1987)

The Latin equivalent of neophyte is *tiro* (also *tyro*).

ne plus ultra
the °ultimate achievement or goal; perfection

Ne is a Latin negative particle. *Plus* is the Latin for 'more'. *Ultra* is a Latin word meaning 'beyond' (so 'ultras' is used as a °synonym for extremists). The expression, supposed to have been inscribed on the Pillars of Hercules, the headlands at the °Mediterranean end of the Strait of Gibraltar, was a command: 'Let there be no more [sailing] beyond this!' Beyond was the edge of the world.

The most famous use of the phrase in °modern times occurred in a declaration by the Irish leader, Charles

Parnell

Stewart Parnell, in 1886 when he was being pressed by Gladstone to declare whether or not the proposed Home Rule Bill would not satisfy utterly Irish °nationalist aspirations:

> No man has the right to fix the boundary to the march of a nation. No man has a right to say to his country 'Thus far shalt thou go and no further'. We have never attempted to fix the *ne plus ultra* to the progress of Ireland's nationhood — and we never shall.

nepotism
a practice whereby those in authority advance their relatives in preference to others

Nepos, nepotis is the Latin word for 'nephew' or 'grandson'. °Political patronage is reprehensible because it is unfair. Nepotism is a form of patronage denounced even by those who enjoy other forms of patronage. Some of the Popes, especially the Borgias, were notorious for their nepotism; so was Napoleon who placed his brothers and sisters on the thrones of Europe. Nepotism may proceed from more than a simple desire to enrich relatives: where a ruler's grip is shaky, he or she may use nepotism to secure loyalty in certain °strategic offices or °localities.

A °democracy favours meritocratic processes. In a meritocracy people gain positions by reason of their ability (*meritum* is a Latin word meaning 'a thing deserved'; the *-cracy* suffix is derived from the Greek word *kratein* 'to rule'). The °Civil Service Commission and the Local Appointments Commission are bodies independent of political °influence which ensure that all appointments to the civil service and the °local authorities are made on merit.

neutrality
a policy, recognised in international °law, of taking sides with neither party in a dispute or war

Neuter is a Latin word meaning 'neither'. The essence of neutrality is not being involved in wars between other °states. A state whose neutrality is °legally recognised has a right to have its integrity respected by the warring states. It in return must perform certain °primary neutrality duties: it must deny the use of its °national territory (including airspace and territorial waters), by force if necessary, to all °belligerents; it must give no support to belligerents although °normal trade may continue; it must apply impartially the rules of neutrality

Major John MacBride holding the sight of a British cannon captured at Colenso, South Africa

under international law.

Neutrality is pursued by a small number of states in Europe. Apart from Ireland, the other European neutrals are Switzerland, Austria, Sweden and Finland. However, about a hundred states throughout the world, including India, Yugoslavia and Egypt, seek to hold themselves aloof from the struggle of the two °superpowers: they follow a policy of non-alignment and belong to the Non-Aligned Movement, started in 1961.

Irish neutrality has its roots in the desire of Irish °nationalists to assert Ireland's separateness from Britain. In the Boer War most Irish nationalists advocated a °*de facto* neutrality (although some, like Major John MacBride, fought on the Boer side). However, during World War I many nationalists fought alongside the British in defence of 'the rights of small nations'. Others subscribed to neutrality under the °slogan 'Neither King Nor °Kaiser'. The British proposal in 1918 to impose conscription on Ireland, °massively rejected, consolidated the neutralist position of Irish nationalists.

Under the Anglo-Irish Agreement of 1921 (the Treaty),

The 200-strong Irish Citizen Army drawn up in front of Liberty Hall, Dublin, the headquarters of the Transport and General Workers' Union. Founded by Larkin and Connolly during the 1913 lock-out to protect the workers, it was committed, along with the Irish Volunteers, to the Easter Rising, 1916

a number of key °naval facilities were retained by the British which made any °credible policy of neutrality impossible. Irish °politicians of all parties subsequently aspired to disentangle Irish forces from those of Britain. In the 1938 Anglo-Irish Agreement the British withdrew from the ports (Berehaven, Cobh and Lough Swilly) — and Eamon de Valera achieved the sovereignty that allowed him to maintain successfully a policy of neutrality throughout World War II ('the Emergency' in Ireland).

Ireland has maintained its neutrality ever since. It is not a member of the North Atlantic Treaty °Organisation (NATO). Its neutral status has allowed it to play an active peacekeeping role in the United Nations, which Ireland joined in 1955. Membership of the °European Community does not involve Ireland in any °military commitments.

Nietzschean
in the manner of the German °philosopher Friedrich Nietzsche (1844–1900)

Nietzsche, the son of a Protestant pastor, became an °atheist early on in life. His thinking led him to proclaim the death of God — which for him meant mankind's loss of belief in any supernatural power to guide and sustain °human life. The death of God implied that man was master of himself and of the world. It is a matter of debate as to whether Nietzsche was °articulating a new philosophy or exploring the implications of a movement which had already begun, namely, °radical individualism, a form of °humanism that put man at the °centre of the world. Nietzsche is sometimes described as a nihilist, that is, someone who denies an °objective °moral order (*nihil* is the Latin word for 'nothing'; the term 'nihilism' was coined by the Russian writer Turgenev in 1861 in *Fathers and Sons*).

Nietzsche suggested that man now had the freedom to become a superman (*super* is a Latin word meaning 'above' or 'beyond'). People were of either of two °mentalities — masters or slaves, an idea Nietzsche explored in his book *Thus Spake Zarathustra*. Religion fostered the slave mentality. Freed from the fetters of religion, man must define his own ideas of nobility and will them. He defined 'will' as power — hence the expression 'will to power' or more accurately 'will as power'. The superman, by °articulating new ideas for himself, charts new avenues of achievement for all—and thereby accomplishes what Nietzsche called the transvaluation (or redefining) of values; that is the eternally recurring task of the great man. Nietzsche, therefore, was not a °hedonist or °amoralist—he simply articulated the idea of man as self-creator, an idea that is °dominant in °modern culture. Some thinkers argue that the pervasive resentment many people feel at having their moral values defined by society for them as traceable to Nietzsche.

Nietzsche

The idea of some existentialists that human life is meaningless and that man must assume responsibility for his °values flows from Nietzsche's individualism and will as power. His ideas about the superman, the master-race, the will to power were seized upon by the °Nazis and made part of their °ideology.

Some scholars believe that the °popular linking of Nietzsche with the bestiality of Hitler's °regime is justified, others vehemently repudiate such an idea.

nomenclature
terminology

Nomen, nominis is the Latin word for 'name' from which we also derive 'nominal', 'nominate', 'nominee', and 'denomination'. *Calare* is the Latin word 'to call'. In Roman times a *nomenclator* was a slave who accompanied a °candidate for office on his rounds and fed him the names of people he was about to meet so that he could address them like long-lost friends. *Nomenclatura*, the word used to describe this practice, transliterated 'nomenclature' in English, has come to mean 'a system of names'. Thus, 'The nomenclature used in °classifying flowers is, as you would expect, colourful. The chrysanthemum — a genus to which the corn marigold and ox-eye daisy belong — derives its name from *chrysos*, the Greek word for "gold" and *anthemon*, the Greek word for "flower". The gentle heliotrope is so called because it turns with the sun — *hēlios* is the Greek word for "sun" and *tropein* means "to turn" in Greek.'

Nomenklatura is a word used for the list of °communist °officials in the Eastern European countries: 'the nomenklatura' is a term used for that privileged group.

non sequitur
a conclusion which does not follow from the argument

Non is 'not' in Latin. *Sequitur* means 'it follows' in Latin. The expression is used in a °logical °context. For example, 'You said John would not hurt a lamb because he is a deer hunter — but that's a *non sequitur*'

obiter dictum
an incidental remark

Obiter is a Latin word meaning 'by the way' or 'in passing'. *Dictum* is the Latin for 'a thing spoken' which, taken over directly into English, is used for 'an authoritative saying'. The expression is used in a °legal °context where a judge in arguing a point may give an opinion not essential to the case. *Obiter dicta* (the plural form of *dictum*) are often cited because they are suasory (from *suadere* the Latin word 'to persuade').

objective
pertaining to a statement, proposition or theory which accords with the known facts or is °verifiable by some accepted standards

Ob is a Latin word meaning 'against' or 'in the way of'. *Jacere* is a Latin word 'to throw'. An object is something thrown in the way of — perceived — by a knowing subject. It is something there to be known. Consequently, in the theory of knowledge, the knowing subject and known object are mutually related terms. The knowing subject is said to be objective when he or she is °focused clearly and fully on the object. The objective °person is one who takes great care to have good reasons for what he or she asserts.

Objectivity is a desirable °value in all areas of knowledge. It is the condition one needs to achieve to arrive at just judgements. 'Subjective', on the contrary, °connotes a person who does not take great care to have good reasons for what he or she asserts and who consequently makes statements without due reference to facts or verification. Used in this sense — to describe the quality of someone's knowledge — it has a °pejorative meaning: there is a suggestion of bias and prejudice. 'Subjective' is also used to connote what is proper or peculiar to a subject, that is, one who is a °centre of knowledge and action. Thus the act of knowing is subjective, feeling is subjective. In these uses, the word is not pejorative.

In grammar and °logic we use the word 'subject' to describe that part of a sentence or proposition which refers to the °topic under discussion to which we apply a predicate — that which is asserted of the object which is referred to by the subject. Thus, in the sentence 'The cat' (subject) 'is lame' (predicate), 'is lame' is predicated (asserted) of the real cat.

We also use the word 'subject' in the same way as we have defined 'object', °e.g. 'the subject under discussion', but this is a derivative use.

In °politics and in °community life we use the word 'subject' to describe those who are under authority, whether it be lawful or unlawful, for example 'a subject people'.

Finally, as a noun, 'objective' means 'something aimed at'.

obscurantist
someone who is opposed to enlightenment

Obscurare is the Latin word 'to cover'. People in authority are often obscurantist so as to lessen their own accountability or to preclude others through ignorance from possible courses of action. °Governments have often been blamed for being more obscurantist than open and therefore less °democratic in practice than they might be. People who do not wish to have their ideas challenged may also resort to obscurantism by, for instance, banning or even burning books.

odyssey
a long, wandering, adventurous journey

The Greek poet Homer wrote the world's two greatest °epics — the *Iliad* and the *Odyssey*. The *Iliad* tells of the capture of Troy (or Ilium) by the Greeks. The *Odyssey* tells of the adventures of Odysseus (known to the Romans as Ulysses) as he made his way from burning Troy to his home on the island of Ithaca, where his wife

The opening lines of the *Odyssey* ('Sing to me, O °Muse, of the much-travelled hero who wandered far and wide after he had sacked the sacred citadel of Troy...')

ἌΝΔΡΑ μοι ἔννεπε, Μοῦσα, πολύτροπον, ὃς μάλα πολλὰ
Πλάγχθη, ἐπεὶ Τροίης ἱερὸν πτολίεθρον ἔπερσεν·
Πολλῶν δ' ἀνθρώπων ἴδεν ἄστεα, καὶ νόον ἔγνω·
Πολλὰ δ' ὅγ' ἐν πόντῳ πάθεν ἄλγεα ὃν κατὰ θυμὸν,

The opening lines of *Ulysses*

Stately, plump Buck Mulligan came from the stairhead, bearing a bowl of lather on which a mirror and a razor lay crossed. A yellow dressinggown, ungirdled, was sustained gently behind him by the mild morning air. He held the bowl aloft and intoned :

— *Introibo ad altare Dei.*

Halted, he peered down the dark winding stairs and called up coarsely :

— Come up, Kinch. Come up, you fearful Jesuit.

Penelope awaited him. James Joyce used the framework of the *Odyssey* in his telling of the wanderings of Leopold Bloom around Dublin on 16 June 1904 in *Ulysses*, regarded by many °critics as the greatest novel of the twentieth °century.

-ology
anthropology, archaeology, biology, cosmology, ecology, epistemology, eschatology, etymology, ideology, methodology, mythology, psychology, sociology, technology, volcanology, zoology — these are all °scientific terms whose common suffix *-ology* comes from the Greek *logos* meaning 'word', 'reason', 'account'

Anthropology means the study of man in the widest sense (*anthropos* is a Greek word for 'man').

Archaeology is the study of °human antiquities usually by excavation (*archaios* is a Greek word meaning 'ancient').

Biology means the study of °physical life (*bios* is the Greek word for 'life').

Cosmology means the study of the °universe (*cosmos* is the Greek word for 'universe').

Ecology is a branch of biology concerned with the study of living °organisms and their relations to their surroundings (*oikos* is the Greek word for 'house').

Epistemology is a branch of °philosophy concerned with the study of the reliability of knowledge itself (*epistēmē* is the Greek word for 'knowledge').

Eschatology is the °doctrine of the last or final things — death and judgement (*eschatos* is a Greek word meaning 'last'). *Scatological* is used to describe obscene literature (*skōr, skatos* means 'dung' in Greek).

Etymology is the study of how words are formed (*etumos* is the Greek word for 'true', 'literal', '°original').

Ideology is a word coined by the French philosopher Destutt de Tracy in 1796 to describe the scientific study of ideas (*idea* is the Greek word for 'idea'). Napoleon attacked the °radical thinking of the Enlightenment (which provided a basis for °democratic °government) as ideological (by which he meant unrealistic and remote from the °concrete realities a man of action like himself had to deal with). The word now °connotes the network of ideas which specifies a particular °historical °social consciousness. It comes close to Plato's understanding of °public opinion as the unconscious °consensus about reality. Ideology is important because by imposing the perspectives within which a community views its °political, social, °economic and °cultural realities, it marshals

'The Death of Cúchulainn' as described in the *Táin Bó Cuailnge*. Ireland has two great cycles of myths—the Red Branch (to which the *Táin* belongs) and the Fenian

support for the structures that maintain those perspectives—and thus is used as an instrument of power. Marx saw that to change a society you had to attack its ideology. Ideology was, he declared, unscientific—it was simply a set of ideas upon which a group or class bases the theory that justifies the pursuit of its own interest—and could be routed by science. Marx, by stressing the scientific basis of his own system, sought to raise it above the sectionalism of a mere ideology ('sectional' pertains to a section of the community—*secare* is a Latin word 'to cut'; 'ism', from the Greek *-ismos*, is a suffix that turns a word into an °abstract noun). However, the basis of science is murky (see 'paradigm') and so nowadays we refer to 'Marxist ideology' without any sense of a °contradiction in terms.

Methodology means the study of methods of doing things (*meta* means 'after' in Greek and *hodos* means 'way' in Greek).

Mythology means either the study of myths or a set of myths, for example Celtic mythology (*muthos* is the Greek word for 'story','myth', or 'legend'; in common usage 'myth' has a °pejorative °connotation of falseness, but scholars also use the word in a °positive sense for any °allegory that gives an insight into an important aspect of human °culture).

Psychology means the study of the mind (*psychē* is the Greek word for 'mind').

Psychiatry is the treatment of diseases of the mind (*iatros* is the Greek word for 'physician'). A *psychosomatic* illness is a physical condition arising from psychological distress (*sōma* is the Greek word for 'body').

Sociology is the study of human society (*societas* is the Latin word for 'society').

Technology is either the science of the industrial arts or the °products of them (*technē* is the Greek word for 'craft').

Volcanology (also *vulcanology*) is the study of volcanoes (Vulcan was the Roman god of fire).

Zoology means the study of animals (*zōion* is the Greek word for 'animal').

ombudsman
an °official appointed by the °Oireachtas to investigate complaints by members of the °public about their treatment by a public body

Ombudsman is the Swedish word for 'advocate' — the Swedes invented the office of *ombudsman.* °Public bodies are staffed with specialists who can appear formidable to the ordinary citizen with a complaint. Such a citizen may find he or she can appeal to an administrative °tribunal, to a minister, or in extreme cases, to the courts (which can be expensive) or to the ombudsman (whose services are free). The ombudsman has all the powers, though not necessarily the resources, he or she needs to ascertain the basis of a complaint but normally only after other remedies have been exhausted. The ombudsman cannot command a remedy. However, his prestige, and the fact that he lays his reports before the Oireachtas, usually ensures a remedy.

ostracise
to °boycott

Ostrakon is the Greek word for a piece of pottery. To deal with a leader of the people thought likely to subvert the °state but against whom there was no evidence, the Athenians introduced a procedure whereby the people could °vote to banish anyone for a period of five or ten years by writing his name on a piece of pottery and placing it in a voting urn.

Ostraka (plural form of *ostrakon*) from the Chester Beatty °Library in Dublin. Pieces of pottery cost nothing and were used in the Graeco-Roman period for the business of ordinary trade, °personal notes, tax receipts and school use. An early cataloguer suggested that these *ostraka* 'can only be the writing exercise by a not very bright student'. Papyrus, the writing paper of the ancient Egyptians, made from the papyrus plant, being a manufactured article was expensive and therefore used sparingly in the ancient world. Papyrus is a Latin word °derived from the Greek *papyros.* From it we derive 'paper'

Plutarch tells us about the ostracism of an Athenian called Aristides The Just. While the votes were being written down, an illiterate countryman handed his piece of pottery to Aristides and asked him to write the name Aristides on it. Taken aback by this, Aristides asked the man what harm Aristides had ever done him. 'None whatever! I don't even know him! I'm just sick and tired of hearing him being called The Just'. When he heard this, Aristides said nothing, but he wrote his name on the *ostrakon* and handed it back to the man. He was subsequently ostracised.

P

pagan
heathen

'The Peasant and his Wife at Market' by Dürer. °Medieval artists tended to emphasise the ugliness of peasants for the amusement of their °aristocratic patrons. In his prints Dürer gave the peasant back his dignity

Paganus is the Latin word for 'country dweller'. Christianity spread from city to city of the Roman °Empire. Eventually, after the conversion of the Emperor Constantine, it became the °state religion. The word 'pagan' is derived from the period when Christianity had not yet reached the country districts.

Country dwellers have always been treated contumeliously by town dwellers. The °sophisticated Athenians called anyone who was rude and unlettered a Boeotian because the Boeotians were dedicated farmers. When Dubliners describe folk up from the country as 'culchies' (from the Mayo town of Kiltimagh), they use a term they clearly think carries no hint of the mores of Versailles (*mores*, the plural of *mos*, *moris*, is the Latin word for 'manners', used in English to mean the customs or °conventions that °characterise a particular °community).

When town dwellers describe someone as 'a boor' (from the Old English/Dutch *boer* meaning 'farmer') or 'a rustic' (from the Latin *rus, ruris* meaning 'country'), they do not intend to flatter. If they did, they would use the word 'urbane' (from the Latin word *urbs*, *urbis* meaning 'city' from which we also derive 'urban').

And so 'by a commodious vicus of recirculation', as Joyce says at the beginning of *Finnegans Wake,* we come to *paganus* once more: from it are derived the French *paysan* and the English 'peasant'.

pan-
a Greek prefix meaning 'all'

Pan, pantos is a Greek word meaning 'all'. It is very usefully deployed to cluster °states within a country or region, for example, Pan-German, Pan-Arab, Pan-European, Pan-American, Pan-African.

Pandaemonium or *pandemonium* is literally 'the place of all the demons' and therefore any exceedingly noisy, disorderly place or condition (*daemon* is 'demon' in Greek, *-ium* is a Latin suffix °indicating place).

A *pantheon* is a °temple to all the gods (*theos* is 'god' in Greek and *-eon* is a Greek suffix °denoting place). It is also used to describe a building dedicated as a memorial to all the great dead — or a notional equivalent of it. Thus, 'In the pantheon of Irish °nationalism there is none more glorious than Wolfe Tone'. (Interestingly, when Tone visited the Pantheon in Paris, he observed: 'If we have a °republic in Ireland, we must build a Pantheon, but we must not, like the French, be in too great a hurry to people it.')

Panorama is literally a complete view (*horama* is a Greek word for 'view') often used to mean a wide view.

Pantheism is a belief that God exists in all the natural world and permeates it (*per* is a Latin word meaning 'through' and *meare* is a Latin word 'to pass').

panacea
a cure-all

Pan is the Greek word for 'all'. *Akos* is the Greek word for 'remedy'. °Modern life is complex and modern man is faced with complex problems to which, almost certainly, he must find complex solutions. People, however, like simple solutions and so they put pressure on °politicians to find a panacea.

paparazzo
a press °photographer who harasses notable people in order to get snaps of them in unguarded moments. The word usually occurs in the plural, the paparazzi, most notoriously in relation to the Italian variety

In his 1960 film *La Dolce Vita* ('The Sweet Life') the Italian director Federico Fellini satirised the °mores of Rome's hedonistic high society (*hēdonē* is a Greek word meaning 'pleasure'; hedonists believe pleasure is the greatest good). In the film the scandal-sheet photographer is called Paparazzo (after a °character in a long-forgotten Italian °opera). Fellini was inspired to use the device of such a photographer by an incident he had witnessed one day in the late fifties on the Via Veneto in Rome. The Egyptian King Farouk was sitting at a table with a girl when some press photographers approached and goaded the °corpulent king sufficiently to make him jump up and overturn his table, and thereby provide the pictures they wanted.

paradigm
an implicit theory or conceptual framework from which other theories or understandings derive their validity

In Greek °philosophy a paradigm is an image or cluster of images which we freely construct in order to reveal the nature of something by seeking correspondences with the image or cluster of images. *Para* is a Greek word meaning 'beside'. *Deignumi* is a Greek word 'to show'. A paradigm then, is literally something you show beside something else to extend your knowledge of it. A paradigm is purely provisional; it may be true or false, well or badly grounded. Its use points to the open-ended nature of knowledge and its °analogical character (the fact that we understand one thing in terms of another). Thus we speak about justice — a °moral concept — in terms of order, harmony, unity between parts (none of which are moral concepts as such).

In °logic, the °primary usage of a word or concept from which our understanding of other usages flows is said to be paradigmatic. Thus we use the word 'healthy' in a wide range of ways — healthy hair, healthy teeth, a healthy respect, a healthy bank balance — but all those usages of 'healthy' derive their meaning from its paradigmatic use in relation to a living body. The first step in debate is to clarify the terms of the proposition — and this entails either the paradigm (implicit theory) out of which we are thinking or the paradigmatic use of the words or concepts we are using, or both. For example, °liberals and °socialists use a different paradigm of °freedom

In the philosophy of °science a paradigm is a set of implicit beliefs assumed to be true (or partly justified) which both °influences our selection of theories and the sorts of facts which might °verify them. It also decides what is to count as a good question or argument, what is or is not relevant, what is significant or insignificant in our thinking about something. It also specifies the practices by which one becomes a member of a particular scientific community, that is, the professional training required. According to some philosophers, all scientific thinking is °governed by a paradigm. Unless one accepts that paradigm, one would not be a respectable scientist in the eyes of fellow-scientists. Scientific paradigms are therefore norms governing the work of scientists and admission to the profession, but norms which cannot be

norm
Norma is the Latin word for 'a carpenter's square' — a *norm* is a standard by which something is measured. A thing is *normal* when it conforms to the accepted standard. A study is said to be *normative* when it lays down standards and prescribes what ought to be done

justified scientifically. Periodically some creative scientist breaks with the prevailing paradigm and works with °hypotheses and theories not justified by it. He is often laughed at by his colleagues and may even be treated as an outcast. But if his hypotheses and theories can be verified (like Einstein's theory of relativity), gradually a new paradigm emerges and becomes the prevailing one (closing down scientific questioning again).

The conquest of an old paradigm by a new one is called 'a paradigm shift'. It is apparent from this °analysis that scientific rationality (the paradigm, as that term is used in logic, of rationality today) is not as rational as it appears. All hypotheses and theories are themselves grounded on beliefs and hunches which cannot be justified by the same sort of rational argument as the theories they spawn. Scientific thinking is °ultimately based on non-scientific thinking.

parameter
a boundary or limit

Para is a Greek word meaning 'beside'. *Metron* is a Greek word meaning 'measure' (from which we also derive 'metre'). The term is derived from °geometry: when a circle must be so drawn that it does not intersect a line °i.e. does not go beyond it, the line is called a parameter. In °public affairs the term is used in relation to problems: the parameters are the boundaries or °major conditions within which a solution must be found. Thus in framing his °budget each year the Minister for Finance usually faces severe parameters such as: the level of °state borrowing cannot be increased, income tax cannot be increased, some concessions must be made to PAYE workers, °social welfare payments must be increased in line with °inflation.

pariah
an outcast

The word is from the Hindi and derives from *parai* 'a large drum' such as was beaten at festivals by low caste servants. The Hindu °population was divided into various classes ranging from the brahmin, the highest, to the pariahs, the lowest — the untouchables, who carried out all the menial tasks. In °democratic °politics it is rather important not to allow yourself to become a pariah.

pari passu
in equal steps or stages

concomitant
means 'accompanying' (*con* is the Latin 'with', *comes* is the Latin 'companion')

Par is the Latin word for 'equal'. *Passus* is the Latin word for 'step' or 'stride'. The phrase is used to describe any sets of moves that are made concomitantly. Thus 'The Americans and the Russians should remove their °nuclear weapons from Europe *pari passu'*.

Virgil, in his great Latin °epic, the *Aeneid*, traces the adventures of Aeneas from his flight from Troy to his eventual landing in Italy where his descendants Remus and the °eponymous Romulus became the founders of Rome. The word *passus* occurs in a celebrated passage that describes the boy-child, Julus, Aeneas's son, hurrying from the burning city of Troy in the wake of his father: 'sequiturque patrem non passibus aequis' — 'and he follows his father in shorter steps' (i.e. because of his short legs he could not manage to move *pari passu* with his father).

Passo is the Italian word for 'step'. When Mussolini visited Hitler in 1937 he was overwhelmed by the sight

A goose-step for Hitler

of the thousands of rigidly drilled German troops goose-stepping past him. He decided to introduce that step into the Italian army, calling it the *passo romano* — the Roman step, 'the firm, inexorable step of the legions for whom every march was a march of conquest'.

parliament
the legislature

Parler is the French word 'to speak' and *parlement* (transliterated 'parliament' in English) means 'speaking' or 'discussion' and by transference 'a meeting for discussion'. Thus the earliest appearance in literature of *parlement* occurs in the eleventh °century °epic, *Chanson de Roland*, where it simply means 'conversation'. In the twelfth century we find that general assemblies of Italian cities are called *parlamenti*.

In England, which has had the longest continuous parliamentary experience, the first parliaments were meetings between the king and his barons to discuss the business of the king and the kingdom. Generally speaking, kings called parliaments not to promote participative °government but to collect money to pay for their expenses. Those who owned or controlled most of the wealth of the country — the land and the °produce of the land — were the lords and bishops, and they were the ones who were first summoned to parliaments. When the shires (counties) and the boroughs (cities and towns) became °officially recognised communities, they were obliged to appoint representatives to attend the king in a parliament to be told what their communities should pay. In time they became the °major suppliers of subsidies to the king.

In parliament the lords and bishops met separately as a House of Lords and the commons — the knights of the shires (substantial freeholders) and the representatives of the towns and cities — met separately as a House of Commons (from the Latin *communis* meaning 'common' from which we also derive 'commune', 'communal', 'communist', 'community').

Parliament's capacity to meet the king's need for money gave it a bargaining power which it used first to have grievances remedied and then to achieve the °law-making power.

However, it was not until the fourteenth century that

petitioners
are people who make requests — they are seeking something (*petere* is the Latin word 'to seek'; a *competitor* is a rival, someone who seeks the same thing with you — *com* derives from the Latin *cum* meaning 'with'; *centripetal* describes a tendency to move towards the centre and derives from the Latin words *centrum* 'centre' and *petere*; its opposite — *centrifugal* — means a tendency to move away from the centre and derives from the Latin words *centrum* and *fugere* 'to flee' (thus a passing bicycle may splash you with mud because the revolving wheels create a centrifugal force)

the House of Commons succeeded in turning itself from a °congregation of petitioners into an assembly that had a part in law-making. Acts of Parliament were the joint products of King, Lords and Commons. To this day, the medieval terminology is still used: 'Whereas it is expedient . . . Be it therefore enacted by the King's most excellent majesty, by and with the advice and consent of the Lord's spiritual and temporal and Commons in this present Parliament assembled, and by the authority of the same, as follows . . .' (We can see the British legacy in the wording of our own °legislation in Ireland: 'Be it enacted by the °Oireachtas as follows . . . ' The Oireachtas, of course, comprises the President, °Dáil Éireann and °Seanad Éireann.) The °monarch, though, was still what we today would call the government. Since the relationship of king and parliament was based on finance, kings could ignore parliament if they did not need subsidies. Thus in times of peace kings often did not call parliaments because they could subsist on the produce of their own properties and on income from sources not controlled closely by parliament such as customs charged on °imports.

By the mid-seventeenth century parliament was challenging the monarch and, after a civil war, beheaded Charles I. Although the monarchy was restored in 1660, parliament soon succeeded in asserting its control over all sources of °taxation. The formal assertion of parliament's control came with the enactment of the Bill of Rights in 1689. This embodied the conditions under which William and Mary were offered the English Crown: parliaments were to be held frequently, freedom of speech in parliament was guaranteed, laws could not be suspended without parliament's consent and parliament's consent was needed for the levying of money or the keeping of a standing army. Within parliament the House of Commons succeeded in asserting complete control over money matters. The House of Lords was denied the power to amend taxation bills and was loath to exercise its power to reject them — a power that in any event disappeared with the enactment of the Parliament Bill in 1911.

The next stage in the °evolution of parliament came when the Commons gained control over the king's ministers. In the reign of Charles II a committee of the Privy Council — the °cabinet — had come into being. This informal group of ministers gradually became the °*de facto* government.

When George I withdrew from government in 1717, one of the members of the cabinet was recognised as the group leader — the prime minister (*primus* is the Latin word for 'first' from which we also derive 'primitive', 'primary', and 'primogeniture' — the feudal right of the first-born son to succeed to his father's offices and property). By the end of the century the king's government was fast becoming government on behalf of the king.

feudal
— relating to the form of government found in Europe in the Middle Ages which was based on the duties of homage and service of vassals to superiors (*feudalis* is a Latin word meaning 'pertaining to a fee')

The °ultimate victory of the Commons in its struggle with the king over his right to appoint and dismiss his government without reference to parliament was signalled by the resignation of Lord North, the prime minister during the American °Revolution, after the House of Commons passed a motion to end the war. It can be said that the power of the king to control the policy of his ministers ceased in 1829 when George IV, after a prolonged struggle, finally gave his assent to the bill for the Emancipation of Catholics.

emancipation
means freedom from legal, political, social, intellectual or moral restrictions. It derives from the Latin *e* meaning 'from', *manus* 'hand' and *capere* 'to take', and described the process by which Roman children became legally independent of their father

The early nineteenth century saw two developments on the road to parliamentary °democracy. During the 1830s the concept of ministerial responsibility with ministers answering to parliament for their departments developed. In the same decade the first Representation of the People Act was passed and the House of Commons was gradually transformed into a representative chamber with successive extensions of the °franchise. It took nearly a century. Young women did not get the °vote until 1928. (Ireland was ahead of the UK in this respect.) The process of democratisation also extended itself in the nineteenth century to °local government which was then extensively reformed.

The British are rightly proud when they proclaim Westminster 'the mother of Parliaments', for the °modern representative parliament is one of man's greatest inventions. However, it can hardly be said that the UK has parliamentary government. For a while in the middle of the nineteenth century this was the situation, but once °mass °politics arrived with the extension of the franchise, governments which could appeal directly to the people began to °dominate parliament and the whole °political process. By the end of the century cabinet government had arrived, that is, a system in which governments have a °monopoly of °legislative initiative and parliament is reduced to appraising, amending and approving the bills and measures proposed to it by the government. It is that system that was inherited by the Irish Free °State in 1922 and which still obtains.

parochialism
an assertion of the °primacy of °local attitudes, perspectives, beliefs, °culture °etc. against the larger world

Parochia is a late Latin word meaning 'parish', the smallest unit of ecclesiastical °organisation (*ecclēsia* is a Greek word meaning 'a °popular assembly', that is, an assembly of the people, derived from *ek* meaning 'out of' and *kaleein* 'to call', which in early Christian times was applied to the Church — the assembly called out of the world).

When the °representatives of the people meet in the °Dáil, they must carry out two °major functions — the first is to make sure that the interests of their constituents are protected and promoted, the second is to pass °legislation for the national good. A conflict of interest often occurs. °TDs may be accused of parochialism if they relentlessly pursue local interests to the detriment of the °national interest. In cultural and °moral °contexts parochialism has a °pejorative sense too, suggesting narrow-mindedness and lack of enlightenment.

However, the poet Patrick Kavanagh, in an essay 'The Parish and the Universe', seeks to establish a °positive aspect of parochialism:

> Parochialism and provincialism are opposites. The provincial has no mind of his own; he does not trust what his eyes see until he has heard what the °metropolis — towards which his eyes are turned — has to say on any subject. This runs through all activities.

Kavanagh

> The parochial °mentality on the other hand is never in any doubt about the °social and °artistic validity of his parish. All great °civilisations are based on parochialism — Greek, Israelite, English.
>
> In Ireland we are inclined to be provincial not parochial, for it requires a great deal of courage to be parochial. When we do attempt having the courage of our parish we are inclined to go false and to play up to the larger parish on the other side of the Irish Sea. In recent times we have had two great Irish parishioners — James Joyce and George Moore. They explained nothing. The °public had either to come to them or stay in the dark. And the public did come.

('Provincial' derives from *provincia*, a large tract or region, outside the °capital or metropolis, controlled not by local °officials but by a Roman official.)

partisan
pertaining to a supporter — usually a vehement one — of a party or cause

Pars, partis is the Latin word for 'part' or 'faction' from which we derive 'partisan' as well as 'party' and 'partial'. *Bipartisan* means 'relating to two parties' (*bi* derives from *bis* the Latin word for 'twice'.) Thus a bipartisan policy is a policy supported by two (usually otherwise opposed) parties.

party whips
°parliamentary party members who ensure their party's °voting strength is available in parliament when required

Each party in each House of the °Oireachtas appoints an °officer called 'the Whip' who is charged with ensuring that the members of the party are available to vote on issues in the House. The term comes from fox-hunting where a 'whipper-in' keeps the hounds from straying from the pack. The term intimates the privileged character of Parliament at the time it was adopted.

patrician
aristocratic

Pater, patris is the Latin word for 'father'. The patricians were the 'fathers' of Rome, the nobility. They were the °senators who, after the expulsion of the kings, held all the power in Rome. The appointment of °tribunes to represent the ordinary people (*plebs*) eroded their power to some extent. They were finally eclipsed by the appointment of °emperors. They reached their °nadir when the mad emperor Caligula reputedly made his horse a consul.

In °modern usage it is apposite to apply the word to someone who lives in a °republic but displays the manners or attitudes of an °aristocrat.

In Ireland 'Patrician' is also an adjective derived from *Patricius*, the Latin name for Saint Patrick. Thus one might refer to 'certain °characteristics of the Patrician Church' (i.e. of the Church system established by Saint Patrick).

patriot
one who loves, serves and defends his or her country

Johnson

Shaw

Patria is the Latin word for 'fatherland'.

A *compatriot* (*com* is derived from the Latin word *cum* meaning 'with') means 'a fellow-countryman'.

An *expatriate* is someone who lives outside his or her own country (*ex* is a Latin word meaning 'from' or 'outside').

Funds invested abroad which are brought home are said to be *repatriated* (*re* is a Latin word meaning 'again').

A *patrimony* is an inheritance from a father or from one's ancestors (it comes from the Latin word *patrimonium*, a °legal term for the will of a *paterfamilias* — a head of a family; it °denotes property inherited by an individual or an °institution — thus 'the patrimony of St Peter' refers to the property passed to a Pope by his predecessor).

The Latin poet, Horace, who was a °contemporary of °Caesar Augustus, gives us one of the most famous observations on patriotism: 'dulce et decorum est pro patria mori' — 'it is a sweet and fitting thing to die for one's country'. The Englishman Dr Johnson gives us another: 'Patriotism is the last refuge of a scoundrel'. The Irishman George Bernard Shaw gave us the wittiest when he declared 'Patriotism is your conviction that this country is the best in the world because you were born in it'.

pedagogic
relating to the principles and practice of teaching

A *pedagogue* was °originally a tutor slave in a wealthy Greek or Roman family (*pais, paidos* is the Greek word for 'boy' and *agōgos* is the Greek word for 'leader' — compare °demagogue). His duty was to guard the sons of the family from evil, both °physical and °moral, rather than to instruct them. In later Roman times the name was given to boy slaves who discharged a variety of °personal services in palaces; later still these were called 'pages' (from a corruption of 'pedagogue'). We might say 'The °primary school °curriculum is strong pedagogically because it seeks, so far as is possible, to °centre learning on the °interests of the child'.

pen-
peninsula, penultimate, penumbra — these are words whose common prefix *pen-* derives from the Latin word *paene* meaning 'almost'

A *peninsula* is a piece of land jutting into the sea — it is almost an island (*insula* is the Latin word for 'island' from which we also derive 'insular' 'insulate' and 'isolate').

Penultimate means 'last but one' — the ultimate is the last (*ultimus* is 'last' in Latin).

Penumbra means the partly shaded area around a darkened °object (*umbra* means 'shadow' in Latin; an *umbrella* provides shade from the sun or protection from rain).

per se
intrinsically, in itself or as such

Per is a Latin word meaning 'through' or 'in'. *Se* is a Latin word meaning 'itself'. Thus, 'Alcohol *per se* is not bad for you — too much of it is!'

persona grata
an acceptable person

Persona is the Latin word for 'a player's mask'. *Grata* means 'acceptable'. In °classical drama each player wore a mask (grave, terrifying, dopey, humorous, as the °character being played required) called a *persona* because it was a thing through which the °actor spoke (*per* is a Latin word meaning 'through', *sonare* is the Latin word 'to sound'). Gradually, *persona* came to mean the character being played and finally it got the °modern meaning of 'individual' or 'person'.

The Swiss °psychiatrist Carl Jung (1875–1961) developed the psychological concept of the persona. The persona is a mask adopted by the person to present to others a particular image, often the one the °public expects because of the person's role in society. The persona is the public personality. It often contrasts with the person's real or °private personality. Thus, 'Nixon presented the persona of an affable, self-confident world leader but the tapes revealed the real Nixon — a bad-tempered, foul-mouthed paranoiac'.

paranoiac — someone with an abnormal tendency to suspect or mistrust others, derived from the Greek words *para* 'beside' and *noos* 'the mind', often used, as here, in a loose, non-clinical sense (*klinē* is the Greek word for 'a bed'; 'clinical' derives from *klinikos* 'pertaining to a [sick] bed')

Jung means 'young' in German. James Joyce used this fact to work into the fabric of *Finnegans Wake* an irreverent reference to the fathers of modern °psychology: pubescent girls were, he observed, 'yung and easily freudened'. ('Pubescent' means 'becoming sexually mature' — *pubes* is the Latin word for 'a grown-up youth'; the *escent* suffix derives from a Latin form that indicates 'becoming', the process of change from one °state to another: an adolescent is someone who is becoming an adult, an obsolescent instrument is one that is becoming obsolete.)

Actor wearing a mask

The phrase *persona grata* is used °primarily in a diplomatic °context where the person so typified is declared to be an acceptable diplomatic °representative by the host country. Someone who is not acceptable or who becomes unacceptable (for example a spy attached to an embassy) is declared 'a persona non grata' and has to leave.

Dramatis personae means the characters in a play (*drama* is the Greek word for 'a play').

philanthropy
love of mankind as shown in disinterested service to the °welfare of all

Philos is the Greek word for 'lover'. *Anthropos* is a Greek word for 'mankind'. Rich individuals who, and °institutions which, °donate money for schools, libraries, irrigation schemes °etc. in undeveloped countries could be °characterised as 'philanthropic'.

A °person is *disinterested* when he or she has no personal advantage to gain from a situation; a person is *uninterested* when his or her attention is simply not engaged by a situation; a person may be interested and disinterested at the same time. A person who characteristically acts in the interest of others is said to be *altruistic* (derived from the Latin *alter* meaning 'other'

Sir Alfred Chester Beatty (1875–1968), American millionaire, mining engineer (he came to be known as 'the World Copper King'), art collector and philanthropist, retired to Ireland in 1950 (he had Irish ancestors) and bequeathed his world-renowned art collections to the people of Ireland

from which we also get 'alternative').

Phile is a particle derived from *philos* which, used as a suffix, °denotes 'lover of ' — thus Anglophile ('admirer of England and things English'), bibliophile ('lover of books' from *biblion*, the Greek word for 'book' from which we also get 'Bible').

Mis is a prefix derived from *misein,* the Greek word 'to hate', which denotes 'hater of'. Thus a *misanthropist* is 'a hater of mankind', a *misogynist* is 'a hater of women' (*gynē* is the Greek word for 'woman'), a *misandrist* is 'a hater of men' (*anēr, andros* is a Greek word for 'man'; but, °anomalously, a *philanderer* means 'a lover of numerous *women*').

Androgynous is used to describe someone who has the characteristics of both a male and a female. *Hermaphroditic* is its °synonym (Hermaphroditos was the son of Hermes, the herald of the gods whom the Romans identified with their Mercury, and Aphrodite, the goddess of love whom they identified with their Venus and from whom 'aphrodisiac' meaning 'sex stimulant' is derived. Hermaphroditos and the °nymph Salmacis grew together into the one person).

Mercury the messenger of the gods with winged feet. *Mercury* was a common name for a newspaper, the speedy bringer of news. People born under the °influence of the planet Mercury were said to be 'mercurial', that is, active and explosively emotional

Phobia is the Greek word for 'fear'. *Agoraphobia* is a morbid fear of open spaces (*agora* is the Greek word for market-place, the equivalent of the Latin °*forum*).

Claustrophobia is the fear of confined spaces (*claustrum* is the Latin word for 'an enclosed space'). Since fear of people provokes hatred of them, 'Francophobe' is the opposite of 'Francophile' and means 'a hater of France and things French'.

philosophy
man's attempt to understand the world by means of °rational argument, discussion and debate

Philein is the Greek word 'to love'. *Sophia* is the Greek word for 'wisdom'. A philosopher is literally a lover of wisdom. °Originally the Greek philosophers were simply called *sophoi* 'wise men' but Pythagoras, one of the greatest of them, felt that that title was too arrogant so he coined the word 'philosopher' instead.

The two Greek philosophers, Plato and Aristotle, are probably the most °influential philosophers that ever lived. It is said that everything written since is a footnote to their writing. For Plato philosophy was an attempt to °articulate the wisdom inherent in the common beliefs of people. For Aristotle philosophy was an attempt to articulate the wisdom inherent in the °phenomena of our everyday experience.

From these two philosophers two great schools of philosophy arose — Platonism and Aristotelianism. They influenced to varying degrees all philosophical and °scientific thinking up to late °medieval times. What we call °modern science saw itself as a conscious break with Aristotle's thinking.

Aquinas

St Thomas Aquinas (1225-74), whose philosophy and °theology are referred to as 'Thomism', was °predominantly Aristotelian but had elements of Platonism. Aquinas sought to articulate his Christian vision of life in Aristotle's categories much as it is said today that °liberation theologians articulate their Christian vision in °Marxist categories. Because of the profound way in which they discussed the °central issues of philosophy the work of Plato and Aristotle is referred to as 'the °perennial philosophy'. It should not be surprising that in °moral, °political and certain areas of philosophic °logic there is a revival of interest in Plato and Aristotle.

It is °traditional to divide philosophy into various segments such as natural philosophy, °epistemology (the study of knowledge), ontology (the study of being), °moral and °political philosophy.

A *sophist* is someone who manipulates words in such a way as to lead to any desired °logical conclusion. Sophists were originally teachers of °rhetoric, a skill needed by the citizen to defend himself in court or to persuade his fellow-citizens to some course of action. The sophists believed that thinking is a technique that can be formalised, taught and learned by people. Their emphasis on technique and on winning an argument at all costs gave the term 'sophist' its °pejorative °connotation. (*Sophister* is an old-fashioned form of *sophist* used most famously by Edmund Burke in *Reflections on the °Revolution in France* where he says that because 'ten thousand swords' did not 'leap from their scabbards' to avenge the smallest insult to Marie Antoinette 'the age of chivalry is gone. That of sophisters, °economists and calculators has succeeded; and the glory of Europe is extinguished forever.')

The term 'sophisticated' is applied to someone who is worldly-wise; applied to things, it means 'elaborate'.

placebo
a medicine given for °psychological rather than °physical effect

Placebo is a form of the Latin word *placere* 'to please' and means 'I shall please'. People often expect a doctor to give them medicine even if he or she feels they do not need it. In order not to disappoint them, a doctor may °prescribe a placebo. People sometimes dourly °characterise an attractive policy proposal made by a °political opponent as a placebo.

platitude
a leaden, commonplace remark

Platus is the Latin word for 'broad' or 'flat'. It is not uncommon for one °political party to attack another party's °manifesto on the basis that it is full of platitudes.

plebiscite
a direct °vote by the °electorate on an important issue

Plebs is the Latin word for 'common people' (as opposed to the °patricians or nobility). The *-scite* formation derives from *sciscere* 'to consult' in Latin. *Referendum*, a Latin word meaning 'a thing to be referred' (to the people), is a °synonym for plebiscite.

pluralist society
a society which respects the °culture and beliefs of the different groups and individuals within it

Plus, pluris is a Latin word meaning 'more'. Human society is fissile (from the Latin word *fissilis* meaning 'tending to split like timber') because pressing issues are constantly cropping up upon which people can strongly differ. Some °states have tended to seek to maintain their unity by restricting the freedom of thought and action of all citizens and, where there were °minority groups, by imposing the °values of the °majority on everyone, particularly through the provisions of their °constitutions. The Islamic states are *confessional* states (committed to a particular religious faith) and therefore the opposite of pluralist.

Until °modern times most European states were confessional (thus, it was not until 1829 that Catholics were given the °franchise in Ireland and Britain).

°Liberal °democratic thinking favours the separation of Church and State in the interest of freedom and tolerance (but this separation is often taken as °synonomous with the separation of °law and °morality—see 'secularism'). °*Bunreacht na hÉireann* embodies °republican and democratic °values but, while liberal in tenor, it is seen by many as embodying the °social and moral teaching of the majority Catholic religion. Dr Garret FitzGerald's 'constitutional °crusade' was concerned to remove what he saw as the confessional °character of the constitution.

Pluralism is a marked feature of modern Western societies that manifests itself in virtually all aspects of life—°politics, religion, law, morality, °economics and culture. In refraining from installing any one idea of the good life as ideal, it creates not only tolerance but also a °productive interaction between people with different ideas and experiences that allows full range to the essentially questing nature of the °human spirit. For °criticism of certain pluralist tendencies see 'liberalism' and 'secularism'.

pogrom
an °organised massacre of a °minority group

Pogrom is a Russian word for 'destruction' which came into use in the late nineteenth °century to describe the sporadic °government-inspired attacks made on Jewish °ghettoes. To deal with the growth of °nationalism among the many non-Russian peoples who had been absorbed in his °empire the °Tsar had decided on a policy of assimilation called 'Russification' — the equivalent of the process of Anglicisation taking place in Ireland at the same time, which Douglas Hyde's Gaelic League sought to counter. The Jews were attacked because they resisted assimilation. The fact that a Jewish girl was among the group of °anarchists who °assassinated Alexander II intensified the animus that found expression in the pogroms (*animus* is a Latin word meaning 'spirit' that in English usage means 'bad spirit' or 'spite'). 'Pogrom' may be applied to attacks on any religious minorities in a community e.g. the anti-Catholic pogroms in Belfast in the twenties and thirties.

polemical
relating to heated dispute

Swift—one of the greatest polemicists

Polemos is the Greek word for 'war' and so 'polemical' suggests a certain fierceness in the discussion or writing. Swift's *Drapier's Letters* was polemical. So was the debate conducted by Irish scholars in the forties about whether there was one Saint Patrick or two Saint Patricks. (*A propos* of this controversy, Myles na gCopaleen observed that it was the singular achievement of the Dublin Institute for Advanced Studies to prove there were two Saint Patricks and no God.)

In a polemical discussion either side is likely to unleash a *diatribe*. A diatribe is a bitter, stinging denunciation (*dia* is the Greek word for 'through' and *tribein* is the Greek word 'to rub'). Someone may even deliver a *philippic* — a speech full of bitter invective, so called after the orations of the Athenian, Demosthenes, against King Philip of Macdedon, father of Alexander the Great, who was establishing his °hegemony over the Greek °states exhausted by the internecine Pelopponesian War (*internecine* pertains to murderous conflict within a group: *inter* means 'between' in Latin and *necare* is a Latin word 'to kill').

politics
all that relates to the °government of °states

Polis is the Greek word for 'city-state'. 'Politics' described the affairs of the city-state. In °democratic Athens every citizen (*politēs*) was expected to play an active part in governing the city by taking part in °public debates, by

Charles J. Haughey, TD, leader of °Fianna Fáil

Alan Dukes, TD, leader of °Fine Gael

Dick Spring, TD, leader of the Labour Party. Labour has participated in government on five occasions (see 'coalition'). In the 1989 general election it won fifteen Dáil seats with almost ten per cent of the vote

°voting, by holding public °office. A citizen concerned only with his own °private affairs, who took no part in public affairs, was called an *idiōtēs* (from which we derive 'idiot').

A *politician* is someone who takes an active part in politics. Everyone in a democracy should ideally be a politician (after the Athenian model). In practice the term is reserved for those who are active in political parties, particularly those who seek election to °local authorities, to the Houses of the °Oireachtas, or to the European °Parliament. Those who win elections are called *public representatives.*

A *political party* is a voluntary °organisation that seeks to gain °popular support for a set of policies. A party with °national appeal will have local party organisations in each constituency to °influence the grassroots and mobilise support at °elections (*mobilis* is a Latin word meaning 'moving', derived from the Latin word *movere* 'to move'; an *automobile* is a vehicle that can move itself — *autos* is a Greek word meaning 'self'). While political parties are not mentioned in °*Bunreacht na hÉireann*, they are vital to the proper functioning of our political system: through them aspiring °representatives of the people first come to notice and through them proposals for °laws are formulated. To get electoral support and keep it politicians in a democracy must be attentive to what ordinary people — the grassroots — are thinking about issues (the term 'grassroots' °originally applied to people living in rural areas).

Whatever interests politicians is *political.* Because of their nature, democratic politicians are likely to be interested in whatever interests significant numbers of people — it might be bank interest rate today, the price of hurleys tomorrow. Broadly speaking, the stuff of politics is woven from five threads. Firstly, politicians are interested in *order.* The °primary function of government is to establish and maintain order within the state and, with that end in view, to seek to secure political stability outside the state as well. Secondly, politicians are interested in °*economic* issues such as industrial development, agriculture, °employment, °imports, °exports, °infrastructure.

Desmond O'Malley, TD, leader of the Progressive Democrats. In the 1989 general election the PDs won six Dáil seats with almost 6 per cent of the vote and entered government in coalition with °Fianna Fáil

Proinsias De Rossa, TD, MEP, leader of the Workers' Party. The party evolved from the split in Sinn Féin in 1970. In the 1989 general election it won seven Dáil seats with 5 per cent of the vote

Roger Garland, TD, won its first Dáil seat for the Green Party in the 1989 general election

Thirdly, politicians are interested in *social* issues such as the welfare of the weaker groups in the state — the sick and the handicapped, the unemployed, the poor, the orphaned, the old (*socialis* is a Latin word meaning 'pertaining to friends or companions' and by extension 'to the °community'). Fourthly, politicians are interested in *cultural* issues (*colere*, the Latin word from which 'cultural' derives, means 'to tend to', 'to cultivate'; 'culture' is sometimes used in a comprehensive sense to mean 'way of life' but here it is used in a restricted sense to cover °education, the arts, language, leisure activities).

Fifthly, politicians are interested in *institutional* issues such as the organisation of the °public service, the efficiency of the courts, the functions of the °local authorities (*instituere* is a Latin word 'to make to stand' — an institution is anything that has been established).

In popular parlance, politics may also refer to any situation in which a group of people seeks to resolve peacefully the what, when, why, how, where issues, for example office politics. It is used in a somewhat °pejorative sense to suggest that the motivation for actions taken against an individual or group is suspect.

Apolitical means 'uninvolved in politics'. (*A* is a Greek negative prefix. It also occurs in the word 'amoral'. *Moral* in its general sense applies to someone who believes in the existence of laws that determine the goodness or badness of human behaviour — *mos, moris* is a Latin word meaning 'custom' or 'manner'. *Amoral*, the opposite of 'moral' in its general sense, applies to someone who does not believe in the existence of such laws and who therefore holds himself or herself aloof from morality. *Moral* is also used in the restricted sense of 'virtuous' — a moral person. *Immoral*, the opposite of 'moral' in its restricted sense, means 'sinful' or 'depraved' — *in* is a Latin negative particle; before b, m or p it becomes *im* — thus also 'imbalance' and 'improper'.)

Realpolitik is a German word meaning 'the politics of realism'. It was introduced in the mid-nineteenth °century to contrast with the lack of realism of the German °revolutionary °liberals of 1848. It survived in usage because it captured the style of Bismarck's politics:

Bismarck sought to assess what his opponents really wanted and based his moves on that rather than on what they said they wanted (because that would almost certainly contain elements they would be prepared to concede in the usual climax of politics — a compromise).

A *political scientist.* is an °academic who has qualified in the study of politics.

pornography
obscene descriptions or depictions

Pornē is the Greek word for 'prostitute'. *Graphein* is the Greek word 'to write'. °Material on sex may be °scientific, erotic (*Erōs, Erōtos* is the Greek god of sexual love called Cupid by the Romans), or pornographic. An °academic, °e.g. medical, °context readily identifies the scientific. However, it is difficult to distinguish between the erotic, which is also regarded as licit (it occurs in love poetry and in the °Bible, e.g. The Song of Songs), and pornography, which is regarded as illicit. For instance, in a permissive age, such as ours, statues of nude °subjects are regarded as a healthy celebration of the °human form (as in °classical times); in a puritanical period they may be fig-leafed. Such °moral relativism bedevils the debate on pornography.

Pornography may, perhaps, be usefully distinguished by the fact that it seeks to give vicarious pleasure to the reader or viewer through subjecting some of those depicted to unloving, violent degradation (*vicarius* is a Latin word meaning 'substituted'.) Such degradation dehumanises. Dehumanisation — the process the °Nazis subjected the Jews to — may lead to violence and murder.

posthumous
after the death of

Post is a Latin word meaning 'after'. *Postumus* is a related word meaning 'coming after'; h was included in posthumous because of a mistaken association with *humare* the Latin word 'to bury' (from which we derive *exhume* 'to disinter' — *ex* is a Latin word meaning 'out' or 'out of'). Used of an author's book(s) 'posthumous' means published after his or her death. Used of a man's son or daughter it means born after his death. Thus, 'Alfonso XII, meanwhile, died in 1885, at the age of twenty-eight, leaving a posthumous son, Alfonso XIII, for whom his mother, Maria Cristina, ruled as °Regent till 1902'. (Hugh Thomas, *The Spanish Civil War*.)

post mortem
an autopsy

Post is a Latin word meaning 'after'. *Mortem* is a form of *mors, mortis,* the Latin word for 'death' from which we derive 'mortal', 'immortal', 'mortality' and 'mortuary'.

postscriptum (PS)
a note written after a letter is completed, a postscript

Post is a Latin word meaning 'after'. *Scriptum* means 'a thing that has been written' derived from the Latin word *scribere* 'to write'.

praetorian guard
the °personal guard of a Roman °emperor or the group of aides surrounding any powerful °politician

Caesar Augustus (31 BC—14 AD). We use 'Augustan' for 'refined', 'classic'

Prae is a Latin word meaning 'before'. A *praetor* was a Roman magistrate next in line to a consul; °originally *praetor* (from *praeire* 'to go before') meant 'headman' and *praetoria* meant 'headmanship'. °Caesar Augustus, the first Roman emperor, established in Rome a praetorian guard of nine battalions of five hundred men each to protect the emperor and act as his orderlies. Subsequently the power of the praetorian guard became notorious. On the death of the Emperor Caligula in 41 AD it was the praetorian guard that proclaimed Claudius emperor. When Claudius died suddenly in 54 AD, it was the praetorian guard that proclaimed Nero as his successor. When in 69 AD the Emperor Galba became °unpopular with the soldiers because of his °economies, the guard acclaimed his °rival, Otho, as emperor, marched in upon the °Forum and unceremoniously °lynched Galba without anyone raising a hand in his defence.

The source of the power of a praetorian guard lies in its ability to control access to the personage it protects.

pragmatic
acting in response to practical needs as they arise

Pragma is a Greek word meaning 'an act'. Pragmatic is opposed to theoretical. It is frequently used of °politicians either in a good sense to suggest they are practical, down-to-earth decision-makers or in a °pejorative sense to suggest they are shallow, non-°ideological and unprincipled.

prerogative
a privilege shared with no one else

Praerogativa is a Latin word meaning 'the act of being asked first' (*prae* is a Latin word meaning 'before', *rogare* is a Latin word 'to ask' from which we also derive 'interrogate'). The Romans, who °voted by tribes or centuries (from *centum* the Latin word for 'a hundred'), had a custom of selecting by lot the tribe or century which would vote first. The other tribes and centuries followed the lead given by that tribe or century because they took the way the lot fell as an °indication of the will of the gods.

president
the °head of state in a °republic

Douglas Hyde

Séan T. Ó Ceallaigh

Prae is a Latin word meaning 'before'. *Sedere* is the Latin word 'to sit'. The president (in Irish *uachtarán*) is the one who occupies the chair of authority. °*Bunreacht na hÉireann* provides for a President who takes precedence over all other °persons in the °state, even visitors however distinguished, but who functions in almost all respects as the °government directs. Every citizen over thirty-five years of age is eligible for the office. A former or retiring President may become a °candidate on his or her own °nomination. Other candidates must be nominated by at least twenty persons, each of whom is a member of one of the Houses of the °Oireachtas, or by the councils of at least four county or county borough councils. The President is °elected for a seven-year term by the same electorate as for °Dáil °elections, and under the PR system. A President may be re-elected once.

The President, with the Dáil and °Seanad, comprises the Oireachtas (or °National °Parliament) because all three °institutions are necessary for the making of °laws. The Oireachtas is summoned by the President, and normally dissolved, on the advice of the °Taoiseach. On the advice of the Taoiseach and with the prior approval of the Dáil the President appoints members of the government. The President also appoints members of the judiciary on the advice of the government. Before a Bill becomes law it must be signed by the President and °promulgated by him or her.

The supreme command of the defence forces is vested in the President but actual control is in the hands of the government through the Minister for Defence. All °executive powers in connection with international affairs are assigned to the President acting on the advice of the government.

The President has certain powers that make him or her the guardian of the °constitution. A Council of State advises the President.

Six men have held the office of President since it was established: Douglas Hyde (1938-45), Seán T. Ó Ceallaigh (1945-59), Éamon de Valera (1959-73), Erskine Childers (1973-74), Cearbhall Ó Dálaigh (1974-76), Patrick J. Hillery (1976-90).

Éamon de Valera

Erskine Childers

Cearbhaill Ó Dálaigh

Patrick J. Hillery

prima facie
at first sight

Prima is a form of *primus*, the Latin word for 'first'. *Facie* is a form of *facies*, a Latin word meaning 'appearance'. The expression is used in a °legal °context. Thus, 'When the police arrived, they found him alone in the house, standing over the body with a smoking gun in his hand. This provided them with a good *prima facie* case that he was the murderer'.

prince
a title applied to the male members of a royal family, apart from the king. A Crown Prince is a king's eldest son, the heir apparent. A

The ancient Romans were once ruled by kings. The last of the kings, Tarquinius Superbus (the Proud), was so cruel that the Romans revolted against him, expelled him and his family, and arranged that in future the °government would be carried on by two °officials called consuls, °elected every year for a one-year term.

The °conspirators who °assassinated Julius °Caesar in 44 BC sought to justify themselves on the ground that

Prince Regent is a prince who acts as king (regent comes from the Latin word *regere* 'to rule') when the king or queen is either too young or incapacitated. The term 'prince' is also applied to cardinals — princes of the Church — because °originally each was head of a Papal °state

he intended to make himself king. Octavian, Caesar's grand-nephew and adopted son, °triumphed in the °civil war that followed. The Romans rushed to heap honours on Octavian but he refused all the titles they offered him, except *Augustus*, which means 'revered', and *princeps*, which means 'first citizen' (it comes from two Latin words — *primus* 'first' and *capere* 'to take'). The word 'prince' is derived from *princeps*.

Caesar Augustus, as Octavian was now called, went on to rule the Roman °Empire brilliantly for forty-five years as *princeps*. In time, the term prince was applied to other sovereigns (in °medieval times °European kings were known as sovereign princes and it is as a sovereign that Christ is referred to as Prince of Peace and Satan as Prince of Darkness). Later, prince declined in prestige as a term and came to be applied to the sons of kings.

privatisation
the process whereby work previously done by °public agencies is assigned to °private firms or individuals

Privatisation has two forms. One is where a public agency hires the services of a private company to do work that is, and remains, the public agency's responsibility. The other is where an activity, carried out by a public agency, is sold off completely to a private company or to a company quoted on the °Stock Exchange. An example is British Telecom. That form of privatisation is the opposite of nationalisation: it is denationalisation.

Privatisation may be an attractive policy to a °government because it may provide cash when cash is in short supply. It may reduce the government's running costs or increase the efficiency of °organisations. °Socialists, who wish to see more rather than less work undertaken by the °state, are °ideologically opposed to privatisation. Privatisation may also be opposed on °technical grounds — where, for example, it is believed the government is selling off an asset too cheaply.

productivity
output per unit of input

Producere is a Latin word meaning 'to lead forward', 'to produce'; that which is produced is a product. Anyone who produces anything, for example, a writer who produces books, may be said to be 'productive'. 'Productivity' is commonly used in relation to industrial or commercial activity because the level of productivity of a firm is vital to its survival. °Private firms compete with one another. The greater their productivity the more cheaply they can offer their goods and services, and therefore the better they can °compete.

Productivity is determined by the quantity and quality of the inputs (land, labour, °capital) and the way they are managed. Is the °labour force skilled and well-motivated? Is the machinery old or °modern? Is the production process managed smoothly? These are the kinds of questions raised by the concept of industrial productivity.

Productivity agreements are agreements made between the workers and managers in an °organisation whereby the managers seek to increase productivity by changes in work practices or by the introduction of new machinery, and the workers agree to this in return for higher wages or a betterment in working conditions, or both.

There are many kinds of work where productivity cannot be directly measured — much of the work of the °public service is of that kind. Thus it is difficult to measure the productivity of a teacher. Teaching inputs can be measured — for example, the amount of time teachers spend preparing for class and the amount of time they spend in class, but how can one measure the output — °education? People tend to settle for indirect measures such as the number of passes and honours achieved by the students. Indirect measures, however, can be misleading. Thus the examination system may reward those who have conformed most to the learning process in the schools rather than those who have increased their creativity, individuality and ability to think for themselves — the qualities most teachers feel are the proper °objectives of education.

proletariat
low-paid wage-earners, the labouring classes

Proles means 'offspring' in Latin. The Romans used the word *proletarius* to describe someone who served the °state not with wealth (taxes or a horse in time of war) but with offspring (to serve as soldiers). For Marx, the proletariat was the °alternative to the °capitalist class. The word is used to describe a key stage in Marxist °revolution — the °dictatorship of the proletariat, that is, the assumption of power by (or at least on behalf of) the proletariat.

George Orwell in *1984*, the novel he published in 1948, uses the diminutive 'the proles' as a dismissive term for his besotted and benighted lower classes.

The *lumpenproletariat* is the amorphous group of dispossessed and rootless individuals at the bottom of the °social heap, despised by °militant socialists because they have no capacity to engage in °politics and promote revolution (*lumpen* is a German word for 'rag'; 'amorphous' means 'without a definite shape' — *a* is a Greek negative particle, *morphē* is the Greek word for 'shape').

prolific
aboundingly productive

Proles is the Latin word for 'offspring'. The particle *fic* is derived from *facere*, the Latin word 'to make'. An 'ideas man' in an °organisation may be described as prolific; and so may a sow.

promulgate
to make known to the °public

The °origin of the word is unclear. It is thought the Latin word *vulgus*, meaning 'crowd' (from which we derive 'vulgar' and 'vulgarity') is present in it in corrupted form. The word is important in °law because justice requires that laws should be known to the public — promulgated — otherwise people would not know whether they were breaking the law or not.

Typically, Bills, before they become laws, are debated in the °Dáil and °Seanad and reported on by the °media. Laws are deemed to be promulgated when, having been signed by the °President, a notice that they have become law is published in the *Iris Oifigiúil*, the °official gazette. Once that is done, a citizen who is accused of breaking the law may not plead innocence on grounds of ignorance.

propaganda
a deliberately distorted presentation of facts or °doctrine to justify one's own actions or to weaken allegiance to one's opponents

Propagandum is a form of the Latin word *propagare* 'to multiply' or 'to spread' and means 'a thing to be multiplied' (or spread). Its use in °communications derives from the establishment in 1622 by the Catholic Church of a °congregation (an °office) concerned with spreading the Catholic faith (*de propaganda fide — fides* is the Latin word for 'faith'). The use of propaganda in war has given it a decidedly pejorative °connotation (*pejor* is a Latin word meaning 'worse'). In war each side seeks to demonise the other. Propaganda, with its lies, distortions, half-truths and invective, is the means to do this.

In the struggle for Independence, a °strategic °objective of Sinn Féin was to win the minds of the °masses of the people. The poster (left) was an early piece of °nationalist propaganda. Joseph McGuinness was imprisoned after the Rising. He was put forward as a °candidate in the North Longford by-°election of 1917. The poster urges the °voters to put him in (to °parliament) to get him out (of jail). He won the election and was released in June 1917. When he went forward in the general election of 1918, his poster proclaimed: 'We got him out — to put him in'.

prophet
a man who foretells events

Pro is a Greek word meaning 'in place of'. *Phētēs* is the Greek word for 'speaker'. A prophet was a man who spoke to the Jews on behalf of God. He told them what God's will was. Since a most effective way of establishing one's °credentials as God's spokesman was to foretell the future, that was the function that came to be associated °predominantly with the word 'prophet'. The word is also applied to a °person who discerns the true °character of events in the life of a religious community before others become aware of it.

Moslems regard Mahomet as The Prophet. The Koran says there have been 200,000 prophets of whom only six brought new °laws or a new dispensation — Adam, Noah, Abraham, Moses, Jesus, and Mahomet.

proscribe
to outlaw

Pro is a Latin word meaning 'before' or 'publicly'. *Scribere* is the Latin word 'to write'. The Roman authorities in the late °Republic would proscribe their enemies, that is, publish a list of their names. Those proscribed were labelled °public enemies: a price was put on their heads so that they could be seized and killed by anyone; their property was confiscated. °Caesar, when he crossed the °Rubicon, was proscribed but he succeeded in routing his enemies.

The great statesman and °orator, Cicero, was not so lucky. When he was proscribed in 43 BC he fled to his villa. His enemies tracked him down there and overtook him as he was being carried in a litter along the shaded walks down to the sea. Plutarch describes his death as follows:

The death of Cicero

> The °tribune, taking a few men with him, ran to where Cicero would come out. Cicero, seeing him hurrying through the woods, ordered his servants to set the litter down; stroking his chin, as he was wont to do, with his left hand, he looked his murderers in the eye, his clothes covered in dust, his beard and hair unkempt, his face creased with strain. Most of those who stood about him covered their faces as the

tribune advanced. Cicero stretched his neck out of the litter and the tribune struck. Cicero was sixty-four.

The tribune cut off his head and, as Antony had stipulated, his hands too, for with those he had written his °Philippics (the name he gave those orations he wrote against Antony).

When these parts of Cicero were brought to Rome, Antony was holding an assembly to choose public officers. When he saw them he declared 'Now let there be an end to proscriptions!' He ordered the head and hands to be nailed over the °rostra where the °orators spoke. The people of Rome shuddered at the sight.

Nowadays harassed parents might declare 'Smoking should be proscribed', that is, solemnly banned. 'Proscribe' is distinguished from 'prescribe' (to lay down rules, or, as in regard to medicine, to give directions for use).

protean
ever changing

Proteus was an old Greek sea-god who had the gift of °prophecy. He told you the future if you could catch hold of him. The trouble was he could change himself into different forms and so escape your grip. Homer tells how one of the Greek leaders, Menelaus, offended Pallas Athene when, after the fall of Troy, he refused to sacrifice to her — she had defended the °Trojan citadel too long, he said. Angrily, the goddess sent storms that prevented him and his crew reaching home.

To find out how to break the spell Menelaus and three companions set out to capture Proteus. They disguised themselves in stinking seal-skins and lay waiting on the shore. At midday they were joined by hundreds of seals. Proteus himself then appeared and lay down to sleep among his flock.

Menelaus and his friends crept towards him and pounced on him. They held on to him firmly though he changed himself into a lion, a snake, a panther, a boar — even running water — and forced him to prophesy.

Proteus told Menelaus that his brother Agamemnon had been murdered and that he, Menelaus, must visit Egypt and propitiate the gods with sacrifices there. Menelaus followed this instruction and, when he had sacrificed, and erected a °cenotaph to his brother, the winds changed and enabled him to sail home to °Sparta. He arrived on the very day that Orestes avenged his father Agamemnon's murder by his faithless wife Clytemnestra and her lover Aegisthus.

°Social problems are frequently protean. When a °government department tackles one problem it often finds it creates another. Thus slum clearance tackles the problem of people who live in unsanitary conditions (*un-* is a Latin prefix that negatives a word, *sanitas, sanitatis* is the Latin word for 'health') but it involves uprooting families and breaking the delicate web of relationships through which they often sustain one another emotionally and financially.

psephologist
one who studies °voting systems and patterns

Psēphos is the Greek word for 'pebble', *logos* is the Greek word for 'word', 'reason', 'account'. In °classical Greece the Athenians were the great practitioners of °democracy. Because they were relatively few in number and lived in a city, they could practise direct democracy — each citizen could vote on issues himself after listening to the arguments for and against, rather than have to elect a °representative to act for him (indirect democracy). The voting procedure was simple. Each citizen was given a pebble and he voted by placing it in the appropriate urn.

public
common to, or shared in by, all

Publicus is the Latin word for 'public', derived from the Latin word *populus* meaning 'people' from which we also derive 'populous', 'popular', 'populist' and 'population'. 'Public' is applied in two major ways. Firstly, it may be applied to anything controlled or owned by the °state — the °public service, the public sector (as opposed to the °private sector — the business conducted by private individuals and firms), public property. Secondly, it may be applied to the people in general as opposed to private individuals. In this sense a public act is something done in public — in the open — as opposed to a private act (*privare* is a Latin word meaning 'to deprive' or 'to separate': *privatus* means 'separated').

A *private company* is one where the number of shareholders is two or more but less than fifty and where the directors have the power to restrict the transfer of shares.

A *public company* is one where the number of shareholders is seven or more and where the directors do not have the power to restrict the transfer of shares.

A *quoted company* is a public company in which the shares are traded on a °stock exchange.

public administration
the management of the affairs of the °state including its subordinate °institutions, or the study of it

Publicus is the Latin word for 'public', derived from the Latin word *populus* meaning 'people'. 'Administration' is derived from the Latin word *administrare* 'to minister to'. Public administration is concerned with the work of °government ministers and °public servants. The subject of public administration is inter-disciplinary, drawing upon other subjects such as °law, ° politics, °history, °economics, °sociology, management.

In the United States, the government is usually referred to as 'the Administration'. In Ireland a °taoiseach's, and in the United Kingdom a prime minister's, term of office is also described as his or her administration, for example people speak of 'Mrs Thatcher's third administration'.

public service
the °organisations engaged in carrying out the work of the °state are collectively known as 'the public service', and the people who work in them are called 'public servants'

Publicus is the Latin word for 'public', derived from the Latin word *populus* meaning 'people'. The public service consists of the °civil service (the civil service departments and the °offices attached to them such as the Revenue Commissioners, the offices that serve the °President, the °Dáil and the °Seanad, and the courts); the °local authorities (°e.g. county councils and boroughs); the regional health boards; the °state-sponsored bodies; the Defence Forces; the Garda Síochána; the prison service; the °universities and other state-funded third level °institutions; first and second level teachers. About 270,000 people are employed in the public service (out of a °total of about 1,100,000 people at work in the state).

The term 'public service' is not defined in °law and so people use it impressionistically rather than exactly. Thus many teachers are employed by °private schools, e.g. secondary school teachers, and therefore are °legally *not* public servants; however, since their salaries in almost all cases are paid by the state, they effectively are.

Pyrrhic
a Pyrrhic °victory is a success won at so great a cost that the victor is grievously weakened

About 300 BC a king called Pyrrhus ruled a small °state in Northern Greece. Courageous and ambitious, he dreamed of matching the success of Alexander the Great. So when the city of Tarentum in Southern Italy invited him to help them fight the Romans, he readily agreed. He landed in Italy with an army of twenty-five thousand men and a herd of elephants.

The two armies clashed outside the town of Heraclea. The Romans fought fiercely until Pyrrhus ordered his elephants to be driven against their flanks. The Romans had never seen elephants before and, terrified by the screeching and roaring of the immense beasts, they panicked and fled.

But the victorious Pyrrhus lost more men in the battle than the Romans. The Romans subsequently defeated him.

Some light relief during negotiations between Pyrrhus and the Roman envoy, Fabricius (an envoy is a representative sent to transact business with a foreign °government, and is °derived from the French word *envoyer* 'to send'

qua
in the capacity of or precisely as

Qua is a form of *qui,* the Latin word meaning 'who' or 'which'. Thus, 'The county manager attended the meeting not qua °public °official but as an interested citizen'.

quid pro quo
something given in return for something

Quid is a form of the Latin word *quis* meaning 'what'. *Pro* is a Latin word meaning 'for', 'in place of'. *Quo* is also a form of *quis. Quid pro quo,* then, is literally 'the what for what'. °Politics is largely based on compromise. Before reaching a compromise one party may demand a *quid pro quo* from the other party before it gives up some privilege or position.

quintessential
relating to the pure concentrated form of a thing or idea

Quintus is the Latin word for 'fifth'. *Esse* is the Latin word 'to be' and so the °abstract noun *essentia* means 'beingness'. In their speculations about what the world is made of, the ancient Greeks (apart from the °atomists) concluded that there were four basic elements (or essences) — fire, earth, air and water — which combined in various ways to make up everything that is. The Pythagoreans (the followers of the Greek °philosopher Pythagoras) conceived of a fifth element — the quintessence — which they called ether. Ether was the most refined element in creation — out of it the stars were made. Transferred to anything in existence, the quintessence is the purest and truest expression of the thing.

Something heavenly or spirit-like may be said to be *ethereal.*

quixotic
lofty but utterly impracticable

Don Quixote is a satire by the sixteenth °century Spanish writer, Cervantes, on the chivalry and romance of the Middle Ages. The madly idealistic knight, Don Quixote, sets out with his faithful squire, Sancho Panza, to rescue damsels in distress and, in one famous scene, tilts at a windmill.

Proposals from a °political party are sometimes declared by their opponents to be quixotic.

quorum
the °minimum number of people who must be present at a meeting before its proceedings can be taken as valid. A *quorum* for meetings should be specified in the °constitution of the body holding the meeting

Quorum is a form of the Latin word *quis* and means 'of whom'. It derives from °government commissions written in Latin (when Latin was the language of the °European °educated classes) where the following words would appear: *quorum vos ... unum* (*duos* °etc.) *esse volumus*, 'of whom we wish that you ... be one (two etc.)'. The purpose was thereby to designate the °person or persons so addressed a member (or members) of an °official body, without whose presence business could not go on.

quota
the proportional part or share needed to make up a certain quantity or number

Quota derives from the Latin expression *quota pars* meaning 'the how manieth part' — *quot* means 'how many'. The word occurs frequently in relation to the number of °persons from a particular country that may be allowed to enter the US in any one year.

It also occurs in relation to our system of °voting — proportional representation (PR) by means of the single transferable vote. The quota is the number of votes a °candidate must get as first preferences or transfers before he or she can be declared °elected. There is an exception to this rule. Where the number of seats remaining to be filled is equal to the number of candidates who have been neither elected nor eliminated, the remaining candidate or candidates are deemed to be elected (without reaching the quota). The quota is the next whole number to the one got when the °total number of valid votes is divided by one more than the number of seats in the constituency. Taking 20,000 as the total number of valid votes and five as the number of seats, the quota, is 3,334 (20,000 divided by 6 = 3333.3).

radical
going to the root

Radix, radicis is the Latin word for 'root'. The term 'radical' may be applied to the following kinds of people: someone who always seeks to get to the root of a problem in the hope of solving it (a radical of this kind, for example, might °analyse crime in such a way as to conclude that poverty is the cause of crime and that crime, therefore, can be abolished by abolishing poverty); someone who believes that his or her particular °community or group has departed from its °original ideals and should now be made to return to them (°liberation theologians speak in that way); someone who believes that present °institutions and people are so corrupt that they must be °totally changed (the atrocities of the Khmer Rouge proceeded from such radicalism); someone who believes that there is a theoretical framework that can solve all problems (many °left wing °politicians are radical in this sense).

A radical approach can be taken within all kinds of political positions and so one can speak of radical °democrats, radical °socialists, radical °communists, radical °conservatives, radical °liberals °etc.

rapprochement
a re-establishment of harmonious relations

The word is French meaning 'a coming together again'. In 1933 the United °States gave °official recognition to the °Soviet °regime, the last among the greatest powers to do so. (In 1919 °Dáil Éireann had greeted the establishment of the Soviet state in a formal message to Moscow — the first °national °parliament to do so.)

In his °autobiographical work *The Invisible Writing* Arthur Koestler describes how he met a black American writer, Langston Hughes, in a remote part of Asiatic Russia just about that time (1933). Hughes had come to Russia on the invitation of the leading Soviet film trust to script a film on the persecution of the blacks. But by the time he reached Moscow a °political *rapprochement* had begun between the USSR and the US. One of the

American conditions for resuming °normal diplomatic relations was that Russia should renounce its °propaganda campaign among the American blacks. Overnight the film project was dropped and the Russians asked Hughes to write a book on the cotton-growing regions of Asiatic Russia instead.

rationale
the set of reasons given to justify an action

Ratio, *rationis* is a Latin word meaning 'reason'. The power to reason differentiates man essentially from other animals: we expect a man or woman to act rationally and therefore to have a rationale for his or her actions. 'Rationalist' refers to a tendency among many thinkers from the seventeenth °century onwards to rely on reason alone to discover the basis for °human society and the principles that should guide behaviour.

reactionary
someone who wishes for, or wishes to bring about, a return to an earlier °political situation or a particular way of acting or thinking; someone opposed to °radical political or °social change

Reagere is the Latin word 'to do in return' from which 'reaction' is derived. Many nineteenth °century thinkers believed social progress, by which they meant reform that would uplift the living conditions of the °masses, was inevitable. Some felt that °modern °technology provided man with a °cornucopia to finance perpetual progress. Others put their trust in °dialectical materialism (which guaranteed progress!). They labelled as reactionary not only those who opposed progress but also those who queried its inevitability.

red-letter day
a very special day

In °monasteries it was the practice to inscribe feast-days in red and other days in black in the calendar. You can see examples of such calendars in the Chester Beatty Library in Dublin.

referendum
a °vote by the °electorate on a °political question referred to them by their elected °representatives

Referendum is a form of the Latin word *referre* 'to refer' and it means 'a thing that must be referred (to the people)'. The referendum as a °modern political device was introduced by the Swiss in the nineteenth °century. °*Bunreacht na hÉireann*, the °constitution enacted by the people in a referendum in 1937, provides that any proposed changes in the constitution must be referred to the people for decision by them. (Some constitutions allow the representatives of the people to change the constitution and are thereby less °democratic.)

A proposal to amend the constitution is first presented in the °Dáil as a Bill. If it is passed or deemed to have been passed by both Houses of the °Oireachtas, it is then submitted to the people. The people decide by a °majority of those °voting validly. *Bunreacht na hÉireann* provides that referenda (plural form) may be held on questions other than proposals to amend the constitution. There have been ten referenda to amend the constitution but none on any other issues.

republic
a °democratic °state which does not have a °monarch at its head

The harp, the ancient °symbol of Ireland, was introduced to Irish coinage by Henry VIII. Note the crown, the symbol of the English °monarchy, which surmounts it. 'The harp without the crown' came to epitomise the demand of Irish republicans (*epitome* °originally meant an abridgement or a summary of a book — from the Greek *epi* 'upon' and *tomē* 'a cut' — and by transference 'something that represents another in miniature' or 'a °person who is the embodiment of some quality'). The harp (without the crown) is the °official logo of the Irish °government

The word, derived from the Latin words *res publica* (*res* means 'thing' or 'affair' and *publica* means '°public' — the public affair or republic), was first applied to Rome after the expulsion of King Tarquinius Superbus and the extinction of monarchical rule there. It was used to unite the Romans around the concept of a state ruled by two short-term elected consuls rather than a king. Since *publica* is a form of *publicus* which derives from *populus* the Latin word for 'people', democracy is inherent in the term 'republic'.

The Roman Republic was so successful — it established an immense and stable °empire — that it became the ideal of later republics. Furthermore the two great values of the Roman Republic — liberty, meaning both freedom from the arbitrary rule of °despots and the right of the citizens to participate in °government, and virtue, meaning the °public spirit that disposed the citizen to pursue the common interest rather than his own °personal interest — became part of republican theory. (*Values* are those things which in a particular °context are thought of as being good; thus equality, justice and freedom are regarded as democratic values; 'value' derives from the French word *valoir* 'to be worth', which in turn derives from the Latin word *valere* 'to be strong'.)

Many states claim to be republics but in fact they are not. They may be °dictatorships like Russia under Stalin or °oligarchies like the °historic Venetian Republic. Not all democracies are republics—there are democratic monarchies (for example the United Kingdom, the

Netherlands). °Modern republicanism, the child of the American and French °revolutions, is closely associated with democratic and °egalitarian values (and claims to be more radically democratic than the ancient republics). Republicans, therefore, abhor distinctions between citizens based on titles of nobility: thus, the French revolutionaries insisted on addressing Louis XV1 as 'Citizen Capet' (from his family name) before they °guillotined him. °Doctrinaire republicans often affect a °Spartan mode of dress and lifestyle: thus the first °Fianna Fáil (The Republican Party) °administrations purposely projected a non-°élitist image through the decision of Eamon de Valera and his ministers to wear ordinary suits at state functions rather than the °conventional °patrician gear with top hats.

Irish republicanism had been developed by the United Irishmen (founded in Belfast in 1791), one of whose leading °ideologists (or ideologues), Wolfe Tone, declared:

> ...to break the connection with England, the never-ending source of all our political evils, and to assert the independence of my country — these were my °objectives. To unite the whole people of Ireland, to abolish the memory of all past dissensions, and to substitute the common name of Irishman in place of the denominations of Protestant, Catholic and Dissenter — these were my means.

This Fenian bond for $20, issued on 17 February 1866, was one of the many such bonds sold in the US from 1862 to 1867 to support the cause of Irish independence. This bond bears the signature of 'John O'Mahony, Agent for the Irish Republic', a prominent member of the Fenian Movement. Many banks honoured these bonds at a later date

Michael Collins, the most prominent leader in the armed struggle against the British, which culminated in the Truce 1921

scenario
— an outline of the plot of a play, °opera or film, scene by scene, often transferred by analysts and planners to mean an outline of one of a number of possible sequences of future development ('scenario' is an Italian word derived from the Latin *scena*, Greek *skēnē*, meaning 'a tent' or 'a stage')

Irish republicanism was revolutionary. Above all it was separatist. However, throughout the course of the nineteenth °century Irish °nationalism found its strongest expression in °constitutional °parliamentary movements, led in turn by two outstanding °public °representatives, Daniel O'Connell and Charles Stewart Parnell. The constitutional process °culminated in the passing of a Home Rule Bill for Ireland in the British House of Commons in 1914, to have effect after the end of the Great War. This would have established an Irish parliament with powers to °legislate on °domestic matters only, which would be under the overall control of the °Westminster parliament; and of course the British monarch would remain °head of state.

However, within a remarkably short time, this scenario was transformed. Republicans, °organised as the Irish Republican Brotherhood (IRB), succeeded in having the Irish Republic proclaimed at the beginning of the Easter Rising, 1916. The backlash against the executions by the British of the leaders of the Rising installed the Republic as the paramount nationalist demand. So when °Dáil Éireann came into being in 1919 it declared °unambiguously for a Republic and its members took an oath 'to support and defend the Irish Republic and the Government of the Irish Republic, which is Dáil Éireann'.

For republicans, the Treaty of 1921, with its provision for Dominion °status, partition, and the retention of the British monarch as head of state, was a bitter

The Proclamation of the Irish Republic, 1916

POBLACHT NA H EIREANN.

THE PROVISIONAL GOVERNMENT
OF THE
IRISH REPUBLIC
TO THE PEOPLE OF IRELAND.

IRISHMEN AND IRISHWOMEN: In the name of God and of the dead generations from which she receives her old tradition of nationhood, Ireland, through us, summons her children to her flag and strikes for her freedom.

Having organised and trained her manhood through her secret revolutionary organisation, the Irish Republican Brotherhood, and through her open military organisations, the Irish Volunteers and the Irish Citizen Army, having patiently perfected her discipline, having resolutely waited for the right moment to reveal itself, she now seizes that moment, and, supported by her exiled children in America and by gallant allies in Europe, but relying in the first on her own strength, she strikes in full confidence of victory.

disappointment — though admittedly a considerable advance on Home Rule. They divided into those who were prepared to accept the Treaty as a stepping-stone to a republic and those who were not. In the °civil war that followed, 1922-23, the anti-Treaty side lost. The defeated republicans held themselves aloof from the °politics of the Irish Free State — the gradualism of W.T. Cosgrave and his colleagues — until 1926 when Eamon de Valera founded the Fianna Fáil party and led most of them back into the political arena.

De Valera, when he came to power in 1932, used the provisions of the °Constitution of the Irish Free State and the constitutional developments within the British Commonwealth to enable him to propose a °*de facto* republican constitution to the people — °*Bunreacht na hÉireann* — in 1937, which they enacted. The small number of republicans who refused to obey the will of the people and who committed themselves to the achievement of re-unification through violent rather than peaceful, democratic means were the °tradition from which sprang today's Provisional IRA.

The Republic of Ireland Act, 1948, which came into effect on 18 April 1949, the thirty-third anniversary of the Easter Rising, 1916, formally described the state as a republic.

revolution
a complete change

Volvere is the Latin word 'to turn', *re* is a Latin prefix meaning 'back' or 'again' from which 'revolution' is derived. The words 'rotate' (from the Latin *rota* 'a wheel') and 'revolve' are often used interchangeably but are distinguished in the statement 'The earth rotates on its axis as it revolves around the sun'. The idea of complete change that 'revolution' now °connotes came from an association with the image of the wheel of °fortune on which men were thought to revolve, being one moment at the top of the wheel, the next at the bottom.

In °politics, 'revolution' denotes a complete change of °government brought about usually by violence as in the American, French and Russian revolutions or a °radical transformation of the beliefs and °mores of a people either by force or °education. Pol Pot attempted such a revolution in Kampuchea as did the Russians after 1917 when they sought to create a purely °secular °culture. In a °social or °economic °context, for example the industrial revolution, there is no connotation of violence.

The word 'evolution' also derives from *volvere*. The prefix *e* means 'out'. 'Evolution' denotes the rolling out (as of a roll of paper) of events, or the natural development of a plant or animal.

Rubicon
when someone makes a °fateful, irreversible move, he or she may be said to have crossed the Rubicon

victorious
derives from the Latin word *vincere* 'to conquer'. A form of *vincere* occurs in Julius Caesar's famous °laconic report to the Roman Senate on his exploits in the field: 'Veni, vidi, vici' — 'I came, I saw, I conquered'

The Rubicon is a little river in Italy. In Roman times it marked the boundary between Italy and the °province of Gaul (France and Northern Italy). Its great moment came in 49 BC.

Julius °Caesar, who had spent the previous nine years campaigning in Gaul, was leading his victorious troops towards Rome. He burned, so his enemies said, to set aside the °Republic and establish himself as sole ruler. The Roman °Senate ordered him to leave his army in Gaul and come to Rome alone — otherwise he would be °proscribed, °i.e. declared a °public enemy.

When Caesar reached the Rubicon, he paused on the northern bank. As he pondered on how much was at stake, he became irresolute. But at last, throwing caution to the winds, he declared 'The die is cast!' and led his troops across the Rubicon, formally breaking the °constitution which forbad a provincial commander to bring his army back to Rome.

He went on to conquer Rome.

Caesar crosses the Rubicon

sabotage
the carrying out of the destruction of °strategic elements in a system; the destruction of property or the disruption of a process in pursuit of some cause

Sabot is the French word for 'shoe'. In the French railway strike of 1910 the workers prevented the operation of trains by cutting the wooden 'shoes' (*sabots*) which held the rails in place. During World War II resistance groups throughout occupied °Europe helped the Allies by numerous acts of sabotage against the Germans. An activist may be said to sabotage talks if at a delicate moment in the negotiations he or she reveals information deeply embarrassing to one or other of the parties. Sabotage is carried out by saboteurs.

scapegoat
someone who bears the blame due to others

The Jews had a custom whereby on the Day of Atonement two goats, one for the Lord and one for the devil, were brought to the altar of the tabernacle. There the high priest cast lots. The goat upon which the first lot fell was for the Lord, and it was sacrificed. The other goat was the scapegoat. The high priest transferred his own sins and the sins of all the people to it, by confession, and then drove the goat out into the desert and let it escape. When things go wrong for a group, such as a °political party, they usually look for someone to blame — a scapegoat. Indeed scapegoating is now recognised as a basic tendency in °human beings: it can intensify the sense of unity within groups while allowing individuals to shed responsibility for their own failures.

'The Scapegoat' by William Holman Hunt, one of the founders of the Pre-Raphaelites, a group of Victorian artists that also included Dante Gabriel Rossetti. Pre- derives from the Latin prefix *prae* meaning 'before'. Raphael (1483–1520) was one of the masters of the classical Renaissance style. The Pre-Raphaelites took their inspiration from the naturalistic Italian painters who flourished before Raphael

Seanad Éireann
the Irish Senate

'Seanad' is a Gaelicisation of 'senate', a felicitous one since *sean* is the Irish word for 'old' and senate derives from *senex, senis* the Latin word for 'old man' ('felicitous' comes from the Latin word *felix, felicis* meaning 'happy'.) The word 'senate' harks back to the early Roman Senate when old age and wisdom were closely associated in people's minds. The Roman historian Livy gives us a glimpse of the senators where he tells of the entry of the Gauls into Rome in 390 BC after their crushing °victory over the Roman army at the Allia river. They found the city silent and deserted until they came to the °Forum, where they found all the grey old senators seated calmly in their togas, waiting. At first the Gauls were awed by the sight; but finally one who was bolder than the rest advanced and stroked the beard of one of the senators; the greybeard resented this liberty and resisted. He was struck down for his trouble—thereby giving a signal for a general slaughter and the pillage of the city. The dignity displayed by the old men, however, °inspired the garrison on the Capitol to hold out for seven months. (The Capitol, from *caput, capitis* the Latin word for 'head', was the citadel of Rome on the Capitoline Hill where the Romans built their °temple to Jupiter. The Romans loved to tell the story of how, one night during the Gaulish siege, a scaling party of Gauls was about to surprise the sleeping garrison when the sacred geese of Juno raised the alarm with their unholy cackling. 'Capitol' is used in the US for the house where Congress or a °state °legislature meets—the American founding fathers reached back to the Roman °Republic for some of their °nomenclature.)

The Sinn Féin °candidates °elected at the general election of December 1918 who were not on the run or imprisoned met in Dublin in January 1919 and constituted themselves as °Dáil Éireann — the °unicameral legislature of the Irish °Republic. The °Constitution of the Irish Free State, approved by the Dáil in 1922, provided for a °bicameral legislature — the Dáil and the Senate. This mirrored Britain's bicameral system. Moreover, there was the intention of positively discriminating in favour of Southern Unionists by providing places for them in the Senate disproportionate to their numerical strength. °*Bunreacht na hÉireann*, enacted by the people in 1937, also provided for a senate — Seanad Éireann.

Seanad Éireann has sixty members. Eleven are nominated directly by the °Taoiseach, three are elected by the °National °University of Ireland and three by the University of Dublin (Trinity College). The remaining forty-three are elected by an electorate consisting of the members of the incoming Dáil, the members of the outgoing Senate, and the members of every council of a county or county borough council. The candidates are grouped in five panels — the °Cultural and °Educational Panel, the Agricultural Panel, the Labour Panel, the Industrial and Commercial Panel, the °Administrative Panel.

Because of its narrow electoral base, Seanad Éireann is given functions that, broadly speaking, restrict its role to that of an advisory body to Dáil Éireann. However, some observers of the time pressure °TDs are under maintain that the work of the Seanad in facilitating the flow of legislation is a significant one. The senate of a °federal state, such as the US, in contrast, is usually a powerful body representing the interests of the various states (each US state irrespective of its size or °population, for example, has two US senators) and has appropriate powers to do so (thus the US Senate has a °major say in foreign affairs and Presidential appointments, which are subject to the advice and consent of the Senate).

secular
pertaining to the present world

Secularis is a Latin word derived from *saeculum*, a Latin word meaning 'an age', 'a generation', or 'a lifetime'. According to the Etruscans, who ruled in Italy before the Romans, a *saeculum* was a space of time of 110 lunar years and therefore beyond the °normal span of life. The beginning of each *saeculum* at Rome was announced by the pontiffs (Latin *pontifex* — plural *pontifices* — from *pons, pontis* 'a bridge' and *facere* 'to make sacrifice': the pontiffs were the °pagan priests who °originally made sacrifice on a bridge across the Tiber in Rome to unite the people living on either side). To celebrate the event the *ludi saeculares* ('the Secular Games' — *ludus* is the Latin word for 'game') would take place.

Like °modern centennials and millennia (*centum* is the Latin word for 'a hundred', *mille* is the Latin word for 'a thousand') the *saeculum* was not always celebrated punctually. The most famous games were held in 17 BC at the request of Augustus. The poet Horace was commissioned to write a poem to celebrate the occasion and it survives — the *Carmen Saeculare* (*carmen* is the Latin word for 'a poem'). Before the games began, a herald proclaimed them throughout Rome summoning everyone 'to view such games as no one alive has seen before and no one alive will see again'.

regular
derives from *regula* the Latin word for 'a rule'. A thing is said to be regular when it follows some rule, principle or pattern — thus regular clergy, regular shape, regular time

In Christian Rome 'secular' came to mean 'of this world' as opposed to the next; secular °clergy were those living in the world as opposed to those living, subject to religious rule, apart in monasteries (*monastērion* is the Greek word for 'monastery' derived from *monos* 'alone'). The latter were called the regular clergy. In common discussion 'secular' contrasts with 'sacred' (derived from the Latin *sacer*).

secularism
a °philosophy of life that precludes all religious and faith experience from relevance to °public life. The Russian °communists embraced systematic secularism, closing churches and promoting °atheism. In Ireland we tend to discuss secularism in terms of Church — °State relations

Secularis is a Latin word derived from *saeculum*, a Latin word meaning 'an age', 'a generation' or 'a lifetime'.

In °modern usage 'secular' contrasts with 'sacred'. Secularist attitudes may contrast or conflict with religious attitudes. Marx developed the most °radical form of secularism in that he sought to reduce all faith experience to some aspect of worldly (°economic, °political °etc.) experience.

The secularist movement in Ireland defines itself in terms of Church — State relationships, holding that the Church should not intervene in public life. Secularists regard religious faith as either false and irrelevant to secular life or °private and divorced from public life. The secular vision of life with its sharp demarcation between private and public derives from certain phases of the °liberal movement. However, the distinction between the secular and the sacred goes back to the early days of the Church.

The State is concerned with the things of this life — it is secular. The Church is concerned with the °redemption of mankind and therefore with all areas of man's experience in this life (*saeculum*), which it views *sub specie aeternitatis* ('from the perspective of eternity'; *sub* is a Latin word meaning 'under', *specie* is a form of *species*, a Latin word meaning 'viewpoint', and *aeternitatis* is a form of *aeternitas*, a Latin word for 'everlastingness' or 'eternity'). The State claims authority over all its citizens. The Church, with its °mandate from Christ to convert the whole world to the Christian way, claims a divine authority. Because of the potential conflict over whether, in a particular case, the Church's °moral view of that case or that of the State should prevail, or whether in a particular situation the State ought or ought not °legislate in a certain way, Church and State have, over the changes of the ages, sought a °*modus vivendi*.

The State into which the Church was born was the Roman °Empire. The Romans were very tolerant of religious diversity but in order to bond every citizen to the State they insisted that the cult of Rome and the worship of the emperor that came to be associated with it should be observed by all. No religion which excluded such observance was tolerated. The only exception the Romans made was for the Jews whose °monotheism ('Thou shalt have no other god but me') — then a unique feature of that race — prevented them from engaging in °polytheistic rituals.

antipathy
means 'a settled aversion' to, for or between persons, derived from the Greek words *anti* 'against' and *pathos* 'feeling'; *sympathy* is the capacity to share feeling with another (*syn* — *sym* before p — means 'with' in Greek); *empathy* is the capacity to project one's feeling into another and so fully understand him or her — thus a good actor has empathy with his audience (*en* — *em* before p — means 'in' in Greek)

At first the Romans did not distinguish between the Jews and Christians. By the time of the Emperor Nero (54-68), however, Christians were known in Rome °*per se*. State °officials now came to appreciate that Christianity as an *international* monotheistic religion posed a threat to the empire and the State religion that bound it together. This consideration, as well as °pagan and Jewish antipathy, led, over the next few hundred years, to sporadic persecution of the Church.

From the beginning there were two schools of thought within the Church over what attitude the Church should have towards the State. In *The °Apocalyse,* Rome (the

State) is called the beast, the great harlot, drunk with the blood of the saints. In St Paul we find the °predominant Christian belief that the State exercises authority under God and should be obeyed — an attitude that persisted through the persecutions (so the Church was not °revolutionary). With the conversion of the Emperor Constantine (312) the Church was granted the same privileges as the °pagan religion (for example, it could hold property and its priests were excused from certain °civic duties). Subsequently paganism collapsed and Christianity became the official religion of the empire.

Under the pagan system the emperor was the chief priest — the °Pontifex Maximus — and was treated as divine. How should he be treated in a Christian system? Constantine and his immediate Christian successors were clear about that: they regarded themselves as God's lieutenants and exercised control over the Church. (Secular control of the Church is, as a result, called *caesaropapism*, from °*Caesar* and *Papa* or Pope: it is exercised nowadays by the °Soviet °government over the Russian °Orthodox Church.) This was not a satisfactory relationship from the Church's point of view because the bishop of Rome, St Peter's successor, was Christ's °vicar.

It was St Ambrose (340-397), the Bishop of Milan, who first enunciated the principles upon which Church — State relations should be based: in matters of faith the emperor must obey the Church, in secular matters the Church must obey the State. The most influential thinker on the subject was St Augustine (354-430 AD) who in his *City of God* sought to reconcile the conflicting roles of the Christian as a °political °actor in the secular world and as a religious pilgrim whose vision transcends the here and now.

Under the °feudal system that developed after the fall of Rome, kings were conceived of as deriving their authority from God (so they were crowned by bishops) and they were bound in conscience to rule in conformity with Christian principles and practices. As a consequence, a king excommunicated by the Church found himself not only a religious °pariah but also a ruler whose people

influential
means having a shaping effect upon a person or thing. It derives from the Latin *in* meaning 'in' and *fluere* 'to flow'. Astrologers thought people's characters and destinies were affected by the °ethereal fluid flowing into them from the stars — hence the concern to find out the star under whose influence one was born. A person whose speech flows smoothly is said to be *fluent*. The point at which two rivers meet to flow together is called the *confluence* (*con* is a Latin particle meaning 'with'). *Affluent* means 'wealthy' as a result of goods flowing towards — Latin *ad* (*af* before f) — one

were no longer bound to obey him.

The relationship between Church and State that developed under the °feudal system was mutually supportive. Out of it secular theorists developed the concept of the divine right of kings which flowered in the absolutism of Louis XIV in France and of Charles I in England. Out of it came the pervasive influence of the Church and the elevation of the Pope to the position of international mediator *par excellence*.

mediator
means someone who seeks to reconcile opposing parties (*medius* is the Latin word for 'middle'; hence also 'intermediary')

The Reformation was the first great attack on the relationship: it divided the Christian world, and in many Protestant countries replaced the Pope with the °monarch as head of the Church. (The Calvinists, however, established a °democratic system for the government of their Church, while being °radically undemocratic in their political attitudes.) The French °revolution was the second great attack on it: it replaced the authority of kings based on divine right with the authority of the people. These changes led on to the development of modern °pluralist societies.

Where radical secularism has been established, religious personnel, practices and images have been banned from public life and places. Any °moral vision derived from religious perspectives is excluded from public life and the only views allowed to have a bearing on °social, political and °legal affairs are the secularist ones. Secularism, then, is radically intolerant in regard to the °criteria which may be used to judge the morality of state actions. It does not escape this criticism by its purported tolerance of private beliefs—these are only tolerated as long as they do not influence legislation.

Where Church and State have been closely allied, the demand for the separation of Church and State has been described by political activists as a demand for secularisation. This demand, however, does not necessarily entail either radical secularism or the demise of religious belief and practice. It is part of what is implied in pluralism.

Even where radical secularism has not been established, sociologists speak of a process of secularisation to refer to the decline in religious beliefs in a particular community and to a °concomitant, almost exclusive concern with here and now issues.

separation of powers
the assignment of the °primary powers of °government to distinct and independent °institutions

°Political scientists identify the primary powers of government as °legislative (law-making), °executive and °judicial. By separating these powers that is, by assigning them to separate, independent institutions, a control is placed on their use. This °doctrine was first elaborated by the French °philosopher Montesquieu in his *Spirit of the Laws* and was embodied in the US °Constitution of 1787.

Under °*Bunreacht na hÉireann* the legislative powers are assigned to the °Oireachtas, the executive powers to the °government, and the judicial powers to the judiciary. In practice, the government dominates the Oireachtas (*dominare* is a Latin word 'to rule over' from which we also derive 'dominant', 'predominant', 'domain', 'dominion', 'demesne', 'domineer' and 'indomitable').

shibboleth
a test word which betrays one's party or °nationality; now usually used for a worn-out °slogan

It is told in the Old Testament that the Ephraimites quarrelled with Jephthah who, gathering the men of Gilead together, fought and routed the Ephraimites. When the fleeing Ephraimites reached the river Jordan they were asked by Jephthah's guards to say the word shibboleth (which the Ephraimites pronounced sibboleth), and in this way were identified. Shibboleth has come to be applied to the cant or slogan that distinguishes any group.

In passing, one might observe that the word 'sixth' would serve as a shibboleth in its °original sense to distinguish people from the North of Ireland from the people of the rest of Ireland: Northerners say 'sikth' rather than 'sikst h'.

sinecure
a paid post for which there are no duties

Sine is a Latin word meaning 'without'. *Cura* is the Latin word for 'care' or 'responsibility'. A sinecure is a °traditional way of rewarding a °political favourite.

sine die
until some other, unspecified date

Sine is a Latin word meaning 'without'. *Die* is a form of the Latin word *dies* meaning 'day'. The expression is used in a °legal or °institutional °context about a court, °tribunal or meeting. Thus, 'The meeting adjourned *sine die*'.

sine qua non
an essential condition

MacEoin

Sine is a Latin word meaning 'without'. *Qua* means 'which'. *Non* is a Latin negative particle. *Sine qua non* literally means 'without which not'.

In 1921 General Seán MacEoin was captured by the British forces in Ireland. 'The Blacksmith of Ballinalee' was one of the most daring of the Irish guerrilla leaders and he was a prized captive. Later in the year, when the British offered to negotiate a truce with the Irish °nationalists, they offered to release all their prisoners except MacEoin. °Dáil Éireann immediately responded that they would not negotiate unless *all* the prisoners were released: they made the release of MacEoin a *sine qua non*. MacEoin was released and a truce — the Truce — was negotiated.

Sisyphean
endlessly laborious

In Greek °myth Sisyphus was the founder of Corinth. He had a dark reputation as an untrustworthy knave. He was the putative father of Homer's hero Odysseus, who was believed to have inherited his cunning from him (*putare* is a Latin word 'to think'; putative means 'supposed' or 'reputed').

He fell foul of Zeus in the following way. Zeus abducted Aegina, the daughter of the river-god Asopus. Asopus came to Corinth looking for her. Sisyphus knew what had happened but he said he would not tell Asopus anything unless the river-god undertook to supply the citadel of Corinth with a °perennial spring (to allow it to hold out indefinitely under siege). When Asopus made a spring rise behind °Aphrodite's °temple, Sisyphus told him all he knew. Zeus, the hot-tempered lover, flew into a rage: he ordered his brother Hades (Death) to seize Sisyphus, carry him down to Tartarus and punish him for betraying the divine secrets. In the underworld Sisyphus was ordered to roll a huge stone up a hill and

Hades
ruled the underworld. He was also known as Pluto ('The Rich One' — compare °plutocracy) because he owned all the gems and precious metals hidden beneath the earth. The most hated of the gods, he was gloomy and heartless

over the far side; but every time he reached the top the stone rolled back to the bottom.

Parts of the °public service face Sisyphean tasks. Thus many harbours have a tendency to silt. To keep the shipping channels of some of the °state harbours open the °Office of °Public Works uses dredgers. Up to a few years ago it had on its books a tired looking dredger called 'Sisyphus'.

slogan
a pithy rallying-call or °criticism of an opponent

The word is derived from two Irish words, *slua* meaning 'crowd' or 'host' and *gairm* meaning 'call' or 'shout' — a slogan was °originally a war-cry. Slogans, shouted, printed or scrawled on walls, seek to rally supporters or attack opponents. Note: Graffiti are often slogans but not every graffito (singular form), °e.g. 'Kilroy was here!', is. An Italian word, graffito is derived from the Greek word *graphein* 'to write'.

social democracy
a °philosophy of the °state, society and the °person which promotes °radical °democratisation as the best way to achieve the °socialist goal of a caring yet free society

Marx asserted that °capitalists would violently resist any attempts by the °proletariat to introduce socialism and that therefore °revolution was necessary. The Social Democratic Party in Germany, founded in 1875, rejected this °dogma. They were democratic socialists rather than revolutionary socialists, and were committed to a programme of gradual social reform to be achieved by °constitutional means. With the failure of Marx's '°scientific' socialism to predict °modern social and °economic °evolution, social democracy has become the ascendant form of socialism in the Western world — and, in the era of °*perestroika*, may prove an acceptable form in the °communist world.

Social democrats believe everyone should be involved as much as possible in deciding those issues that concern him or her. They would like to see all our °institutions democratised, that is, they would like to see all the decisions made by institutions arrived at by democratic means. This form of participatory democracy goes well beyond °representative democracy, which gives the people the power to °elect those who form the °government and to change them periodically, if they wish.

Social democrats stress the social nature of the °person, our mutual inter-dependence, our responsibility for each other and the responsibility of groups and society as a whole to foster the personal development of each member of society. It places great stress on equal °educational opportunities. Social democrats stress harmony, dialogue and sharing as opposed to individualistic °competitiveness and acquisitiveness. They see the state as intervening to promote wealth creation, to redistribute wealth, and to ensure equal social and °cultural conditions for all. Unlike Marxists and many democratic socialists, they do not require that the means of °production should be owned by the state. They favour in fact the mixed economy because it makes for a plurality of subordinate groups, with their own identity and °culture, and the freedom to live their own form of life.

Social democracy might be contrasted nowadays with °liberal democracy which lays great stress on the rights and freedom of individuals and the many °pressure groups which they develop to foster their own interest (rather than that of society).

socialism
a body of °political beliefs that stresses that man is a social being and achieves his full °humanity in and through authentic relationships with others. Hence the stress on the responsibility of the community to meet the needs of its members. Some argue that this can be done only by °public, that is, °state, ownership of the

Socialis is a Latin word meaning 'pertaining to friends or companions' and by extension 'to society in general'. 'Social' may be used to refer to any aspects of the life of a community. It contrasts with 'individual' or '°private'. Socialism, which came into use as a term in the early nineteenth °century, stresses the responsibility of the °community to care for its members and opposes the °competitive, individualism favoured by °liberals.

As the industrial °revolution worked its way through Europe in the nineteenth century, it presented the grim prospect that the means of production (and therefore wealth) would be concentrated in the hands of fewer and fewer owners of °capital and that the bulk of the °population would be transformed into a °proletariat forever struggling on subsistence wages. Socialism sought to contend with that development. It appeared first, therefore, in the three countries that were first to

means of °production and public control of distribution (thus °communists and democratic socialists); others argue that it can be achieved best by social control of the free market of production and distribution (thus social democrats)

industrialise — France, Germany and the United Kingdom.

Socialists argued that industrial capitalism, by grossly over-rewarding the owners of the means of production and grossly under-rewarding the labour which made them productive, was fundamentally unjust, that by creating classes within society it perpetuated inequality, that by making the worker an extension of a machine, it robbed him of his dignity, that by rewarding self-interest, it frayed the social ties that made co-operation possible.

Socialists demand °communal action which would make wealth and power serve the interests of all. For them, social equality and justice are the °predominant °values. Socialists have elaborated a great number of means by which their °objectives might be achieved. Broadly speaking, two systems have been put into practice. The system employed in °communist countries places the means of production and distribution into the hands of a °central planning agency. The result, as is now evident, has been to stultify the °economies of those countries. The other is the system employed in those Western European countries where socialist parties have gained power.

The work of Labour °governments in the UK is most familiar to us. To bring industry into communal hands they used nationalisation. To distribute the fruits of production equitably to all the citizens they developed the °welfare state. To prevent large-scale private accumulation of wealth they imposed death duties and restrictions on gifts and inheritances. They invested surplus state wealth in communal °cultural and leisure amenities. However, such centralised socialism is also currently under fire because of its failure to provide °dynamic growth in the economy. Social democracy, with its reliance on the °mixed economy, is increasingly being favoured.

Socialism is internationalist in sympathy — it sees workers everywhere as having a common interest in overthrowing capitalism — but in practice socialist parties, like the British Labour Party, may be °nationalistic. Socialism expresses itself in many forms ranging from Marxism to °social democracy. It is an important °political movement in Western °Europe. Indeed the variegated Socialist group is the largest group in the °European °Parliament. Socialism which seeks to achieve its goals through the parliamentary, multi-party system — democratic socialism — contrasts with °revolutionary socialism, which insists that socialism can only be achieved by force. Marxism, the only form of revolutionary socialism to be tried, stresses the role of the state controlled by the proletariat as an agent of transformation from capitalism to socialism. It regards socialism as only the °penultimate stage in the progress to communism when the state will wither away and everything will be administered by experts. (Note that the USSR is the Union of Soviet *Socialist* Republics).

In Ireland the °electoral support for the socialist parties — Labour, The Workers' Party and the Democratic Socialists — is almost fifteen per cent.

the social partners
the employers, trade unions, farmers and °government

°Modern °democratic governments seek to rule by creating consensus in the community about how °major °social, °economic, °cultural and °legal issues should be tackled (*consensus* meaning 'agreement' derives from *con* a Latin prefix meaning 'with' and *sentire*, a Latin word 'to feel'; it °connotes °unanimity and therefore the expression 'general consensus' is °tautologous). Governments pursue consensus by involving the major °interest groups — the employers, the trade unions and the farmers — in the making of policy. They invite them to submit proposals and meet with them to agree °national plans. In view of the consensus being sought, these interest groups, along with the government, are called 'the social partners'.

soviet
a °political assembly in the Union of Soviet °Socialist Republics

Sovet, transliterated 'soviet' in English, is a Russian word for 'council' like the French *conseil* and the German *Rat*. In °Czarist Russia it was applied to any political or °economic advisory body. In the °revolution of 1905 in Russia, workers' councils called 'soviets' were formed out of strike committees. In February 1917, after the overthrow of the Czar, workers' and soldiers' soviets mushroomed in Russia to take over all political, °administrative and economic functions. The soviets in turn °elected °delegates to an All-Russian Congress. Lenin and his Bolsheviks (*bolshevik* is a Russian word for 'majority'), with the °slogan 'All power to the Soviets!', used the soviets to gain control of Russia in the October Revolution of 1917.

Each of the fifteen constituent °republics of the USSR has a Supreme Soviet. Above these is the Supreme Soviet of the USSR itself.

Spartacists
a group of German °revolutionary Marxists, founded in 1916 and called after Spartacus, the slave who led a revolt against the Romans (73-71 BC)

The Romans trained slaves to fight one another to the death as gladiators in the arena (*gladius* is a Latin word for 'sword'). Spartacus was among a group of gladiators who escaped from a training-camp in the Italian town of Capua. A °charismatic leader and shrewd °tactician, Spartacus succeeded in drawing thousands of other slaves, and even poor shepherds and herdsmen discontented with their lot, to his standard; he armed them and led them to °victory against the forces sent out by the °Senate against him.

Alarmed at the revolution spreading through the countryside, the Senate eventually appointed Crassus, one of their wealthiest and most °influential men, to lead a large army against Spartacus. Crassus doggedly stalked Spartacus and his slave army, eventually defeating him. Plutarch, in his *Lives of the Noble Romans* (one of Shakespeare's sources) describes the death of Spartacus as follows:

> Before the battle began Spartacus's horse was led up to him whereupon he drew his sword and killed it on the spot, saying the Romans had plenty of fine horses which would be all his if he won the coming battle, while if he lost, he certainly would have no need of a horse. After this, in the battle itself, he made a beeline for Crassus, thrusting through the weight of weapons and wounded soldiers. He failed to make it through to Crassus but managed to down two °centurions who fell on top of him. At last, deserted by those who were about him, he stood at bay, surrounded by the

enemy. Bravely defending himself, he was cut to pieces.

The Spartacists worked for a °proletarian revolution and became the °nucleus of the German °Communist Party. They opposed the first world war. Their leaders, Rosa Luxemburg, and Karl Liebknecht, were murdered in Berlin in 1919 by the °right wing Freikorps, the loosely °organised movement of ex-soldiers who felt they had been betrayed in 1918, and who were one of the elements from which Hitler later drew support for his °Nazi Party.

Spartacus is recalled in the ballet *Spartacus* (1956) by the Soviet composer Aram Khatchaturian and in a Hollywood film, *Spartacus* (1960), in which Kirk Douglas plays the °eponymous hero and Laurence Olivier plays Crassus.

Spartacus kills his horse in front of his army

Spartan
exceedingly austere in the manner of the ancient Spartans

The Spartans were the greatest warriors of ancient Greece. Their system of °government depended on the existence of a form of serfdom. The serfs, far more numerous than the Spartans, were called helots. They were kept subdued through an efficient secret police service *(krupteia)* and the timely °assassination of any promising helot leaders. The country they controlled was called Laconia and their city, Sparta, was the only unwalled city in Greece.

The Spartans built their whole life-style around their need to excel in war. They lived absolutely equal and °communistic lives. Each Spartan had his plot of ground and a number of helots to till it. The men lived in barracks and had their meals served at common mess-tables. They had no home or family life. They visited their wives by stealth and returned to barracks. They practised °eugenics. When a child was born the mother brought it to a hall where the elders sat to examine it. If it was healthy they said 'Rear it!' If not, it was exposed to die in a cleft of the mountain.

excellent
means 'surpassing' from the Latin *excellere* 'to surpass'. The word does not admit of degrees — a thing is excellent or it is not excellent: 'more excellent' is a °solecism. (However, custom allows the usage 'most excellent majesty') Likewise, since *unique* (from the Latin *unus* 'one') means 'without a like', only a citizen of Soloi would say 'very unique'

The °education of the boys was aimed at making them excellent warriors. They followed a °regimen that made them strong, able to bear pain, despise luxury and be resourceful (they were kept half starved so that they developed great skill in stealing food — something that could be °critical in a protracted campaign by land). Their intellectual development was functional too — they were taught to answer questions briefly and to the point, so famously so that terse speech is still called 'laconic' (from Laconia).

luxury
derives from the Latin *luxuria* which itself derives from the Latin *luxus* meaning 'excess'. *Sybaris*, a Greek city in ancient Italy, was so noted for its wealth that 'sybaritic' became a °synonym for 'luxurious' or 'opulent' (from the Latin *opulentus*)

The Spartan government tended towards the °aristocratic model. They and their allies engaged in a great war against °democratic Athens and its allies. The Spartans won but the war so weakened the Greeks in general that they could not resist the outsider, King Philip of Macedon, the father of Alexander the Great.

The practices of the Spartans had a large °influence on the thinking found in Plato's °major work *The °Republic*.

state-sponsored bodies
broadly speaking, agencies other than the °civil service, °local authorities and health boards, established by the state to carry out certain functions for the °community

Status is a Latin word meaning 'state'. *Spondere* is a Latin word meaning 'to promise' from which 'sponsor' is derived: to sponsor is to go surety for.

There are about ninety of these bodies. Among the best-known are Aer Lingus, Bord Fáilte, Bord na Móna, CIE, ESB, IDA, the Industrial °Credit Corporation, An Post, RTE, Irish Sugar Company, Telecom Éireann and VHI. State-sponsored bodies carry out a very wide range of functions such as °export promotion (Córas Tráchtála), research (Eolas), °production (Nitrigin Éireann Teo), °regulation (The Medical Council). They tend to be set up because they can operate with greater freedom than other parts of the °public service. They employ about 96,000 people.

Aer Lingus

The term 'state-sponsored bodies' is not defined by °law. We rely on °conventional usage to let us know what agencies fall within it.

The °government divides state-sponsored bodies into commercial bodies (ones that trade like commercial bodies) and non-commercial bodies. The government has to meet the salaries of people working in non-commercial bodies from °taxation. That is primarily why it makes this distinction.

State-sponsored bodies are sometimes referred to as 'semi-state bodies' (*semi* is a Latin prefix meaning 'half'; *hēmi*, as in 'hemisphere', is its Greek equivalent). The use of this term should, however, be discouraged because on °analysis it is meaningless. State-sponsored bodies are also being increasingly referred to as *parastatals* (*para* is a Greek word meaning 'beside'; prefixed to a noun it means 'closely resembling': thus *paramedics* are such people as nurses, physiotherapists and ambulance drivers who help doctors, *paramilitaries* are armed civilians °organised as a °military force either to help or fight the professional armed forces).

status quo
the existing situation

Status is a Latin word meaning 'state', 'condition' or 'rank in society'. *Quo* is a form of *quis* meaning 'in which'. °Conservatives tend to wish to maintain the

symbol
Symbolon is the Greek word for 'a token'. A symbol is an emblem, something taken by convention to represent something else

status quo. The *status quo ante* — the pre-existing situation (*ante* is a Latin word meaning 'before') — is the state two parties in an inconclusive conflict may wish to return to. A *status symbol* is something its owner believes to declare his or her desirable rank in society. For many people a sports-car is a status symbol; and, interestingly, throughout °history another form of transport — the horse — was a status symbol.

statute
an °Act of the °Oireachtas

Statutum is a Latin word meaning 'a thing established (by law)'. A statute is a °law passed by the Oireachtas as opposed to a law arising from customary practice or the decisions of judges. A provision described as *statutory* is one that proceeds from an Act. A *statutory instrument* is a set of detailed rules issued by a minister under the general provisions of an °Act. The Oireachtas later examines these instruments, through one of its joint committees, to ensure they comply with the Act. By allowing the use of statutory instruments the Oireachtas avoids getting bogged down in the minutiae ('small details', the plural form of the Latin word *minutia* meaning 'smallness') of °technical °legislation.

the stock exchange
the building in which people buy and sell stocks and shares or the association of people who engage in that business

Before the London Stock Exchange came into being in 1773, rich people often met in the coffee houses there and put their money together to buy ships to send around the world to trade with other countries. When a ship returned after a successful voyage, the profits were shared out among the speculators in proportion to the amount they invested in the ship. A merchant who had invested in a ship but wanted his money back quickly before the ship returned would go to the coffee houses to see if anybody wished to buy his share and, if they did, at what price. Other businesses, such as factories and mines, came to be financed in the same way.

The Stock Exchange was established to provide a single place where all the buying and selling of shares could be done efficiently. The Dublin Stock Exchange — now the Irish Stock Exchange — was established in 1799, the year after the Rebellion. It is part of The

Stock Exchange centred in London. The American Stock Exchange is known as Wall Street, the French as *La Bourse*. The Amsterdam Effectenbeurs is the oldest stock exchange in the world. It began in 1602 with trading in shares of the Dutch East India Company.

The Stock Exchange enables companies to raise money for expansion or to °produce new products by selling shares in the companies. It enables the °government, °local authorities, °state-sponsored bodies and health boards to borrow money to build roads, hospitals, airports °etc. by offering securities on which a certain rate of interest is paid each year.

People who save in such °institutions as building societies, banks, insurance companies (as many as nine

The Irish Stock Exchange, Dublin

out of ten adults, it would seem) deal indirectly in the Stock Exchange because those institutions invest the money lodged with them in securities and shares. A smaller number of people deal directly in the Stock Exchange through professional advisers and dealers called stockbrokers.

The value of shares fluctuates as the trading experience of the various companies fluctuates. Speculators who seek a profit by selling a security in the hope of buying it back later at a lower price are called *bears* (and thus a bear market is one that would favour bears — a falling market). Speculators who seek a profit by buying a security in the hope of selling it later at a higher price are called *bulls* (and thus a bull market is one that would favour bulls — a rising market). A *stag* is someone who applies for *new* issues in the hope that they will rise immediately and provide an opportunity for a quick profit.

An index representative of industrial and commercial shares (such as the Dow Jones Index in America, the Financial Times Index in Britain, ISEQ — the Irish Stock Exchange Equity Index — in Ireland) indicates each day whether the market overall is rising or falling (*index, indicis* is the Latin word for 'the forefinger', which is used to indicate).

A *gilt* or *gilt-edged security* is one where interest and °capital are guaranteed by a government. An *Irish gilt* is one guaranteed by our government. A *blue chip* investment is one in the most highly regarded industrial shares (the term is American, derived from the highest valued chip used in poker).

stoic
indifferent to pleasure or pain; courageous in the face of danger or adversity

In ancient Athens there was a decorated portico (the Stoa Poikilē) famous for its °historical and °mythological pictures. Here in the fourth °century BC a °philosopher called Zeno held lectures. His °doctrine came to be called Stoicism from the name of the portico.

According to Zeno, the divine mind, which produced the °cosmos, is itself present in every part of it. Man by his possession of reason shares in the divine nature. But his nature also has lower elements that often oppose his reason. Virtue consists in living at one with the divine mind which expresses itself in and through the world, °i.e., in living in accordance with the °natural law which is discoverable by reason. (This idea of a natural law was incorporated in the Roman and Christian °legal systems. These systems were taken over by the °barbarian kingdoms of °Europe after the fall of Rome; as a result the Stoic natural law doctrine lies at the heart of the legal systems of Europe today.)

The Stoics placed great emphasis on doing one's duty. Because pleasure, praise, the fear of pain and death were obstacles to the performance of one's duty, the Stoics sought to make themselves indifferent to those conditions through stern, sustained exercises. An important tenet of Stoicism was that reason must manifest itself in action. Stoics, therefore, were °politically active whereas Epicureans, who sought happiness or pleasure, were politically inactive: the latter believed political activity would not normally °contribute to the individual's happiness because it would not assist 'repose of the mind'.

('Epicurean' is frequently used to describe someone who single-mindedly pursues °physical pleasure, that is, as a °synonym for 'hedonist', even though the Epicureans opposed excess.)

synonym
An *antonym* is the opposite of a synonym — it is a word opposite in meaning to another (*anti* is a Greek word meaning 'against') — thus good and evil are antonyms. A *homonym* is a word that has the same sound as another but a different meaning (*homos* is 'same' in Greek) — thus 'peace' and 'piece' are homonyms

The Romans were strongly attracted to Stoicism because of its exhortation to contribute to the °state. Indeed many of Rome's earliest heroes such as Brutus and Cincinnatus were later felt to have been natural Stoics before the Stoic philosophy was formulated in Greece—*avant la lettre* as the French put it. Some °historians believe that Stoic qualities inherent in many early Roman leaders such as Appius Claudius, Fabius Cunctator and Cato the °Censor played an important part in Rome's eventual supremacy. The Stoic qualities referred to would be *pietas* (love of god, country and family) and *gravitas* (a general seriousness of outlook; *gravis* is the Latin word for 'heavy' — hence also 'grave' and 'gravity'; we still use the word 'gravitas' in such expressions as 'He has not the gravitas to be a judge'). Aeneas, the hero of Virgil's *Aeneid* and the ancestor of

Romé's founders, is in essence a Stoic—thus while he dallies with Dido in Carthage awhile, his sense of duty soon drives him back to his ship to continue his arduous mission.

In common usage, we might say of a man who endured with courage a series of calamities 'He remained stoical throughout'.

strategy
the series of steps needed to win a campaign or other °major °objective

Stratēgos is a Greek word for 'a general' so strategy is concerned, as a general is, with the overall objective. At a lower level of concern the general must decide the *tactics* (from the Greek word *taktikos* meaning 'fit for arranging') to be employed in gaining each strategic position. Thus to capture a strategic city he may decide to besiege it or try to scale the walls; or he may come up with a *stratagem* as the Greeks did when they built a wooden horse outside Troy, filled it with soldiers and left it—an irresistible trophy—for the °Trojans to haul inside the city themselves.

sub judice
before the courts

Sub is a Latin word meaning 'under'. *Judice* is a form of the Latin word *judex, judicis* meaning 'a judge'. When a matter is *sub judice* it is before the courts and therefore not yet decided. While a case is *sub judice*, the °media must not discuss it so as to avoid prejudicing the °legal process. If they did so, they would place themselves in contempt of court and subject to heavy penalties.

subpoena
a summons to appear in court under threat of a fine or imprisonment

Sub is a Latin word meaning 'under'. *Poena* is a Latin word for 'punishment'.

sub rosa
in strict confidence

Venus and Cupid

Sub is a Latin word meaning 'under'. *Rosa* is the Latin word for 'rose'. For the Romans, Cupid was the god of love (*cupiditas* is the Latin word for 'desire'), represented in art as a chubby child (his mother was Venus, the goddess of love). Venus had many lovers and Cupid once gave Harpocrates, the god of silence, a rose as a bribe to keep quiet about his mother's indiscretions. Ever since, the rose has been a °symbol of secrecy (as well as being associated with love!). The ceilings of Roman dining-rooms were often decorated with roses to remind guests to keep *sub rosa* what was said *in vino* (under the °influence of drink).

Veneris is a form of *Venus* from which we derive 'venereal' as in 'venereal diseases', that is, sexually transmitted diseases (STD).

subsidiarity
the principle whereby a lesser body which is carrying out its functions efficiently and effectively should be allowed to continue in being by a superior body

Subsidiarius is a Latin word meaning 'supplementary'. °Modern °history is largely the story of how certain °dynasties succeeded in concentrating power in their own hands and thereby established the various °states we know today. °Central authority has a drive to increase its powers. Often, it tries to do this by absorbing or destroying lesser bodies, frequently on the grounds of efficiency. The principle of subsidiarity is a good appeal against centralism because it, too, is based on efficiency — the fact that service can be delivered best by those closest to the people or bodies to be served.

The term *subsidiary* is used in business — a subsidiary company — to describe a company operating its business with a significant degree of freedom and discretion but subordinate to the overall policies of an owning company.

sui generis
unique

Sui is a form of the Latin word *suus* meaning 'his', 'her', or 'its'. *Generis* is a form of the Latin word *genus* meaning 'kind' or 'class'— *sui generis* means 'of a class of its own'. The birth of Christ was *sui generis*.

sycophant
an ingratiating flatterer

At one time it was forbidden by °law in Athens to °export figs. Someone who laid information against another for exporting figs was called a *sukophantēs* (*sukon* is the Greek word for 'fig' and *phainein* is the Greek word 'to show' or 'to expose'). It is not clear how the word came to have its °modern meaning. Presumably the reason people often informed on others was to ingratiate themselves with the authorities.

Phantasm (a fancied vision), *fantasy, phantom,* and *phenomenon* (the appearance anything presents to the mind) are all derived from *phainein.* So is *diaphanous* meaning 'transparent' — *dia* is a Greek word meaning 'through'. ('Transparent' itself derives from the Latin words *parere* 'to appear' and *trans* 'through'.)

symposium
a formal °academic discussion of, or set of papers on, a single °topic, by a number of specialists

Sun is a Greek particle meaning 'with' transliterated *syn* (*sym* before a word beginning with p). *Posis* is a Greek word meaning 'drinking'. A symposium — the Latin transliteration of the Greek *symposion* — was °originally a Greek drinking party, heightened by agreeable conversation, music and dancing. The °philosopher Plato liked to enliven his treatises by casting them in the form of dialogues (*dialogos* is a Greek word for 'conversation'). The setting for one of his most famous works is a symposium — it is called *The Symposium* — thus beginning the formal connection between the word and a conference to present varying academic views about a topic.

A Greek symposium. A favourite amusement at symposia (plural form) was telling riddles. If you solved a riddle, you could expect a reward of a cake or a kiss. If you failed, you were likely to be condemned to drink in one breath a jug of wine, sometimes mixed with salt water. The Greek word for a riddle *ainigma* transliterates into English as 'enigma'

syndicate
a combination of people for some common purpose

Sundikos (transliterated 'syndic' in English) is a Greek word that °originally meant 'a defendant's advocate' (*sun* is a Greek word meaning 'with', *dikē* is a Greek word meaning 'justice'). It later came to mean 'an officer of °government'. A *syndicate* was a group of such officers entrusted with the affairs of a city or °community. *Syndicate* came to be applied especially to a combination which °capitalists entered into for the purpose of prosecuting a scheme requiring large amounts of capital, often one having the aim of cornering the market in a particular commodity — see Rembrandt's painting 'The Syndics of Amsterdam'.

A *syndicated column* is an article carried by a combination of newspapers. In France the adjective *syndical* is applied to combinations of workers — trade unions.

Syndicalism is a development of trade unionism that originated in France which aims to put the means of °production into the hands of unions of workers.

T

Tánaiste
the °Taoiseach's deputy

rival
is said to derive from the Latin *rivalis* 'pertaining to a river' (Latin *rivus*): a rival draws water from the same river

Under the Brehon system succession to the kingship was usually decided after the king died. The great weakness of this arrangement was that an enemy could take advantage of an undecided succession and of a °community divided between rival claims. As a result the custom of 'tanistry' or preliminary °election of a successor (*tánist* or *tánaiste*) before the kingship became vacant developed. It is likely that tanistry received a fillip following the Norman invasion and the introduction of the °feudal system: the feudal system provided for succession in advance through the °law of °primogeniture.

The post of °Tánaiste is provided for in °*Bunreacht na hÉireann.*

Taoiseach
prime minister

De Valera

Taoiseach means 'chief' or 'chieftain' in Irish (its plural form is 'taoisigh'). The word was introduced in °*Bunreacht na hÉireann* to name the head of the °government or prime minister. Under the °Constitution of the Irish Free °State (1922-37) the prime minister was known as °President of the °Executive Council.

The Taoiseach, who must be a member of the °Dáil, is appointed by the President on the nomination of the Dáil. The Taoiseach nominates the other members of the government for appointment by the President with the prior approval of the Dáil. The Taoiseach assigns

Costello

Lemass

Lynch

Cosgrave

FitzGerald

Haughey

each member of the government to a particular department. He or she appoints one member of the government to be °Tánaiste who acts as Taoiseach if the Taoiseach becomes incapacitated or is unavailable to act.

The Taoiseach nominates the Attorney General (the government's adviser on °legal matters) to the President, who must appoint the Taoiseach's nominee. The Taoiseach may advise the President to accept the resignation of a member of the government. He or she may request a member to resign. Should the member fail to comply with the request his or her appointment is terminated by the President if the Taoiseach so advises. If at any time the Taoiseach resigns, the other members of the government are deemed also to have resigned.

The Taoiseach manages the progress of the government's °legislative programme through the °Oireachtas, co-ordinates the work of departments through °regular °cabinet meetings and other contacts with ministers, takes part in EC meetings of heads of state or of government, represents the government abroad on other occasions, holds discussions with the °social partners, presents the government's °major policies to the °media, promotes the °organisation and morale of the party, and deals with the problems of his or her own constituents.

Those who have held the office of Taoiseach are: Eamon de Valera (1938-48; 1951-54; 1957-59); John A. Costello (1948-51; 1954-57); Sean Lemass (1959-66); Jack Lynch (1966-73; 1977-79); Liam Cosgrave (1973-77); C. J. Haughey (1979-81; 1982; 1987-); Garret FitzGerald (1981-82; 1982-87).

tautology
saying the same thing twice in different words

Tauto is a Greek word for 'the same'. *Logos* is a Greek word for 'word', 'reason', or 'account'. 'They were looking for a °panacea for all their troubles' is tautologous and should read '... a panacea for their troubles'.

taxation
the system of °contributions exacted by the °state from individuals and °organisations to pay for the services provided by the state

Taxare is a Latin word 'to value' or 'to charge'. °Governments levy taxes on incomes, on property and on the °production and retail sales of goods and services. Taxes on incomes include *Pay-As-You-Earn* (PAYE) and taxes on the self-employed. °*Capital taxes* include taxes on inheritance and on residential property above a certain value. Production gives rise to company profits and these are liable to °*corporation tax*. Certain types of production are separately taxed, for example whiskey distilling, which is subject to *excise duties*. The retail sales of goods and services are also taxed, particularly by means of *Value Added Tax* (VAT).

VAT is an example of an *ad valorem* tax because it varies according to the value of the goods or services being sold (*ad* is a Latin word meaning 'to', *valor, valoris* is a Latin word meaning 'value').

Taxes are called either *direct* or *indirect* depending on how they relate to income. PAYE, levied directly on income, is a direct tax. VAT, levied on one's expenditure on goods and services, is an indirect tax. The amount of direct tax one pays is outside one's control; the amount of indirect tax one pays can be controlled by controlling one's expenditure.

Taxes are also °classified by whether they are *progressive*, *proportional* or *regressive*. Progressive taxes take proportionately more from the rich than the poor. An income tax structure with increasing rates of tax for increasing income is progressive. Proportional taxes take exactly the same proportion of the incomes of the rich as of the poor. An income tax structure with the same rate of tax (say twenty-five per cent) for all income is proportional. Regressive taxes take proportionately more from the poor than from the rich. Thus a £1 duty on a gallon of petrol will take a higher percentage of a poor °person's income than of a rich person's.

In Ireland in 1988 the °total tax revenue gathered by the Revenue Commissioners was £7.3 billion. Income tax (mainly PAYE) yielded forty-two per cent of the °total, VAT twenty-five per cent and excise duties twenty per cent.

The newest tax to be introduced is Deposit Interest

Retention Tax (DIRT). It is levied on the interest earned by invested money and is withheld from the investor by the bank or other financial °institution on behalf of the state. It yields two to three per cent of the total tax raised.

tele-
telecommunications, telegram, telegraph, telepathy, telephone, telescope, television — these are all words whose common prefix *tēle* means 'afar' in Greek

Telecommunications is the transmission of messages over long distances by electronic means — radio, television, cable, telephone, telegraph (*communicare* is a Latin word 'to communicate').

Telegram is a written message received by telegraph (*gramma* means 'writing' or 'letter' in Greek).

Telegraph is an °apparatus for sending messages or signals over long distances by electricity (*graphein* means 'to write' in Greek).

Telepathy is the act of communicating thoughts and feelings to another over a distance without the use of a telephone or other apparatus (*pathein* is 'to feel' in Greek).

Telephone is an apparatus for speaking to another over a long distance (*phōnē* is the word for 'voice' in Greek).

Telescope is an instrument for making distant °objects appear closer (*scopein* is 'to look at' in Greek).

Television is an apparatus for receiving sound and pictures broadcast from a distant place (*videre* from which 'vision' derives is 'to see' in Latin).

theist
a believer in God

Theos is the Greek word for 'a god'.

An *atheist* is someone who does not believe in God or who positively denies the existence of God (*a* is a Greek negative particle). An *agnostic* is someone who professes not to know for certain in some particular matter. An agnostic in religious matters professes not to know for certain whether God exists or not—and thus is distinguished from an atheist (*gnostikos* is a Greek word 'having knowledge').

A *monotheist* is someone who believes in the existence of one god only (*monos* is the Greek word for 'alone').

A *pantheist* is someone who believes God exists in all of nature (*pan* is the Greek word for 'all'). A *pantheon*, however, is a °temple to all the gods, and by extension to the illustrious dead who are °immortal in °memory.

A *polytheist* is someone who believes in the existence of many gods (*polus* is the Greek word for 'many').

theology
°rational discourse about God and man's relationship to God

Theos is the Greek word for 'a god'. *Logos* means 'word', 'reason' 'account'. Theology is the systematic study of every source of knowledge about God, but particularly of the sacred revealed writings, °traditions and practices of a particular believing community. Its purpose is to enrich the life of that community and the lives of its members in their endeavours to achieve both °communal and °personal unity with, and witness to, God. Christian theology takes as its chief source God's revelation of himself in the Old and New Testaments and in Christ, and the Christian community's developing understanding of that revelation. Theology has been defined by St Augustine as 'faith seeking understanding'.

Dogmatic theology is the continual effort to re-articulate the basic truths about God in language which is appropriate to the believing community and in a way that integrates a developing understanding with the tradition of that community (*dogma, dogmatos* is a Greek word meaning 'opinion' — in English a settled opinion, hence a principle, a tenet, a °doctrine laid down with authority; in everyday use 'dogmatic' has a °pejorative sense — thus a dogmatic person is someone who believes his or her opinions are incontrovertible). Dogmatic theology is also called speculative theology as opposed to practical theology or °moral theology.

integrates — 'combines various elements into a whole'; *integral* means 'whole', 'complete' or 'forming a whole'; an *integer* is a whole number (from the Latin *integer* derived from *in* a negative particle and *teger* from *tangere* 'to touch' — an integer is something untouched and therefore whole)

Moral theology is the same faith seeking understanding of the implications of these truths for the daily living out of the faith in God by the community and the person ('moral' is derived from the Latin word *mos, moris* meaning 'custom' or 'conduct'). It tries to articulate in a theoretical way an account of those practices which will bring the community and the person into a deeper union with God. ('Articulate' means 'to express oneself coherently', achieved by joining statements together in a way that makes sense; 'articulus' is the diminutive form of *artus* the Latin word for 'joint'; *arthron* is the Greek word for 'joint' from which we derive 'arthritis', inflammation of the joints.)

Whether it is dogmatic or moral theology, the aim is

always understanding with a view to a life lived in union with God here and hereafter. (Different faiths have different theologies because their sources of knowledge about God are different but all theologies have as their common purpose the leading of persons towards union with God.)

Liberation theology is an attempt to articulate the demands of the Christian faith for a particular Christian community where its members and fellow °human beings are the victims of oppression and degradation. It faces such practical issues as whether, and to what degree, Christians should involve themselves in °radical, even °revolutionary, endeavours to free themselves and their fellow-citizens from °political, °economic and °social servitude. It developed in Latin America where great contrasts exist between the wealthy ruling classes and the oppressed °masses. Liberation theology has created tension in the Catholic Church in Latin America and elsewhere, and has divided the Christian communities there.

servitude
-tude is a Latin suffix indicating a state or condition. *Servus* is the Latin for 'slave' — servitude means slavery or subjection. Thus also fortitude (*fortis* means 'strong' in Latin), multitude (*multus* means 'many' in Latin), altitude (*altus* means 'high' in Latin), certitude (*certus* means 'certain' in Latin)

Some forms of liberation theology justify violence in the interest of justice and thereby come into conflict with the Vatican's °proscription of violence. Some forms accept a Marxist °analysis (on the principle that theological problems should be translated into economic and political ones) and thereby come in conflict with the Church which rejects this kind of reductionist analysis. (Reductionism is a theoretical understanding of human affairs which commits one to a search for antecedent causes of a particular problem. These causes may be of a different °character to the event to be explained or understood. Nonetheless, reductionists believe that unless those causes are understood the °original complex problem cannot be properly understood and solved. *Reducere*, the Latin word from which reductionism derives, means 'to lead back'.)

However, not all liberation theologians are believers in violence or Marxism. *Liber*, from which 'liberation' derives, is a Latin word meaning 'free'.

the Third Reich
the Nazi regime 1933–1945

Reich is a German word meaning '°empire' or 'kingdom'. It is related to the Latin word *regere* 'to rule' (from which we derive 'regime' meaning 'administration' or 'course of treatment' and 'regimen' meaning 'course of treatment'). It is also related to the Irish words *rí* and *ríocht* meaning 'king' and 'kingdom' and the Hindi words *raj* meaning 'kingdom' and *rajah* meaning 'king' or 'ruler' (the British °government of India, 1858–1947, was known as 'the Raj').

Hitler receiving an ovation at a youth rally in Berlin, 1938. The Romans publicly acclaimed their victorious generals in either of two processions. In a *triumph* the general entered Rome in a magnificent chariot drawn by four horses, preceded by the captives and the spoils of war. The magnificence of the display and the adulation of the crowds were so heady that a slave accompanied the general in the chariot to shout occasionally in his ear: *Hominem memento te!* ('Remember you are only a man!'). In an *ovation*—a lesser triumph—the general entered the city on foot, he did not wear the gorgeous gold embroidered robe, nor did he carry a sceptre; and the ceremonies concluded with the sacrifice not of a bull but of a sheep (*ovis* is the Latin for 'sheep'—hence 'ovation')

The first reich was the °medieval Germany-°centred Holy Roman °Empire. The Holy Roman Empire, a revival of the ancient Roman Empire of the West, came into being with the coronation of Charlemagne as Emperor by Pope Leo III in 800. It fell into decline for a period but was revived by the coronation of the German Otto I as emperor in 962. It continued in being until it was dissolved by Napoleon in 1806.

The second Reich was the German Empire established by Bismarck in 1871, which ended with the abdication of °Kaiser Wilhelm II in 1918.

The Third Reich, °inaugurated in 1933 when Hitler gained °dictatorial powers following his appointment as Chancellor, would last, the °Nazis boasted, a thousand years. It lasted twelve.

The idea of a golden age of a thousand years occurs in *The °Apocalypse* — it was the period Christ would reign on earth following His second coming; people who believe in such a °doctrine, taken literally, are called millennialists or millenarians (*mille* is the Latin word for 'a thousand') or chiliasts (*chilias* is the Greek word for 'a thousand'). The writer Arthur Moeller van den Bruck applied the concept to the developing °political state of Germany in a book published in 1923 called *Der Dritte Reich* (*The Third Reich*), and the Nazis gladly seized upon it for °propaganda reasons.

the third world
the underdeveloped countries

The first and second worlds are the two °major groups of developed countries — the free enterprise countries led by the US and the °socialist countries led by Russia. Third world countries are marked by an extremely low level of °economic activity, dependence on one or a few °primary commodities (food or minerals), a poor °infrastructure, illiteracy, poor °social °welfare and health services. Third world countries desperately need help from developed countries, often to meet °disasters such as famine, flooding and earthquakes, but persistently to help them develop their own economies. The internationally accepted target for °official (as distinct from voluntary) aid from developed countries is 0.7% of °gross national product (GNP). Some of the oil-rich

The greening of Africa. Irish horticultural specialist, John Hegarty, with students at the Farm Training Centre, Ndola, Zambia ('horticultural' derives from the Latin *hortus* 'a garden' and *colere* 'to cultivate')

Arab countries exceed the target, a few countries such as the Netherlands and Norway reach it, but the average response is 0.36%.

In 1987 Ireland's official aid was IR£39 million (0.226% of GNP). Of this, IR£21 million was °multilateral assistance through the °EC, UN and World Bank, and IR£18 million was °bilateral assistance, such as development projects in Zambia, and °personal service on projects by some four hundred and fifty Irish specialist/development workers °organised by the Agency for Personal Service Overseas (APSO). IR£1 million was devoted to various items such as the administrative costs of Gorta, the Refugee Resettlement Committee and the Advisory Committee on Development Cooperation. Ireland's voluntary assistance, through bodies such as Trócaire, is substantial — about IR£20 million in 1986, not including °donations of clothes, food, books °etc., and the services of some 5,000 missionaries (working mainly in Africa but also in Asia and Latin America) which, if valued at a low average of IR£10,000 yearly, would amount to IR£50 million.

titanic
immensely powerful

Atlas was condemned by Zeus to the eternal labour of holding up the sky. He is often represented in art

In Greek °myth, at the beginning of all things Mother Earth emerged from °Chaos and bore a son Uranus. Uranus fathered the Titans upon Mother Earth. The Titans were giants, the best-known being Cronus and Atlas. Cronus and his brothers attacked Uranus and killed him. Cronus then became the chief god. Subsequently Cronus had a son called Zeus who in turn engaged in a great struggle with Cronus and his brothers, eventually overcoming them. The Titans were banished and Zeus became the chief of the gods. 'Titanic', then, is aptly applied to a struggle between mighty forces — the struggle between the °superpowers is titanic.

Gigas, gigantos is the Greek word for 'giant' from which 'gigantic' is derived (the Greek word for 'earth' *gē* lurks in the word 'giant' because the giants, like Adam, came from the earth).

The *Cyclopes* were a race of giants who had a single eye in the °centre of their foreheads. They lived °barbarous lives in caverns by the sea. (They were troglodytes —

as bearing the earth on his shoulders. In the sixteenth century printed collections of maps often featured Atlas as a frontispiece. The Flemish geographer Mercator (1512-94) first used the term 'atlas' for a collection of maps itself

Odysseus blinds Polyphemus ('the eye sizzled', says Homer) in one of the most famous episodes in the *Odyssey* (an episode is an interesting incident in a story and derives from the Greek *epi* 'upon' and *eisodos* 'a coming in')

Odysseus escapes from the Cyclops's cavern by clinging to the belly of a ram: for when they blinded Polyphemus, the Cyclops made his way to the mouth of the cavern and groped about to catch any Greek who tried to escape. At dawn, as he let his sheep out to pasture, he stroked their backs to make sure no one was astride them

the Greek word *troglodytēs* means 'cave-dweller'.) In the *Odyssey* Odysseus puts out the eye of the Cyclops Polyphemus with a burning stake. 'Cyclopean' is aptly applied to °massive walls made from large, rough-hewn stones because the ancient Greeks associated that style of masonry with the Cyclopes.

Colossal is a °synonym for 'gigantic'. It derives from the Greek word *kolossos* (Latin *colossus*) meaning 'a giant statue'. The most famous colossus was the Colossus of Rhodes — a bronze statue of the god Apollo that stood over one hundred feet high near the harbour. (It was wrongly thought to have stood astride the entrance to the harbour allowing ships to pass full sail between its legs — hence Shakespeare's description of Julius °Caesar '... he doth bestride the narrow world/ Like a Colossus; and we petty men/ Walk under his huge legs, and peep about....'). It was one of the seven wonders of the world. The Colosseum in Rome was a huge amphitheatre — a building with tiers of seats around an open space like a modern football pitch — opened in 80 AD by the Emperor Titus. Beside it stood a massive statue of Nero as the sun-god, the colossus from which the building took its name. The Colosseum itself was colossal — it had seats for 45,000 spectators (*eum* is a Latin suffix °denoting place — compare °museum). Both 'gigantic' and 'colossal' are aptly applied to °physical things. Losses, too, may be gigantic or colossal (but not titanic or Cyclopean).

Gargantua, the Rabelaisian hero, was a giant with an enormous appetite. 'Gargantuan' is aptly applied to a huge meal. (We use the term 'Lucullan' to describe a lavish °epicurean feast, after a first °century BC Roman general called Lucullus, who was famous for his banquets.)

Hercules was a giant son of Zeus. He was most famous for the twelve labours he performed: these would easily have defeated any °normal man. His fifth labour, for instance, was to clean out the Augean stables in a single day. King Augeas of Elis, one of the wealthiest men on earth, had huge herds of cattle and flocks of sheep. But his stables, where he kept the animals, had not been cleaned out for years and the stench carried across the whole of Greece. Eurystheus, who set Hercules this task, cackled gleefully as he pictured the hero piling the noisome filth into a basket and carrying it away in a °state of near asphyxiation ... and then haring back for more. Hercules, however, made two gaps in the stable walls and diverted two neighbouring rivers so that they streamed through the stables and swept them clean. 'Herculean' is aptly applied to a spectacularly difficult task.

Hercules's First Labour was to kill the Nemean lion, a fearsome beast invulnerable to arrow, spear or stone. Hercules went straight into his den, caught him by the neck and strangled him

traumatic
pertaining to an emotional shock of such violence that it causes recurrent °psychological reactions

Trauma is the Greek word for 'a wound'. °Psychoanalysts seek to treat traumata (plural form of *trauma*). The word is often used to describe any severe shock. Thus, 'The defeat of Fine Gael in 1969 — its fourth successive defeat in a general °election — was a traumatic experience for the party'. The Latin word for 'wound' *vulnus, vulneris* gives us *vulnerable* 'open to being wounded'.

tribune of the people
a champion of the ordinary people

The Latin word *tribunus* °originally meant 'a tribal commander'. In the early days of the Roman °Republic there was a class struggle between the °aristocratic party, who ruled through the consuls and the °senate, and the ordinary people, the *plebs*. The *plebs* eventually won the right to °elect a number of °representatives to protect them from abuse of power by the senate and the consuls.

They were called *tribuni plebis* 'tribunes of the people'. The expression is now used of any defender of the people — thus one of the titles given to Daniel O'Connell was 'Tribune of the People'.

Caius Gracchus (154–122 BC), Tribune of the People, was ranked by °historians of Rome as a °public speaker second only to Cicero. He asserted the rights of the *plebs* over those of the °patricians to an unprecendented extent (from *plebs* we derive °plebeian' meaning 'pertaining to the lower class'). When he slipped from power, he escaped the wrath of the °Senate only by persuading his slave to stab him to death

In °modern times the word 'tribune' is much favoured as a title for a newspaper: it promises the excitement of °crusading journalism to the readers and of big circulation to the publishers.

In time the Roman tribunes acquired the °veto over Senatorial appointments and acted as judges in certain cases. It is from their °legal functions that we get the word 'tribunal' meaning either a place where a case can be heard or a process of formal enquiry, as in 'The °government has set up a tribunal of enquiry into the price of petrol'.

THE SUNDAY TRIBUNE

INTERNATIONAL Herald Tribune®

Published With The New York Times and The Washington Post

-type
archetype, prototype and stereotype are words whose common suffix *-type* derives from the Greek word *tupos* meaning 'stamp' or 'model'

Archetype means the °original model (*archos* is a Greek word meaning 'first' or 'chief' — hence archbishop and arch-enemy). It is usually applied to people. Thus Cain is the archetypal °fratricide.

Prototype also means the original model (*prōtos* is a Greek word meaning 'first'). It is usually applied to things. Thus before a new line of aircraft is put into °production a prototype is built to test the design.

A *stereotype* is a fixed set of °characteristics that is applied by °convention to certain kinds of people. Thus the stereotype salesman is young, nattily dressed, excitable and fast talking. *Stereos* is a Greek word meaning 'solid'. A stereotype was originally a solid metal plate developed in printing to ensure an even, clear image on all the sheets of paper. It was made from a cast of the movable type (the type had to be movable so that different words could be made from its different letters). A solid has three dimensions — height, width and depth. Sound reproduced with three dimensions is stereophonic (*phōnē* is the Greek word for 'voice' or 'sound').

ultra vires
beyond one's °legal authority

Ultra is a Latin word meaning 'beyond'. *Vires* is a plural form of the Latin word *vis* meaning 'power'. °Governments give specific powers to certain bodies — for example county councils — to carry out functions for the °state. Cases often arise in the courts on the issue of whether or not these bodies have exceeded their powers in particular instances. A body that has so acted is said to have acted *ultra vires;* one that has acted within its powers is said to have acted *intra vires* (*intra* is a Latin word meaning 'within').

unemployment
lack of paid occupation

Employer is a French word meaning 'to employ' derived from the Latin word *implicare* 'to enfold' (from which we also derive 'implicate' and 'implication'). People lay claim on some of the goods and services made available in the country each year through the payment of money. Most adults obtain money from a paid occupation that involves the °production of goods and services: employment is the means most people have of making a living. A small number of people are wealthy enough not to need employment. Adults who are incapacitated or who cannot find employment must be provided for by the °state (from taxes gathered from those employed and those who are rich). Or by relatives. Or by charity.

Unemployment is a term covering the condition of those who would like a job but do not have one. We derive the numbers of unemployed from the °labour force. The *unemployment rate* or rate of unemployment is the percentage of the labour force without a job. In Ireland in 1988 the unemployment rate was nearly eighteen per cent.

The rate of unemployment is a more important measurement than the number unemployed. If we are told the number unemployed in Ireland is about 230,000 we have little idea whether this is big or small. It would appear small by °comparison with the 2.3 million unemployed in the UK. However, if we use the rates of unemployment we see that the Irish rate of nearly eighteen per cent is big by comparison with the UK rate of about eight per cent.

The term 'the unwaged' is sometimes used to embrace the unemployed, dependent groups such as the elderly, the young, the handicapped who are unemployed, and certain people who work but recieve no pay such as most housewives.

universe
the whole creation

The Latin equivalent of the Greek *cosmos* is *universum*, literally 'the whole thing', the °totality of the physical world, in English 'the universe' (*uni* is a Latin particle meaning 'one' and *-verse* derives from the Latin word *vertere* 'to turn' — the universe is that which has been turned into one by divine order). *Universal* is used to describe something that applies to everything or everything in a class, °e.g. universal °suffrage (as opposed to limited suffrage where, for example, only men or property-owners have the right to vote). *Universitas* is a Latin word meaning 'the whole', which came to be applied to a society. 'University' now denotes a learned society or °institution which is authorised to confer degrees. There is a °connotation of universality in the range of its interest in study.

utopian
pertaining to an imaginary °state of perfection

Utopia (from the Greek *ou* meaning 'not' and 'topos' meaning 'place') is the name of a book written by Sir (later Saint) Thomas More in 1516 which describes an imaginary island of that name where everything is perfect — °laws, °morals, °politics °etc. Aldous Huxley's *Brave New World* is a °modern example of the genre (°originally a French word meaning 'type' or 'kind' derived from the Latin word *genus, generis*; a genus — plural genera — is a class of °objects containing a number of subordinate groupings called 'species'). 'Utopian' is often used to describe schemes that are well-intentioned but utterly unrealistic.

vandalism
wanton destruction of property or other amenity

The Vandals were one of the fiercest of the °barbarian tribes that fell upon the Roman °Empire in its decline — they sacked Rome in 455 AD. They were notorious for their delight in destroying churches, books and works of art. The word 'vandalism' was coined in °modern times by a French °cleric to °characterise the destruction of works of °art by French °revolutionary °fanatics. It is applied nowadays to the destruction of °public °telephone boxes, bus shelters, trees °etc. It is done almost invariably by young people in towns and cities. °*Institutional vandalism* is a term applied to the destruction of beautiful things or amenities by a public or °private °organisation, for example the demolition of an °historic building to make way for a car-park.

veto
the power to reject

The °tribunes of the people in Rome had the power to prevent a judgement from being carried out. They exercised it by uttering the word *Veto!* ('I forbid!' in Latin). The word entered the °modern °political vocabulary at the beginning of the French °Revolution when the °constitutional issue arose as to whether the king could veto the decisions of the °National Assembly.

The veto may be a formal power. Thus in the United Nations Security Council each of the five permanent members (China, France, USSR, UK and US) can exercise a veto to prevent the Council from taking action on any matters other than procedural ones. In the °European Community most of the decisions of the Council are made by a °majority °vote; in the voting the larger °states have more votes than the smaller ones and a qualified majority is needed for a decision, that is, a greater number of votes than a minimal absolute majority (a half plus one). On the most important and far-reaching questions, including the admission of new members, there must be °unanimous agreement. That means that each member state in theory has a veto in regard to those issues. However, the Community always works in such a way that no single member state ever finds that the disadvantages arising from any one proposal decisively outweigh the basket of benefits it gets from membership.

The veto may also be informal. Thus Northern °nationalists have frequently complained that successive British governments have allowed the unionists to exercise a veto over all proposals for °governmental change in Northern Ireland.

viable
capable of maintaining independent life

Vita is the Latin word for 'life' from which is derived the French *vie*, the immediate source of viable. °Originally applied to the foetus — a viable foetus is one that is capable of independent life — the word is now often transferred — a viable project, a viable °economy.

(*Via* is the Latin word for 'way' or 'road'. In the expression 'She came home from Germany via London', via means 'by way of'. To take the *via media* is to take a middle course between two extremes — media is a form of *medius* the Latin word for 'middle'. A *viaduct* is a structure that carries a road or railway over a valley, formed by °analogy with *aqueduct*, a structure built by the Romans to carry water — Latin *aqua* — over a valley.)

vice versa
the other way round

Vice is a Latin word meaning 'turn'. *Versa* is a form of the Latin word *vertere* 'to turn'. The expression literally means 'the turn having been turned'. Thus, 'The °Czar relied on the army and vice versa'. The word 'vicissitude' meaning 'turn of fortune' is derived from the Latin *vicissitudo*. Thus, 'He remained °stoical in spite of all vicissitudes'.

Vichy France
that part of France (and its °empire) not occupied by the Germans in 1940, which had a °government whose seat was in the town of Vichy. The Vichy

France was shattered by the German °blitzkrieg of May-June 1940 which carried German forces up to the Channel and precipitated the British withdrawal through Dunkirk. France's leaders had two choices. They could acknowledge the German °victory, seek an armistice and negotiate a peace or they could flee °metropolitan France and continue the war from the French territories overseas. The vast °majority supported Marshal Philippe Pétain, the legendary defender of Verdun in the first world war

government collaborated with the Germans and disappeared with the °liberation of France in August 1944

(*'Ils ne passeront pas!'* — 'They shall not pass!' — from his Order of the Day, Verdun, 26 February 1916), and made the first choice. A small number, led by General Charles de Gaulle, made the second. Pétain successfully negotiated a peace with the Germans who were content with access to French agricultural and industrial °production and did not wish to get bogged down in controlling the French °population. He also succeeded in commanding the loyalty of almost all the French territories overseas. He established his °government in the town of Vichy.

Pétain

De Gaulle

emigration
Migrare is a Latin word meaning 'to go from one place to another' from which we derive 'migrate', 'migrant', 'migration' and 'migratory'. *E* is a Latin prefix meaning 'out of' — 'to emigrate' is to move out of one country into another. *In* (*im* before m) is a Latin prefix meaning 'in' — 'to immigrate' is to move into one country from another

Vichy is famous for its natural spring water. A southern mountain spa town, it had the spare accommodation to meet the needs of a °bureaucracy. It was favoured before the southern cities because some, like Marseilles, were too close to the temptation of emigration and others, like Lyons and Toulouse, were the °political power-bases of opponents of the Vichy °regime.

The Vichy government never achieved its aims of negotiating the °reintegration of France and of installing itself in Paris.

vigilantes
a self-appointed group of citizens who band together to maintain order in a °community

Vigilare is the Latin word 'to watch' from which 'vigilantes', °originally a Spanish word, derives — vigilantes watch for criminals. But they also catch and punish them and thus usurp the proper functions of the Gardaí and the courts.

Vigilantes tend to appear whenever the °law is failing to protect the community. They mete out justice in a rough and ready manner. In the absence of the formal processes of law, gross injustice is sometimes perpetrated. In Ireland in recent times there has been evidence of vigilantes at work in certain areas of Dublin to deal with drug-pushers.

vote
a registration in some agreed way of one's opinion about a °candidate or on an issue

Votum is a Latin word for 'a wish' or 'vow'. You cast a vote in an °election by marking a ballot-paper and placing it in a ballot-box (*ballot* derives from the Italian *ballotta* meaning 'a little ball': little balls placed in an urn or box were used for voting). The °law provides for °*universal suffrage*, that is, it enables everyone to vote (*suffragium* is the Latin word for 'vote'), for a *secret ballot* so that voters will not be intimidated (*timidus* is a Latin word for 'fearful'), and for the division of the country into *constituencies* so that °representatives will be returned by the different parts of the country. To have the *franchise*, that is, the right to vote, is the mark of a free man (*franc* is an Old French word for 'free').

The *poll* at an election is the total number of votes cast (*poll* derives from a middle Dutch word *polle* meaning 'head' and by extension 'the counting of heads'). Some voters spoil their votes from ignorance or in protest. The *valid poll* is obtained by excluding spoilt votes. (The word 'poll' is also used in relation to attitude surveys — opinion polls — and to poll tax or head tax.)

Those who do best at the *hustings* win the seats (the husting was a °temporary platform on which the nomination of °parliamentary candidates was made before the Ballot Act, 1872, and is now applied to any platform where election speeches are made and, by extension, to the election campaign generally).

vox pop
the opinions of people in the street

Vox, vocis is a Latin word meaning 'voice'. *Populi* is a form of *populus*, a Latin word meaning 'people'. *Vox pop* is a short form of *vox populi* 'the voice of the people'. (The Latin phrase 'vox populi vox dei' — 'the voice of the people is the voice of God' — has been used by leaders down the ages to cloak abject submission to the will of the mob.) Vox pop is often used in radio and °television circles for a sequence presenting the views of members of the °public randomly chosen.

Wall Street
the American financial establishment

The American °Stock Exchange is °located in Wall Street, New York. Wall Street is used as a °synonym for that stock exchange and by extension for the financiers and the financial specialists from the American business world who conduct their business there — the financial °establishment.

welfare state
a °state in which the °economic and °social needs of dependent groups such as the poor, the sick and the elderly are met by the state

Welfare means well-being. For our well-being we need to be able to avail ourselves of a wide range of services, from womb to tomb. The full-hearted welfare state seeks to provide such services as health, housing, °education, °unemployment assistance, family allowances, widows', orphans' and old age pensions.

The first notable step in welfare °legislation was taken in Bismarck's Germany. Other European states followed. In Britain the welfare state was greatly advanced under Clement Attlee's Labour °government, 1945-51. The system was based on recommendations in a report by the economist, Sir William Beveridge, who had been commissioned to prepare it by the war-time °coalition government.

Because of the close relationship between Ireland and Britain, especially the ease with which Irish people can move to and from Britain, Irish welfare legislation has tended to mirror Britain's. Most °modern states might be called welfare states, even the US (beginning with Roosevelt's New Deal) whose political °culture favours rugged individualism and therefore self-sufficiency.

White Army
the °Czarist anti-°revolutionary forces defeated by the °communist Red Army in the Russian °civil war 1917-21

When the revolutionary °government in Paris introduced conscription in 1793 to deal with the external threat, parts of the west of France — called La Vendée — revolted. The movement was taken over by the Royalists and it was from their emblem the *fleur de lys* (the white lily of the °monarchy) that the largely guerrilla forces got their name 'The Whites'. It was from them in turn that the Russian °reactionary armies got their °popular collective description. There was not, therefore, an °eponymous relationship between White Russia (or Byelorussia), one of the fifteen constituent °republics of the USSR, °located in the west close to Poland, and the White Army.

Whitehall
the °centre of British °government

Whitehall is a street in London where a number of important government offices are °located, including the Treasury. The °media use the term 'Whitehall' to refer to thinking on policy (rather than °political) matters at the highest levels of British government. (Downing Street, a small street off Whitehall where the British premier resides, is used to refer to thinking on party political matters at the highest level.)

The °Cenotaph is located in Whitehall.

Whitehall, London

the White House
the °official residence of the American °President in Washington, DC, the °capital of the US

In 1790 a decision was made by the first US congress under the new °constitution to establish a °federal capital on the Potomac river. In a °public °competition to choose a design for the President's residence, an Irish °architect from County Kilkenny who had settled in Philadelphia, James Hoban, was the winner. It is said that Hoban

The Hoban stamp issued jointly by An Post and the US postal service in 1981

derived elements of his design from that of Leinster House, the residence of the Duke of Leinster in Dublin and now the seat of the °Dáil and °Seanad.

Work on the new capital — and the President's house — went slowly and Washington never lived there. When the °government finally moved to the new city in 1800, President Adams took up residence in the still unfinished building. The building was partly destroyed in the course of a war with the British in 1814. Afterwards, it was found impossible to clean the walls blackened by smoke, so Hoban suggested that the entire exterior be painted white. This solution was accepted — and gave the house its name.

White Paper
a statement of °government policy published by the Stationery Office

The term — a colloquial one — is derived from British °parliamentary experience. During the nineteenth °century the practice arose of printing °official reports, °statistical and other government publications, which were to be presented to parliament, on white °paper and of covering them in a heavier blue-coloured paper. Those publications became known as 'blue books'. Short government policy statements did not need a special cover and were printed entirely on white paper. Such documents became known as White Papers. That term, from 1945 on, came to be applied specifically to documents that contained government *decisions* on a °major area of °public policy.

In 1967 the Labour government in Britain decided, in the interest of open and more participative government, to publish a consultative document *The Development Areas: A Proposal for a Regional °Employment Premium* so that interested parties could make their views known before the government made its decisions. That document was issued with a green cover. Such consultative documents have ever since been called Green Papers.

The colours white and green are no longer material to the nature of the documents they describe.

xenophobia
morbid fear and dislike of foreigners

Xenos is the Greek word for 'stranger'. *Phobia* is the Greek word for 'fear'. °Politicians sometimes whip up xenophobia to strengthen the internal cohesion of their countries — or to seek °scapegoats.

zeitgeist
the spirit of the times

derive
Rivus is the Latin word for 'a river', *de* is a Latin word meaning 'from' — 'to derive' is to draw from a source

Zeit is the German word for 'time' or 'era'. *Geist* is a German word for 'spirit'. The term is often used in its ostensible sense (*ostendere* is a Latin word meaning 'to show' — ostensible means 'outwardly showing'). Thus, 'Jazz, booze and playing the stockmarket — these manifested the zeitgeist of the twenties'. But the word, derived from the writings of the °influential German °philosopher Hegel (1770–1831), has a much deeper import.

Thinkers address themselves perennially (constantly — *per* is a Latin word meaning 'through' and *annus* is the Latin word for 'year' which in the form *ennial* also occurs in 'centennial') to the problem of the meaning of °human °history. Does it follow a divine plan? Is it simply the process through which the fittest survive? Is it meaningless? Hegel believed the movement of history was dialectical (*dia* is a Greek word meaning 'through', *lektikos* is a Greek word meaning 'spoken'). For Socrates and Plato the dialectic was simply a form of discourse designed to force people to acknowledge their true beliefs. Hegel transformed the idea of dialectic to explain and understand the historical process.

Each era of this process and each phase of development of each era generates its own negation (from *negare* the Latin word 'to deny'; 'negation' is a °synonym for 'contradiction' which is derived from the Latin words *contra* 'against' and *dicere* 'to speak'). A new era emerges when the °synthesis of the °positive and °negative forces is realised. All that is good and true is preserved and enriched in the new era; nothing is lost. (Thus the Greeks discovered the principle of freedom but it was negated by further °political developments, to re-emerge in a new and richer light in the French °Revolution.) Contradiction is at the heart of reality; contradiction is the moving principle of the world and Reason is its agent.

The °subject of this historical process is Spirit and through history it is seeking self-understanding. Man is the vehicle of this self-understanding and there can be no further development beyond man. Hence all expressions of the human spirit — religion, °art, politics, philosophy — are expressions of, and a moment in, this endeavour by Spirit. History ends when Spirit, through the human spirit, will have achieved full self-knowledge, that is, will have become Absolute Spirit.

Marx seized upon Hegel's idea of the dialectic for his theory of history. Since he did not believe in Hegel's notion of Spirit, he sought the explanation of the historical process in the dialectic between man and the material conditions of his existence. Marx's theory of history is therefore called 'dialectical materialism'.

zenith
the highest point

Zenith derives from the Arab word *samt* meaning 'way' (of the head). Zenith is the point of the heavens directly above the observer's head. It is opposed to the *nadir,* the diametrically opposite point of the heavens — *nadir* means 'opposite to' (the zenith). Both words attest to the °primacy in °astromony attained by the Arabs in the ninth, tenth and eleventh °centuries. The words often appear in connection with the lives of °public figures and soldiers. Thus, 'This campaign marked the zenith/nadir of his career'.

Zionism
the Jewish movement to establish and develop a Jewish homeland in Palestine

Zion is a °synonym for the Holy Land and so Zionism is an apt name for the movement that re-established the Jews in Palestine and continues to help the °state of Israel by gathering funds and enlisting diplomatic support for it (mainly in the US) and promoting the °emigration of Jews to it.

Following the destruction of Jerusalem by the Romans in 70 AD, most of the Jewish °population of Palestine fled abroad. It was only °natural that a yearning to return to the Promised Land should be a feature of the °culture of the Jews of the °diaspora — they prayed for it three times a day. However, the first real steps to achieve the aspiration were taken when the Hungarian Jew Theodor Herzl (1860-1904), moved by the °anti-Semitism revealed by the Dreyfus Affair in France, convened the first World Zionist Congress in Basle, Switzerland in 1897. Some Jews did not agree (as some still do not) with his °strategy of setting up a Jewish homeland — they felt Jews should seek to be good Jews and good citizens of the states they lived in. Most Jews felt it was necessary for their protection as a race to establish a state (though a small number of these felt the state need not necessarily be in Palestine).

Of those who felt a state should be established in Palestine, Herzl and his supporters felt the task was urgent; others favoured a gradual building up of the Jewish °population in Palestine by small-scale °immigration first. (The °total population of Palestine at the turn of the century was small. It built up rapidly thereafter with immigration of Arabs from the surrounding states and of Jews from Europe.)

Chaim Weizmann

It was Chaim Weizmann (1874–1952) and his followers who decided these issues. They won the Balfour Declaration (1917) which committed the British °government to support the establishment of a Jewish °national home in Palestine. The British, who controlled Egypt, were expected to control Palestine if the Ottoman Empire did not survive the Great War. As it happened, the Balfour Declaration was included in the °mandate for Palestine given by the League of Nations to the British after the war.

The Declaration, however, had also contained a guarantee not to interfere with the °civil and religious rights of the °majority non-Jewish population of Palestine (the half million Moslems and 60,000 Christians). Understandably, the Palestinian Arabs were opposed to Jewish immigration and the establishment of a Jewish state. The British found themselves in a difficult situation over a commitment made for °propaganda reasons at a °critical point in a great war.

In 1924 America closed its door to °mass immigration.

David Ben Gurion

This was a momentous event in the °history of Zionism because it diverted the massive Jewish °emigration from Poland and Russia to Palestine. (By 1931 the Jews in Palestine numbered about 175,000.) Another momentous event was the accession of Adolf Hitler to power in Germany in 1933: in spite of a restrictive immigration policy imposed by the British, the Jews in Palestine, swelled by those who managed to flee °Nazi °anti-Semitism, numbered about 400,000 in 1937. (The Arabs then numbered about one million.)

The Holocaust — the terrible destruction of the °European Jews by the Nazis (*holokauston* is a Greek word for 'whole-burnt sacrifice' from *holos* meaning 'whole' and *kaustos* meaning 'burnt') — cost six million Jewish lives and reduced the world Jewish population by as much as a third to twelve million. It built up an

Belsen concentration camp after the fall of the Third Reich

irresistible pressure for the establishment of a Jewish state through which the Jews could defend themselves. Immediately after the war Jewish refugees from Europe streamed into Palestine, most of them °illegally. By 1948 there was a million Jews there.

The UN solution to the Palestine problem, at that stage erupting in violent clashes between Jewish guerrilla forces and the British, was partition. Partition was accepted by the Jews but rejected by the Arabs. In May 1948 the British withdrew and the Jewish leader David Ben-Gurion proclaimed the State of Israel. The Israelis beat off the attacks immediately mounted on them by the surrounding Arab states. Some half-a-million Arabs fled the Israeli-occupied territories: these displaced people and their children are at the heart of the Middle Eastern problem today. Indeed it is often said that the Palestinians have paid the penalty for Europe's, especially Nazism's, crimes against the Jews.

INDEX

The page numbers in *italics* indicate where the major reference to the word or concept will be found. The complete references for rarer words are given to enable the reader to explore the various usages found in the text. For common words such as 'public', 'social', 'national', 'economic', 'government', only the major reference is noted.

Index

T